Born to be Happy
Enjoy life to the full

Born to be
Happy
Enjoy life to the full

Prasanna Rao Bandela

NEW DAWN PRESS, INC.
USA • UK • INDIA

NEW DAWN PRESS GROUP
Published by New Dawn Press Group
New Dawn Press, Inc., 244 South Randall Rd # 90, Elgin, IL 60123
e-mail: sales@newdawnpress.com

New Dawn Press, 2 Tintern Close, Slough, Berkshire, SL1-2TB, UK
e-mail: salesuk@newdawnpress.org

New Dawn Press (An Imprint of Sterling Publishers (P) Ltd)
A-59, Okhla Industrial Area, Phase-II, New Delhi-110020, India
e-mail: info@sterlingpublishers.com
www.sterlingpublishers.com

Born to be Happy: Enjoy life to the full
Copyright © 2005, Prasanna Rao Bandela
ISBN 978 1 84557 442 0
Reprint 2006, 2008

All rights are reserved. No part of this publication may be reproduced, stored in a retrieval system or transmitted, in any form or by any means, mechanical, photocopying, recording or otherwise, without prior written permission of the publisher.

PRINTED IN INDIA

Dedicated to Dhimathi

Acknowledgements

This is a product of the synergy of many minds. Numerous authors contributed most of the ideas included in this book. I admire their wisdom and insight into the complexities of human life. I am greatly indebted to the publishers of *Reader's Digest*, for I have researched old issues for the material required for this project and quoted them profusely.

I am thankful to late Dr E G Parameswaran Emeritus Professor of Psychology Osmania University, Hyderabad, for his encouragement.

My friends K L Narasimha Rao and CH S Madhava Rao stood behind me at every stage of this project. I am grateful to them for their solid support and suggestions.

Thanks to K Rajni Kanth who has done commendable work in preparing the manuscript.

I gratefully appreciate love, understanding and support of my wife Dhimathi and my children Srikanth, Sridhar, and Vandana.

Preface

The main idea in this book is that we human beings have only one life to live; then why not celebrate and enjoy life! Happiness of course seems to be elusive, yet we all seek happiness as if it is out there in the world. The truth is, it is hidden in our feelings. All of us are born with valuable gifts of life to make our lives happy; but we hardly make use of their full potential. If only we realise this all of us can enjoy life. The main thrust is in the direction of positive psychology. That's the view in this book.

A unique feature of this book is the introduction of a new paradigm of experience. It is based on the fact that the divisions of the *past, present* and *future* of man do not really exist in the passage of time. In fact, they are created by human mind. Yet, paradoxically, our thinking about past and future makes a considerable impact on our present. Our life is influenced by memories of the past and concerns about future. Human mind always wanders in the microcosm it has created. It plays with ideas, creates beautiful dreams and wonderful visions. It is totally committed to help us in our struggle to be happy in life. In the process it raises hopes of bright future of sunny days and addresses fears of future uncertainty.

Another special feature is the use of "quotes as heuristic devices." This is because, quotations have profound impact on people. They have inspiring value, persuasive influence, motivational force and the credibility of authentic people—some times great persons. Any thing in excess may cause digestive problems, we know; but when we play host we would like to provide the best food (for thought) we can.

Let the discerning gourmets enjoy what they like. The author takes the responsibility for certain words made italics within the quotes.

"A book ought to be an ice pick to break up the frozen sea within us," says Franz Kafka. In a similar vein, Christopher Morley says, "The real purpose of a book is to trap the mind into doing its own thinking." I shall be too glad, if this little volume serves that purpose.

Hope this will delight you. Enjoy reading.

Hyderabad
June 1, 2004.   Prasanna Rao Bandela

Contents

	Acknowledgements	vi
	Preface	vii
1.	Introduction: Showers of Blessing on the Stream of time	1
2.	Mystery of the Wandering Mind	11
3.	The Past : That Never Comes Back	21
4.	The Future: That is Not Yet	30
5.	The Present: The Only True Reality	38
6.	Precious Gifts of Life: Unwrap Joy	60
7.	Gift of Unique Body and Wonderful Self	63
8.	Gift of Marvellous Brain and Fantastic Memory	74
9.	Great Gifts of Knowing, Thinking, and Learning	85
10.	Delightful Gift of Communication Skills	103
11.	Emotions and Feelings : Exclusive Gift to Humans	118
12.	One Life to Live Joyfully	125
13.	Sanity in Accepting Reality	163
14.	Happiness in Satisfying Needs	168
15.	You Need Money: Not the Craze	177
16.	Joy of Realising Dreams and Achieving Goals	182
17.	Fun in Capturing Opportunities	189
18.	Cheerful Actions Lead to Accomplishments	196
19.	Thrill of Success In Spite of Failures	216
20.	You Can Harness Anger and Stress	233
21.	Take Charge: Win Your Emotional Battles	255
22.	Choose to be Happy: Living is Joy Enough	277
23.	Enjoy Life to the Full	306
	References	

> *I know there is nothing good for man except to be happy and live the best life he can while he is alive.*
>
> Solomon (970-928 BCE)
> King of ancient Israel
> In *Ecclesiastes*

Chapter 1

Introduction: Showers of Blessing on the Stream of Time

It's not the river that runs, but water. It's not time that passes, but us.

Herve Bazin (1911-96)
French author

Let your life lightly dance on the edges of time like the dew on the tip of leaf.

Rabindranath Tagore (1861-1941)
Indian poet,
Nobel Prize for literature 1913.

"How are you doing?" "Good, how are you doing?" These are just formal greetings. But when we ask any one informally, "How is life treating you?", we get different answers: "Well, getting along," "It's okay," "Not so bad." We rarely hear, "I'm happy" or "very happy." The undertone in all these responses invariably revolves around the state of well-being or otherwise. This is because we all cherish happiness and do not want suffering in our lives. It looks as if we run our very lives around these emotional states. Momentary feelings of sadness or happiness may cloud our judgement of overall quality of life. An objective appraisal of our life's trajectory is important in making decisions about our life. Before we do that we must understand and appreciate our place in this world.

Life on earth is a miraculous exception in the entire universe; and the evolution of man is indeed an awesome wonder, beyond the comprehension of any human mind. It is delightful to imagine how thrilling it is to visualise billions of living cells dancing in concert in every human being on earth—a small stage in the heavenly theatre of infinite space. Human beings are like meteor showers that dazzle in the boundless sky. In another dimension they are like showers of blessing that float for a while on the eternal stream of time. "I think it's a very happy accident," wondered Miguel de Cervantes, a Spanish philosopher. It is perhaps the most exciting event in the world worth rejoicing. In fact, all the things in life are no less than blessings—blessings and opportunities to learn, to love, to rejoice, and celebrate living and share our joy with other fellow beings.

It is mind boggling to know, from Professor Carl Sagan of Cornell University, New York, that the universe is in existence for the last 15 thousand million years(or at least in the present incarnation since the "Big Bang"). He says, "if we compress this vast time of the universe into one year, men and women originate at 10.30 p.m. on New Year's eve; and all the recorded history occupies the last ten seconds of December 31. Yet despite the insignificance of the instant we humans have so far occupied in the cosmic time, it is clear that what happens on earth at the beginning of the new cosmic year will depend very much on the scientific wisdom and the distinctly human sensitivity of mankind."

Scientists explain that there are millions of galaxies like our Milky Way galaxy in which our sun is but a tiny star; the earth is one of the planets that revolve around the sun; that the earth is the only place in the universe where life exists; it took millions of years to evolve complex intelligent beings capable of thinking on their own. Will Durant, an American historian, says, "we are such microscopic particles in so immense a universe that none of us is in a position to understand the world, much less to dogmatize about it." Pascal trembled at the thought of man's bewildered minuteness between the immensity of the whole and complexity of each part. "These infinite spaces," he said, "frightens me." Let us be careful how we pit our pitiful generalisations against the infinite variety, scope and subtlety of the world." So much, to remind the minuteness of man in the universe.

Introduction: Showers of Blessing on the Stream of Time

"When we are mindful of every nuance of our natural world we finally get the picture," says Elizabeth Gilbert, "that we are only given one dazzling moment of life here on earth, and we must stand before that reality both humble and elevated, subject to every law of our universe and grateful for our brief but intrinsic participation in it." We, the humans are given tiny bits of space and time, with a choice to make a life of our own.

Life at the longest is amazingly short. But when compared to other life forms with a short life-span, we are deluded into believing that a hundred years is a very long time. Ralph Waldo Emerson tickles us with a dialogue in an interesting story. An elderly ephemera, ripe in age, says, "young man, you have a long life to go." We are instantly amused, because we know the life-span of this insect is hardly a day! The Zen intuition comes to mind. At this moment, some one like Phaedrus must be laughing at us!

"What is funny about us is precisely that we take ourselves too seriously," says Reinhold NEIBUHR. Yes, we ask serious questions about this ephemeral life of ours and we make elaborate plans. "It is not how many years we live, but rather what we do with them," asks Evangeline Cory Booth. That perhaps is a question that is being asked today by many thinking people. No doubt, what we do with our lives is our choice; but the truth is, whatever we do, we invariably look forward to the ultimate goal of happiness in life. Sometimes we succeed and some times we fail. That's life! Perhaps that is why Elbert Hubbard warns, "Never take life seriously, you will never get out of it alive."

We know that this awareness comes from our mind, where our thinking takes place. But we are not sure how it works. Many things happen in this world without our knowledge. For example, we are part of the dynamic movement of the earth, yet we don't realize how fast it is whirling around the sun. We are all travellers on the spaceship called the earth! Stephanee Gregory and Brad Wetzler tell us that it is moving at an incredible speed: "To some one standing next to you at the equator, zero degree latitude, you'd appear stationery. To a Martian hovering over earth, however, you'd appear to be spinning at 1041 mph. From the sun, it would look like you are riding a terrestrial Tilt-A-Whirl and orbiting the home star at 60,000 mph. From the edge of Andromeda galaxy, Earth would be seen spinning, orbiting and finally spiraling through the Milky Way at an average speed of 530,000 mph. Add all this up, you are travelling at a top speed of 591,041 mph. But not so fast—the universe itself is expanding, so it's not possible to know how fast we are really going." But the fact remains that we, the earthlings are moving in space at an incredible speed, quite unaware of this! No wonder, we don't realise how fast our minds are working, while moving in space at such a great speed! Though the mind is part of us we hardly know what it does and how fast it works. Neuroscientists tell us that the brain of a human being has 100 billion cells; and his mind can make learning connections at an incredible rate of 3 billion per second! That is the amazing power of our thinking mind! It is one of those things we take for granted without ever realising the might of human mind. "The stars are no strange as the mind that studies them, analyses the light, and measures the distance," says Henry Emerson Fosdick.

We hardly notice how our mind works day and night. What happens to it, when one is sleeping, is anybody's guess. What all we know is that our mind does not take rest, it wanders without our knowledge. Fortunately we remember some of the dreams created by the mind. But they hardly give us any clue as to its ramblings. From the content of our dreams we come to know that it shows a lot of concern for our life on earth. Our dreams are knit around the past events, future concerns and present happenings. From these dreams we infer that our mind is wandering all over the past, the future and the present. That is, our mind is wandering in the microcosm it has created! Of course it has a purpose: to help us live a happy life, the way we want.

"Time has no divisions to mark its passage," says Thomas Mann in *The Magic Mountain*, "there is never a thunder storm to announce the beginning of the new year. It is only we mortals who ring bells and fire off pistols." Man is a very insignificant speck in the vast universe; and human life is indeed a very short voyage in the eternal stream of time that runs infinitely. Yet, for the convenience of man, his mind has divided time into the past, the present and the future.

To him it looks as if this dynamic movement of life is caught between his past and future. In reality they don't exist, but nonetheless they appear real to him. He takes it as the universal truth. His mind operates on that premise. As he believes in this kind of axiom, his experience follows this belief. It looks as if this kind of thinking is the prime mover of his life. It is almost the sole basis of his actions. All this is because he believes in his mind, which believes in the past, the future and the present.

Our mind knows we are serious about our lives. It is trying to help us out in our struggles and sufferings in life. It appears that it knows that we are seeking happiness in the pleasant experiences of life. Perhaps, that is the reason why it evaluates every experience and segregates the pleasant experiences from the unpleasant ones.

It continues to work with the purpose of finding avenues for our happiness. That is why it visits the memories of our past experiences, the happy and unhappy memories, and brings them back to our awareness. When we remember past successes we are pleased with ourselves; we gain a lot of confidence in our capabilities. We look at ourselves with a sense of personal worth and pride. If we stretch it to the extremes we are deluded into believing that we are invincible and even develop superiority complex. We start thinking no one can beat us. When we remember our mistakes and failures, two things can happen. We may become depressed and develop inferiority complex. On the other hand, we may ponder over the mistakes and failures and try to learn from them. We know this is going to help us in our future endeavours.

When it visits the future concerns, we get into our fantasies and dreams. When our imagination is at work, we build up our aspirations and ambitions in life. We usually raise hopes for a bright future and try to foresee what it would be like. We make plans to achieve whatever goals we set. When our imagination trespasses the thin red line border of reality we land into trouble. We may develop distorted thinking and may even become schizophrenics. On the other hand we may be swayed into thinking the possibility of a frightening future. Brave hearts make necessary preparations to counter the danger, if it should happen. The feeble hearted lose hope, and cry today for tomorrow's woes. They may develop anxiety syndromes and experience bouts of depression. This is how our past and future affects the present.

This is the basis of a new paradigm of experience that is being introduced here. Consider the elements of this conceptual framework:

	Past	Time Present	Future
Experience Pleasant	Memorial House	Life	Dreamland
 Unpleasant	Cemetery	Here and Now	Dark Zone

Human life: Time between birth and death.

Experience: Knowledge and wisdom derived from the changes and trials of life.

The Past:

Pleasant experiences

Memorial House: It has two important halls. Hall of Fame is a place where achievements of people are displayed and honoured. Hall of Shame is the place where the most despicable deeds of people are displayed to invoke their conscience.

Unpleasant experiences

Cemetery: This strange burial ground has two important places of interest.

Burning Pyre is a place where the negative feelings generated by failures, disappointments, and unpleasant experiences in life keep on burning. Kind Garden is a place where a person's failures, mistakes, disappointments, defeats, and setbacks are forgiven and forgotten. It also has a Kindergarten where lessons from unpleasant experiences, mistakes and failures can be learned, so that they can be used in our efforts to be successful and happy in our lives.

The Future:

Pleasant experiences
Dreamland: It is the nurturing place of dreams, hopes, and future plans.

It has two important places of interest. Creative Realm is a place where we dream. All our dreams, day-dreams, fantasies, imaginations, hopes, aspirations, ambitions originate from this place. Futuristic Domain is a place where every thing concerning future is entertained. All our future visions, future hopes, future plans, future projects come from this place.

Unpleasant experiences
Dark Zone: It is the dwelling place of our future fears. It is also the place where our endurance, fortitude, resilience develop. It has the House of Horrors where the best horror movies are shown to amuse the brave hearts and to haunt the feeble hearted. It also has the House of Torture where the people are tortured at their will to give them the imaginary experience of pain and suffering, while the machos enjoy the pleasure of torturing others.

Axioms:
1. Every human being has only one life to live.
2. Every human being can live the way he /she wants to live.
3. Time and experience are the essential ingredients of human life.
4. As the wandering mind swings between the past and the future, human life is caught in between, in the present.
5. Human experience can be either pleasant or unpleasant.
6. Every human being has needs to satisfy and goals to achieve.
7. Every human being has the potential to satisfy personal needs, achieve life goals and be happy.

Hypotheses:
1. Human life has become complex with memories of the past experiences, future concerns and a lot of things to do in the present.
2. Every human being is born with valuable gifts of life that can help satisfy needs, achieve life goals and make life happy.
3. Every human being is capable of making one's own life happy.

Message : We can be what we desire to be. With determination and effort we will be, what we can be. The choice is ours. If we want, we can always be happy and make others happy. Remember, we are born to be happy and therefore can live a joyful life.

Every human being is aware that death is inevitable; but there are many people who fear death. "You can not conquer death, but you can conquer the fear of it," says Elizabeth Coatsworth. Every man struggles to satisfy his needs and achieve personal goals during the short span of life. In the process he looks for opportunities and earns money for survival. He decides his destiny and works strenuously towards its end. He tries to find what gives him happiness; and strives to get it by any means. Success or failure, no matter what, he is destined to work hard till the end of his life. Man has the desire to seek pleasure, but often he can not avoid miserable pain. The more he seeks happiness, the more he gets suffering. He cannot escape this predicament in life. That is his lot. As Jean Paul Sartre rightly said, "There is no exit from human dilemma." "It is a sorry business that God has given man to busy himself with," says king Solomon. "I have seen all the deeds that are done here under the sun, they are all emptiness, and chasing the wind." After thoroughly examining human life on earth, he came to the conclusion: "I know there is nothing good for man except to be happy and live the best life he can while he is alive." Yes, we know that we all have to live short lives, all have to face death one day or the other. Then, why not we try to be happy as long as we live?

"Only one life to live!" reminds Anna Robertson Brown. "We all want to make most of it. How can we accomplish the most with the energies and powers at our command? What is worthwhile?" This is the kind of thought that reverberates in most of us. Man's struggle to find happiness is the main theme of his life. The *mind*, our life partner and friend, struggles to help us in all our endeavours. Keeping the above conceptual framework in mind, we shall consider where it wanders and how it works to help its master (you). This knowledge has the potential to help us understand the undercurrents of our own behaviour which is being directed towards achieving happiness in our lives. "Humanity does not ask us to be happy," says Orson Scott Card, "It merely asks us to be brilliant on its behalf; survival first and then happiness as we can manage it."

Another important aspect is the hidden potential in all of us. It is like having a diamond mine which becomes beneficial only when precious stones are dug out and the value realised. But we do not know the value of the various faculties with which we are endowed. We shall examine how best we can make use of them in our struggle to make a happy living on Earth.

In the beginning of the 20th century people talked of Industrial Management; and then came Product Management and Brand Management. In the new millennium experts are talking of Management of Perceptions. It's a new science "that depends on image matrices that can leverage attitudes and subsequent behaviour." Marketing people are trying to create critical attitudes that lead to purchase decisions, and more importantly an attitude that fosters the brand in a positive mindset for years to come in the minds of consumers. They are trying to influence our minds for their benefit. "So even with all advances, anthropology will be your problem. Not technology—human nature will be your problem," says Scott McNealy, CEO and Co-founder of Sun Microsystems. Sir Winston Churchill forewarned us : "The empires of the future are the empires of the mind." We have seen the advent of Knowledge Management. Soon, it is going to be the dawn of Mind Management. We may have to be prepared for it. Most important thing is, we have to learn to manage our minds before others do.

"An unexamined life is not worth living," said Socrates. So, in our struggle to find happiness, let us consider various aspects of human life. Is there any expert who can tell us all the things we want to know about human life? The answer is, none. But then our *mind* tells us we can learn a lot of things from the experiences of other human beings. A great number of living people, and those who lived before, have left for us a great treasure of knowledge, wise teachings and sayings. They contain the quintessence of their rich experiences that can teach us the complexities of life on earth. That perhaps is a proper recourse. Let us consider them for whatever they are worth. We may not be able to follow all of them; but we can take a view that is convincing to us.

Chapter 2

Mystery of the Wandering Mind

Mind is the limit. As long as mind can envision something, you can do it.

Arnold Swarzenegger (1947-)
Champion body builder, three time
Mr. Universe, Actor, Governor of California.

It is not the place, nor the condition, but the mind alone, that can make any one happy or miserable.

Sir Roger L' Estrange (1606 – 1704)
Englishman of letters

Unique existence of man in the vast expanse of the universe is still a mystery. Another mystery is the presence of the invisible mind in the three-dimensional space of his brain. It is the mind that creates the world about us. Awareness of its existence is awareness of life itself. The dictum of Rene Descartes –*Cogito ergo sum* – "I think therefore I am," reiterates this truth. Then, wandering nature of mind is, indeed, the mystery of the mysteries!

Do you know that the average person can only keep his mind on one thing for six to eleven seconds at a time? The average used to be eleven seconds about twenty years ago, but psychologists think that —due to social pressures, chronic television watching, and drug damage—the average concentration span is now only six seconds; and it is getting worse. So, even when you are thinking about something you choose to think about, your mind will tend to wander every six seconds if you are average. You will have to consciously make an effort to bring it back. A sense of well-being and the ability to think clearly is destroyed whenever thoughts or feelings are turbulent. Concentration becomes difficult when we face problems in life.

What is the purpose of this wandering? Just curiosity or is there any objective? Observe your wandering mind. You can know its movements. It's not rambling with no fixed course. It moves in its own microcosm with a serious purpose. There is a definite purpose for its wanderings. Its fundamental nature is to create order out of disorder and chaos. Even if the available information is scanty, it comes to an understanding of what is in focus in the present. That is why it looks as if it makes meaning out of nothing.

Mind produces creative ideas and dreams

Mind is the store house of all our experiences; it draws upon its stored information and always plays with ideas. John Pfiffer says, "Imagination is a kind of mosaic process, the "pieces" being already-formed memory traces which are assembled into new patterns—similies, metaphors, scientific theories, utopias." Ideas are products of your mind. Remember, your ideas are your assets. It all depends on how you make use of them. "Nothing is as powerful an idea whose time has come," said Victor Hugo. Believe in your ideas and hold on to them until their time comes.

Our mind always plays with ideas and creates wonderful visions and dreams. Our dreams reveal the creative genius of the mind. They are an enduring source of fascination. Socrates looked on them as representatives of the voice of the conscience. Voltaire dismissed them as random products of physical dispositions. Sigmund Freud called them as "the royal road to unconscious." Carl Jung, accepted Freud's view that dreams are messages from the unconscious, but rejected the idea that they all go back to infancy and sex. He believed that the dreams were concerned with present problems; they were revelations rather than disguises of what was going on below the surface of the mind. Today, many psychotherapists are coming to believe that any intelligent person can successfully interpret his own dreams to acquire new insights into his own character and nature of his relationships with others.

"A dream that is not understood," says The Talmud, "is an unopened letter." Every night we have important messages from our unconscious. Dr Ann Faraday, a psychotherapist and dream researcher, goes even further in urging people to interpret their own dreams. Her book *Dream Power* spells out three stage process by which any dreamer can examine his dreams for different kinds of meaning. In the first stage, you can examine your dream for its objective content; tremendously important messages can come on this level. If nothing obvious appears in your dreams, she says, then look to them next as a mirror of your attitudes and prejudices, your opinion of yourself and others. A third way of exploiting dreams is to probe for hidden sources of your personality problems.

In recent years popular interest in dreams is quite visible in the best-selling books on dreams, proliferation of dream-workshops and dream-therapy groups. Even scientists are interested in investigating this fascinating phenomenon. A new general dream theory is now being talked about. Much simplified, the theory sees human beings as information processors equipped with two ways of dealing with an infinitely complicated world. "The first, which involves the left hemisphere of the brain, is the one we usually use during our waking hours," says dream researcher Laurence Cherry. "It deals most effectively with the constant bombardment of facts that must be judged as meaningful or irrelevant. The second, which involves the right brain, is concerned more with perceived feeling than objective fact and seems the mode of dreaming mind. The stray feelings and random bits and pieces of emotion that are recognized and unexamined during the day must be dealt with during sleep to see how they fit our most interior, most intimate conceptions of ourselves."

"Every night," says psychologist Paul Balkan, "for a brief duration of dream, the illogical, the emotional, highly visual right brain is almost completely freed from the dominance of the left brain, and the result is the torrent of images, sounds and feelings known as a dream." Images of striking colour (all dreams are colour) jostle each other in a "dream stream," while the laws of logic are often casually ignored. In this strange world lofty pine trees grow in the bottom shelf of the refrigerator and timid kittens turn into three-metre monsters. Moods of giant terror and giddy happiness are common, which often seem unrelated to the events taking place. But behind all this processing of mental images into creative dreams, there is a definite purpose. But even our mind, the director of this dream show, does not know what it is until the processing of information is complete.

"This sort of processing of information is our regular night shift work," says psychologist Rosalind Cartwright. "Mostly it concerns the personally relevant information that has to do with who we were. At night we reconcile the new information to our old self, and put it all together so we can get up and fight another day." It is now evident that this processing of information is the genius of our mind that works indefatigably, day and night, to help us out in our daily life. Apparently the process helps us cope with problems that we face every day.

Mind day-dreams during waking hours

Day-dreams play vital role in all our lives. "Clinical and experimental research has confirmed that day dreams are normal to all active minds," says Jerome Singer, professor of psychology at the Yale University, in an interesting article "Don't Be Afraid to Day-dream." "Through day- dreams our brains put us through mental rehearsals and keep us aware of the unfinished business in our lives. They are a very real part of our growth and self development—an asset we can make use of to help us modify a dull situation, plan for the future, or try out new ways of relating to people around us – day-dreams add colour and intrigue to our lives, make them more exciting—provided, of course, we do not escape at inappropriate times such as during an important business conference or driving in heavy traffic." Consider the specific advantages and uses of day dreaming: They help make your life more creative and original. Help you to use the past and to explore your future. Help develop your personality. Help calm and soothe yourself. Help overcome your loneliness. Provide useful insights into your behaviour. Strengthen yourself in adversity.

David McClelland, professor of psychology at Harvard University has shown that day dreams of achievement will be reflected in a-person's actual striving to get ahead. Day dream, your fantasies, enjoy-the ecstasies. Think differently, imaginatively. Think of creative ideas, and innovative applications. Know what hopes to raise, aspirations to cherish, ambitions to fulfill. Dream unfulfilled desires first, you can realize them later in life. Don't be afraid to live your dreams. If you can discover your dreams and truly believe in them, you can help yourself to become the person you are designed to be. They can make your life happy. Make list of your life goals, and get moving towards them. Anticipate change, and imagine how best you can adjust to the expected changes. Construct various scenarios, make future plans, implement them in small steps, one after the other. Review progress, supplement with whatever is needed to do.

W. Kingston explains in his book *Innovation,* that there are many people between the dreamer and the mandarin—the artist, inventor, innovator, entrepreneur, trader. What makes them different is their mental make up. Dreamers and artists use imagination rather than verifiable facts; ideas rather than concrete realities. Inventors and innovators go a step ahead. They see new things rather than familiar things; world as it might be rather than world as it is; they like to take chances rather than depend on predictable things; like to depend on spontaneity rather than learned behaviour; driven more by emotion rather than intellect; they think of revolution rather than evolution; concern with future rather than past or present. The entrepreneur, trader and the mandarin also see these things, but their interests revolve around application of these inventions and innovations, business ventures, profitable opportunities, and profits.

Mind wanders in the world of dreams

Psychologists have studied the process of dreaming under laboratory conditions.

A dream researcher Laurence Cherry says in his article "Why You Need to Dream" (*Reader's Digest* Sept. 1978) "dreams punctuate our sleep several times. Four to six times a night, at an interval of about an hour and half, a sleeper enters the REM (Rapid Eye Movement) stage of sleep, which has been found to be closely related to periods of vivid dreaming. Each period becomes longer until, by the fourth or fifth dream, it may last as long as an hour. This 90-minute rhythm seems to be a basic pulse of human life. More than a hundred body functions, from stomach contractions to hormone secretions—and many mental activities as well—follow a cycle that repeats itself every 90 minutes."

Cherry says that

> "Most dreams follow a standard, highly organized sequence. The first and the shortest dream, usually set in the *present* is a kind of overture; it often revolves around a problem occupying our mind before we fall asleep, and sets the basic theme for the dreams to come. The next two dreams, though they incorporate feelings from the *present* usually deal with the *past*. The fourth dream is often set in the *future* and concerns some kind of wish fulfillment (What if I didn't have this problem?"). The fifth, and for the most people the final dream of the night, builds on material from all the previous dreams, forming a grand finale set in the *present*." (Italics are mine).

That the dream is a product of mind is self-evident. The proof of the wandering mind comes from the sequence and pattern of dreaming. If we look at the sequence, focus of our mind is first on the *present* with its endless problems. And there after, it browses through millions and millions of files of stored memories of our *past* experiences, obviously looking for relevant information, lessons from similar experiences, clues, methods, skills, to solve the current problems. Further it visits the *future* via the unexplored route of fantasies, dreams and imagination. It tries to apply unconventional theories, discover new methods, invent novel techniques, to find creative solutions. After exhausting the vast resources of stored information of our *past* memories, and considering the dreamy *future* possibilities, imaginative alternatives, and creative solutions, the mind returns to the *present*. That is when the mind blends and transposes all the relevant information and refocuses on the current problems. This reflects the grand finale of its efforts to search for solutions for the current problems. And understandably it ends up with dreams concerning the *present*. Our mind is concerned about our success, our future and our happiness in life. Since all this happens without our awareness we are surprised to know from dreams what solutions our mind has worked out for us. Thus the dream research has provided us with a solid proof about the wandering nature of human mind! It lends credence to our paradigm of experience discussed earlier. Yes, indeed, our past experiences and future concerns do influence our present behaviour! We shall consider this aspect in detail in the following chapters.

Mind is your problem solver

Psychoanalyst Eric Fromm says that we are often more intelligent, wiser and capable of better judgement when we dream than when awake, and spectacular examples support his view. "During sleep, dreams seem to take over the work of constructive problem solving," says psychologist Rosalind Cartwright, director of Sleep Disorder Services and Research Centre at Rush Presbyterian, St. Luke's Medical Centre in Chicago.

"The ability of the dreaming mind to pose solutions to unresolved problems has intrigued dream researchers for years," says Laurence Cherry. Creative people often harness their dreams to solve problems. Albert Einstein, Mozart, Edgar Allan Poe, among scores of highly creative people, regularly relied on their dreams for new insights. Chemist Friedrich August Kekule had visualised that the atoms of a benzene molecule are arranged in a straight line. Dreaming, he saw them as a dancing snake which suddenly caught its tail in the mouth, forming a circle. Waking up, he recognised that the formation made by the snake was a hexagon and saw that the molecule's actual structure was a hexagon, a flash of insight usually considered as one of the most brilliant pieces of prediction in the history of organic chemistry. It was said that Kekule once ended a speech to a scientific congress concerning his discovery of the structure of benzene by telling his special audience, "Let us learn how to dream, gentleman, and then perhaps we will discover the truth."

Our dreams produce new ideas. They discover new things hither to unknown. Sometimes they invent new applications and innovations. Blake Clark gives the example of physiologist Otto Loewe. He had been thinking of transmission of nerve impulses, when one night he dreamt of an experiment which would determine if his hypothesis was correct. Though it was 3 a.m., he hurried to the laboratory, set up the experiment exactly as he dreamed it—and it worked! This inspiration established the chemical transmission of nerve impulses and gained its creator the Nobel Prize.

According to Naomi Epel, author of *Writers Dreaming*, when some writers, artists and scientists go to sleep, they ask their subconscious for a dream that will help them with unresolved issue. "Your unconscious knows things your conscious doesn't," says Epel. "It can be an ally with new insights."

Mind is concerned about your well-being

Recent research affirms that state of the mind has definite influence over your health. A positive attitude really can be good for what ails you. Contact with others seem to contribute to health and longevity as well. Sharing the feelings may also help. Confiding in someone else can have long term physical as well as psychological benefits. Optimism is another strong factor; optimistic attitude can be valuable in fighting diseases. There is a relationship between psychological factors and susceptibility to cold.

A new field of research called psychoneuroimmunology (PNI) reveals a link between the brain and the immune system. According to this, our thoughts can influence our health or sickness. PNI experts have uncovered hard evidence demonstrating that the brain and the immune system communicate with each other. In the late 1970's, Karen Bulloch, director of Neuroimmune Programme at the University of California, found nerve fibres in the thymus gland, an organ found under the breast bone that produces immune blood cells or T-cells. In a recent work Bulloch and psychiatrists Denis Darko and Michael Irwin identified receptors on the cells that receive signals from the nervous system. David Felton at the University of Rochester School of Medicine also traced nerve fibres to the thymus, spleen, lymph nodes, and bone marrow—all parts of the immune system. Since all nerves are ultimately linked to the brain, the work of these scientists documents clear connection.

Continuing research has further identified the 'chemical' links between the brain and the immune system. Bit by bit our scientists are assembling data suggesting that our anatomical systems communicate with each other. There are hundreds of bio-chemicals carrying messages back and forth. These substances, many of which are known to have a powerful effect on mood and emotion, provide a molecular way to understand the long suspected connection between state of mind and the state of health.

While at the National Institute of Mental health in 1987, Candace Pert and her colleague Michael Ruff announced that monocytes—immune cells that help heal wounds, repair tissue and ingest bacteria—are sensitive to chemicals produced in the brain called neuropeptides. There is particularly strong concentration of neuropeptide producing cells in the brain's limbic system, which controls emotions.

What all this research has established is that there is the molecular equivalent of telephone lines between brain and the immune system, in which the white blood cells receive messages directly from the brain.

Mind wanders in the past and future, to help you in the present

We know, mind always wanders, but it is difficult to explain. We introduced a 'paradigm of experience' as a heuristic device for a meaningful understanding of this phenomenon. We believe that the mind segregates our pleasant experiences from the unpleasant ones; they are housed in Memorial House. It has two special halls. Hall of Fame is designed as a gallery for the display of the achievements, successes, memorabilia, souvenirs, personal effects of great people. Hall of Shame displays the shameful deeds behind the success stories of great people.

Mind buries all its unpleasant experiences in the Cemetery. It has two interesting places. Burning pyre is one, where memories of failures and disappointments keep burning till such time they are forgiven and forgotten. Kind garden is the place where unpleasant memories of failures, are forgiven and forgotten before they are buried. It has a Kindergarten where important lessons are taught from the failures, mistakes and set backs. All the necessary lessons for achieving success are taught.

Mind always plays with ideas, and produces pleasant dreams. They are housed in Dreamland. It has two divisions. Creative Realm is a place where sweet dreams, day-dreams, fantasies are stored.

Futuristic Domain is a place where concerns about our future are entertained. Future is visualised, and future plans are entertained. It is here that future hopes are raised, aspirations and ambitions are built.

Mind is also concerned about fears of uncertainty in future. In the Dark Zone, it apprehends fears of dangers. It has the House of Horrors where fears about future uncertainty are exaggerated through illusions and delusions. In the House of Torture, it gives experiences of pain and suffering imagined in future.

Mind wonders in the microcosm it has created. It's main concern is about the *present* – its problems and issues. For this purpose it wonders in the past experiences and future dreams and visions. From the past it brings out the self-confidence, and lessons from our successes and failures. From the future, it brings back, dreams to be realised, and the future plans, to work out strategies to achieve goals. Mind also brings back to the present, the imagined uncertainties in the future. It prepares you in advance as to how to deal with anticipated problems, dangers, and sufferings.

It is mainly concerned about your life here and now. It is fully engrossed over your day to day problems. It tries to help find solutions. For this purpose it loves to wander in the world it has created: your own world of past, present and future. Your past experience can be a great source of strength. The mind believes in your dreams, and creative abilities. It believes in your ability to foresee future and works for it. It has tremendous confidence in your abilities to deal with current problems. It is totally committed to help you achieve a happy fulfilled life.

Our purpose here is to ponder over the human predicaments, and examine how we can make our lives happy. Just before that let us visit the secret world of our mind — the past, future and present of our lives.

Chapter 3
The Past: That Never Comes Back

The past is malleable and flexible, changing as our recollection interprets and re-explains what has happened.

Peter Berger (1925 —)
Professor Emeritus of Religion, Sociology and Theology, Director, Institute for the Study of Economic Culture, Department of Religion, Boston University.

Forget your past circumstances whether they be sorrows or joys. The one is not without remedy, the other not perfect. Both are past, why remember them. Why should you carry about parched corn when you dwell among fields white unto harvest? Why carry putrid water in the bottom of a rancid skin, when living in a land of fountains and brooks that run among hills? Why clasp a handful of withered flowers, when the grass is shown with their bright eyes opening to the sunshine.

Alexander MacLaren (1826- 1910)
British preacher, Union Chapel, Manchester

Mind, our friend, is keen on showing the microcosm it has created. *I* volunteered to come along with *me* to give company. We agreed that we should visit the two most important places in the great network of our memory which stores all our experiences. Most of our memories fall into two categories : the pleasant and the unpleasant. The pleasant memories are generally associated with our successes and achievements; and the unpleasant ones with failures, disappointments and painful sufferings.

Memorial House

The Memorial House is the place where the mind stores all the things associated with our achievements and the delightful feelings associated with pleasant experiences. Most desirable deeds are exhibited in the Hall of Fame. Undesirable deeds are exhibited in the Hall of Shame.

The Memorial House is a lofty building on a small hill in a green valley. Red woods around are singing softly as if welcoming the visitors. Subtle touch of the cool breeze is pleasing to the senses. Look at those delightful lights! Everything is brilliantly illuminated, beautifully decorated—purple curtains, golden hangings, colourful festoons all over the place. Oh, what a sight! People are waiting to welcome you with garlands of roses.

Hall of Fame

The Hall of Fame looks like a museum of sorts. A gallery for the exhibition of eminent deeds of great people. Many of their achievements are on display: outstanding achievements, significant contributions, acclaimed successes, and the honours bestowed upon them. Big successes, small achievements, patents, medals, certificates, testimonials, everything connected with their success finds a place here. Biographies of successful people, albums of their photographs, writings, diaries, memoirs, even personal effects and memorabilia acquire the status of valuable artefacts. They are carefully preserved and displayed for the visitors to see. Portraits of great achievers are hung on the walls, just six feet above the floor so that everything gets attention. There are two brass plates with shining letters displaying two famous quotations:

> *"A good name is more to be desired than great riches. Esteem is better than silver and gold"*—Solomon.
>
> *"The way to gain reputation is to endeavour to be what you desire to appear."*—Socrates

Look at that portrait of yours, in the central hall. A life-sized oil painting with a beautifully carved gilded frame. It is indeed a magnificent painting. Did you see that? You are looking straight into the eyes of the audience. Your image is looking at you with great admiration, as if saying, "but for you this painting wouldn't have been here." And *mind* is also saying, "all this is because of your achievements. What a stupendous work you have done! Congratulations. Keep it up".

Look at that bronze statue! It's indeed a beautiful replica of yours. One of your admirers made it. He needs appreciation too. Tell him, he had produced a great work of art. That way, you will learn admiring the work of others as well as yours.

You must be wondering why you are led to this counter first, when there are so many great people who deserve to be admired. That's because people are self-centered, and you are not an exception. You like to be appreciated and admired first; others take the next priority. Now, you have the choice to visit other counters to know more about them. If you don't have time, you may skip them for now. Some other time, you may like to know more about them; and refer to their biographies, encyclopedias or video clippings and whatever.

Delight yourself with the memories of your successful experiences. Sweet memories of your achievements are like honey to the palate. Relish and enjoy whenever you want. You have succeeded in the past; and you have a considerable number of achievements to your credit. But remember, no achievement is too small to enjoy. It will certainly boost up your self-image and enhance your feelings of self worth. It will build up your self-confidence—an absolute requirement for success in life. It is a product of your past successes. Therefore you should visit the Hall of Fame every now and then and remind yourself of your triumphs to cement your feelings of personal worth. Delightful feelings associated with your successes will generate more self-confidence that triggers your success mechanism.

But don't try to show off yourself at this place. You might as well face an awkward situation like Charlie Chaplin. He once entered a Charlie Chaplin look-alike contest in Monte Carlo—and came in *third*! You never know what will happen to you.

Hall of Shame

It is located just behind the Hall of Fame. This place looks like a junk yard. All the untold flip side stories of achievers are exhibited here for the benefit of the visitors. The most despicable deeds of great people are on display. "Did you see what I saw?" *I* asked *me*. "How come there is a statue of Alexander the Great?" Yes, yes, we remembered. *I* think it was in *Encyclopaedia Britannica* (10:618) that we read about Seleucus Nicator: "Of all the Macedonian generals, he was the only one who did not repudiate his wife after Alexander's death." What the statement did say, in not saying what it did not say? What does that mean? Oh! my …. What a shame on this man! What kind of greatness is this? Of course, we read that he was "not without romantic impulses;" but we are not aware of this disgraceful side of his character. That perhaps is the reason why he did not live his full term. He lived only for 33 years (356-323 BC). What an irony of fate!

Again there is a passage about his capture of Thebes. Every able-bodied man except the family and the descendants of poet Pindar, was sold into slavery. What a shame for the great conqueror! His supporters explain that he needed money to pay salaries to a great number of his soldiers. Is that believable? If he needed money, why in the first place, did he burn the riches of Athens? Did he forget the teachings of great philosopher Aristotle, his personal tutor? In the royal parlance, perhaps, the ends justify the means. Any way, does that make anyone great?

How come Ashoka, one of the greatest emperors of India is here? Yes, we remember, he invaded Kalinga in 261 BC. A replica of his edict at Shahbazagrahi is installed right beside his statue. It says, "In this war in Kalinga, men and animals numbering one hundred and fifty thousand were carried away captive from that country." What the edict did not say was the shameful act: they were sold away as slaves. It continued, "as many as one hundred thousand were killed there in action, and many times that number perished." What a misery for the innocent folks of Kalinga! It proclaims the royal repentance. "After that, now that the country of Kalinga has been conquered, the beloved of the gods is devoted to an intense practice of the duties of *Dhamma,* to a longing for *Dhamma* and to the inclination of *Dhamma* among people. This is due to repentance of the beloved of the gods on having conquered the country." What if a great emperor repents for his heinous crimes? The religious principle of *Dhamma* is certainly not a magic wand. The guilt of causing untold misery to millions of people does not vanish just like that by waving the wand. Does it? What a farce?

Did you recognise this statue? Is it not the image of Julius Caesar, the greatest ruler of the Roman Empire? How come? The explanation is implicit in the golden letters, written below the statue: "When Caesar is in Rome no man's wife is safe." What a reputation! What a shame!

Of course we were not surprised to see Adolf Hitler. Look at that maniac! He had the ambition to rule the world at the cost of millions of innocent people killed. See those pictures of his shameless campaigns, ethnic prejudices, concentration camps, gas chambers. Millions of innocent Jews were mercilessly killed. Is it possible for a single man to bring so much misery to so many in the world?

We were wondering how could men do such disgusting things. Then I saw a quotation of Harry Truman written on a wall: "Men often mistake notoriety to fame and would rather be remarked for their vices and follies than not be noticed at all." But the truth remains, nothing can right the wrong they have done. "Seldom are we given a chance to right a terrible wrong. Once done, a wrong shapes us in ways we don't understand. Even when we think we have buried it in our memory, the wrong is there, festering, waiting to be righted," says George Orick

What! Isn't it your statue? *I* asked. Immediately the *mind* told *me* even my statue is there. "Don't be surprised," *mind* explained, "almost every body is represented here; one only has to look for it. Every shameful thing you did is recorded here. *I* was wondering why my shortcomings were not shown first. Immediately *mind* gave the explanation: "Oh! That's because every body hates to know one's own faults; and would like to be the first to know other's shortcomings."

Just before leaving the hall, *I* saw a beautiful plaque with golden letters: *"Blessed are the people whose names are not found here"*!

Cemetery

The Cemetery is associated with our failures, disappointments, setbacks and all the unpleasant feelings in life. It's a strange burial-ground. Looming black clouds above are fast covering the sky, as if in a hurry to provide a cool shade. Silver lines at the fringes are gleaming hopefully once in a while. A low-pitched groan is audible from the great elms and oaks around. Barren trees that lost the autumn leaves are nodding with empathy at the bereaved visitors. They seem to be saying "your pain is in my heart". Dry leaves on the ground started rolling slowly with a subtle rustle, like the unwelcome memories. Windy draft is yet to come, but the comforting cool breeze is visible in the waving blades of sighing grass. Every other thing stood still. Silence here is so profound that it was like being here in the void before the beginning of time. The mood is serene and the feelings compassionate. Here we come with our condolences to pay our respect to the dead—failures, mistakes, disappointments, insults, humiliations, unhappy experiences.

When we feel sorry for the failures and mistakes we are engulfed by depressing emotions. When our *mind* expressed compassion for our failures, it is heartening to hear those soothing words of support and encouragement. It is indeed a very bitter-sweet occasion, because we are going to examine and review both these aspects.

Burning Pyre

Yonder is an eternal burning pyre of miserable feelings that remind half-hearted attempts, miserable failures, utter disappointments, deplorable results, and humiliating defeats, insulting comments and all the unpleasant experiences. Once in a while the flames flare up, like the churning of burning heart. That is the way some people prefer to set fire to their feelings caused by their failures. Perhaps that is the reason why they like cremation by fire rather than the burial. But unfortunately there is no end to that. Hot coals here never become ashes. The burning feelings continue to flare up as long as they are remembered. Psychotherapist Bill Little says, "Burning your self at the stake is not only useful in generating bad feelings in your self, it also disgusts the people around you—which enables you to feel even worse." Many people who suffer from burning feelings are not aware of this.

Kind Garden

Kind garden is an interesting spot. At the entrance we find an archway with its motto written in large letters: 'Learn, forgive and forget'. That's how it has got its name. Its main attraction is Kindergarten. This is where the visitors learn important lessons from their mistakes; and how to convert a failure into a success. Thereafter people forgive themselves, and others for their failures, mistakes, setbacks, and disappointments. They bury all those dead bodies right here and forget them for ever.

After all progress in every thing involves setbacks. And failures and losses are inevitable in life. "Every one gets a chance. No one lives a fail proof life forever," says Amitai Etzioni, a professor of Social Economics in Washington. Success and failure are the part of life of every human being. No one can achieve success in every attempt. Failures are not permanent; and the same is true of successes. One must accept the fact that every one is imperfect. And you are not an exception. Ann Landers says, "It's done. Finished. Over. There is nothing you can do about it. Take heart from the knowledge that something good can come of it if it teaches you a lesson. Profit from it –then forget it."

That's right. Why carry those bitter memories of the past failures. We don't know really why. This is particularly not justified when we are hale and healthy, reaping plenty of successes whenever we harvest. Learn to be kind to yourself and show compassion for your mistakes failures, setbacks, disappointments. Compassionate attitudes toward other people—and most important, toward yourself—are necessary to understand people and yourself. Psychologist Robert Staub, believes the no. 1 cause of failure is a lack of self awareness.

"Our mistakes are easier to forgive than the means by which we try to whitewash them," says Markus M Ronner. Be kind to your self and adopt the 'learn forgive and forget' policy of this garden. "Not that we deny our failures; this would be unrealistic," says, Maxwell Maltz. "We should use our blunders as guides to learning, then forget them." Bury those mistakes and failures that burn our hard feelings and give them a final funeral. "Keep a fair-sized back yard in which to bury the faults of your friends," says Henry Ward Beacher. You must put the injury out of your mind, refusing to dwell upon it. You must forget them along with the incessant psychic burns and the unhappy feelings. That is, you must not dig them up every time you remember them. If they show up by any chance, lead them to the Kindergarten. That is where they can pick up some important lessons useful in future. Marlon Brando is said to have wandered so much on the way to kindergarten that, his sister Jocelyn eventually had to take him to school on a leash. May be, you need such a leash to take your unwieldy failures to the kindergarten here.

Kindergarten

This is where we learn from our mistakes and failures. We can learn many things, if only we have the curiosity of a child to learn. Important lessons of life are taught here with object-lessons, toys and games. Look at those innocent children playing with blocks of failures and toys of mistakes. Mr Froebel ponders over their ignorance, and teaches them what they can learn. They teach the most unforgettable lessons of knowledge about the realities of this world. They teach that failures are one's attempts to succeed; and they help to know individual limitations. They remind us that our mistakes are new lessons for success. They teach what is needed to succeed in life. Most important lessons are those that bring out the insights from our failures and mistakes. They teach here, how to see the failures as stepping stones and convert a failure into a success. They keep telling everyone, *Successful people are not the people who don't fail, they are the people who learn from their failures.* Every child is taught to imbibe the qualities of successful people, and work hard to learn and achieve whatever they can. A wall-hanging says, "The world is a kind of kindergarten where millions of bewildered children are trying to spell SUCCESS with wrong blocks."

Every person who wishes to achieve success should be willing to make honest mistakes. A failure "teaches something about your strengths and acquaints you with your limitations," says Rabbi Harold

Kushner, "That is an important part of maturity." Many psychologists confirm that people who willingly risk failure and learn from failures have the best chance of succeeding whatever they try. On the other hand, the unsuccessful people instinctively avoid risk due to fear of failure, even when a smart gamble might pay off. Vic Sussman says, "do not fear failure. It is the normal way to map the unknown—and can be your greatest tutor." You should try to reduce your fear of failure. You must accept the fact that every one is imperfect. Therefore you must accept your mistakes and failures and try to learn from them. They can lead you to the royal road to success.

Happy memories can create a paradise on earth

Remember, "The past is malleable, changing as our recollection interprets and re-explains what has happened," as explained by Professor Peter Berger. The past is like a kaleidoscope; every time you tilt it, its colourful reflections change. Every time, your mind re-explains your past experiences, your interpretations take on different meanings. That is the inevitable problem with our memories.

Whatever they are, heed to the advice of Alexander Mac Lauren:

> "Forget your past circumstances whether they be sorrows or joys. The one is not without remedy, the other not perfect. Both are past, why remember them. Why should you carry about parched corn when you dwell among fields white unto the harvest? Why carry putrid water in a rancid skin when living in a land of fountains and brooks that run among hills? Why clasp a handful of withered flowers, when the grass is shown with their bright eyes opening to the sunshine."

Why not learn to live in the present where happiness is waiting for you! Don't forget to remember that your happy memories can always create a virtual paradise on earth!

Chapter 4

The Future: That is Not Yet

I feel that you are justified in looking into the future with true assurance, because you have a mode of living in which we find joy of life and joy of work are harmoniously combined. Add to this the spirit of ambition which pervades your being, and seems to make the day's work like a happy child at play.

Albert Einstein (1879- 1955)
Physicist, Philosopher, Nobel Prize for physics 1921.

When you relinquish the desire to control future, you can have more happiness.

Nicole Kidman (1967-)
Oscar winning Best Actress, Producer.

"Future is that period of time in which our affairs prosper, our friends are true, and our happiness is assured," said Ambrose Bierce. When we think of future, it is an exciting time but it is also one that is fraught with peril. We don't have to worry about it immediately though. Because, as Dean Acheson said, "the best thing about future is that it comes one day at a time." Albert Einstein goes one step ahead, "I never think of future, it comes soon enough." But then, we mortals cannot just relax and postpone our thinking about future. It may not be urgent but it is very important. Just think, when you think all is lost, the future remains in our minds.

Dreamland

We went on a conducted tour of the Dreamland. Behold, it's the world of your dreams. Every thing here is fantastic. Look at the warm sun of pure gold; and the backdrop of incredible velvet-blue sky with an elusive streak of rainbow path. Acquaintance of the wind here is a kind of wisdom. It is an understanding of the boundless horizons. Fly on the magic carpet. Take a view of the panorama that awaits you. Look at the deep blue sea of infinite hope— gigantic, limitless, blazing with splintered sunlight—it curved away to infinity, dwarfing the land, rivaling the sky. Below were tops of trees queerly inverted, and—even more unimaginable—the backs of gulls in flight. The meandering path through the dunes was mere thread. Dew drops on the evergreen trees shimmered iridescent light. Look at the sprawling gardens laid with carpets of green grass, exotic plants in a riot of colours and the trees in bloom with fragrant flowers. Experience the tingling touch of the affectionate breeze, musical notes of the nightingales, beautiful dancing peacocks, innocent children playing make-believe games. All this in one glance!

This is a virtual heaven. This is the world of fantasies, dreams, day-dreams, imaginations, hopes, aspirations, and ambitions. It is like a dream and vision put together. We have realistic dreams, and intuitive visions of prophecy. Here, at your wish, beautiful palaces rise in a second. Floating above the clouds, they will come to you at your command. Wave your magic wand. Create all the wonderful things you want. You can travel in time machines and visit people who lived in the past and those that would live in the future. You will meet strange and funny creatures. Your mighty genie is at your service. It can do great things for you which you have neither imagined nor expected. Make your wishes known. Thy will be done! Tall and hefty men, looking like champion body builders, move around to protect you. Heavenly fairies, merry maidens, lovely ladies, and beautiful girls are at your service. Relish this wonderful world of your dreams. Enjoy the exhilarating exuberance to your heart's content, before you switch over to the mundane world on earth. You can return to the present, any time you want, but remember your future concerns will always remain. Still need a reason to visit Dreamland?

Mind told us that Dreamland is the playground for your ideas. People who visit this place produce great ideas. They play with them and dream fantastic things; and they try to live up to their dreams. In real life dreamers grow up to become doers and achievers.

Creative Realm

Children make castles in the sand; grown-ups build castles in the air. There are no limits for our creative imagination. Absolutely true. "Our castle is psychological, nonetheless real," says John Goodwin. Our dreams and visions are imaginary, yet they have tremendous impact on our lives here and now. "We would still be in dark ages were it not for wishful thinking," says Alex Osborn. "Without it most of the achievement of mankind would never have been started,". Remember, "first must come the dream and then the reality, as without dream there will be no launching of the missile," says Arthur Lipper III.

A dream is most frequently, a wish for that which is not presently available. A dream does not have to be inflexible, unmoving or static. A dream should, to be healthy and constructive, reflect that which is just beyond reach, but still be available predictably possible, otherwise the dream becomes a fantasy to the point of becoming a nightmare.

Jerome Singer, a professor of psychology at Yale University says that clinical and experimental research has confirmed that "daydreams are normal to all active minds" and they "make our lives more creative and original". Creative scientists, artists, and writers are greatly given to indulging their fantasies and engaging in playful mental explorations of the most odd and outlandish possibilities that come to mind. Some of the greatest scientific discoveries arose from the willingness to daydream. If you can discover your dreams and truly believe in them, you can help yourself become the person you are designed to be. Discover your dreams and get moving toward it. Any movement will be progress only if it is in the direction of the destination. That is the first step in realizing your dreams.

Futuristic Domain

"Futurology" was coined by Ossip Flechtheim a German historian in 1949. It is a science of visualising and predicting future. "The best way to predict future is to create it" said Peter Drucker. Make plans for your future and implement them in small steps, one after the other. Review progress and supplement with whatever is needed to do. Everything is within your powers.

Mind, our friend, reminded the words of Charles F Kettering: "We should be concerned about the future because we will have to spend the rest of our lives there." Concern for future necessitated the creation of a different world. Futuristic Domain is a heavenly abode that helps us dream and expect great things in future.

"It is indeed an exotic place where your imagination is at work, guessing what the future is like," says our friend. "Daydream your fantasies, enjoy the ecstasies. It can add a little bit of magic in your life. Think differently, imaginatively, creatively. Know the hopes to raise, aspirations to cherish, ambitions to fulfill and dreams to realise. Dream unfulfilled desires first, you can realise them later in life. Imagine how best you can adjust to the anticipated changes in life. Foresee the future. Make a realistic picture, examine various scenarios. Make a list of your future goals, and make your plans – short-term and long-term. Foresee future problems and make contingency plans to deal with anticipated risk. Think of your strategies."

Leonardo da Vinci did visit this place several times. He made here, all his designs of the flying machines, the parachutes, armoured tanks, and other scientific inventions. Wright brothers who wanted to fly, finally realised the moment of magic when their dream became a reality on the historic day of December 17, 1903. Recently, we have seen the computer revolution. Jay Forester invented the magnetic memory for computers. Bill Gates showed his computer wizardry. Tim Berners-Lee invented here world wide web in 1991. Marc Andreeson invented the Internet browser in 1994. We are now enjoying the fruits of their ideas. Who knows what discoveries and inventions you will make?

It is here Alvin Toffler foresaw the coming disease of change. In *Future Shock* he tells us how it can be averted. In *The Third Wave* he tells us in advance the revolutionary things that are going to invade the world; and how we should be prepared to live with them.

Dark Zone

The Dark Zone is a dreadful domain that apprehends future shocks and helps us cope with threatening situations. "The courage to imagine the otherwise is our greatest resource adding colour and suspense to all our life," says Daniel Boorstin. These dreams and visions of fears of future uncertainty have tremendous impact on our lives.

At the outset, the *mind* warned us about the frightening things in the Dark Zone: "It is pitch dark out here. The strange light here is as dark as darkness itself. To see things, you require special glasses that are used for night vision. Curiosity may lead you here but be prepared to expect the unexpected. Unfamiliarity and ignorance of the place may induce nyctophobia—the fear of darkness. This may start a chain reaction of other fears that include the fear of death."

Fear of the unknown may frighten you more than the dangers you imagine. Silence here is somewhat deafening, neither hard hitting nor subtle. Once in a while you will hear high-pitched whine from the pines around. Bizarre wind sounds cruel, reminding the curse of this place. Ambience here is eerie and experience could be scary. Slug-like creepy animals with slimy tentacles and stinging flies will scare you like hell. White ghosts and black witches frighten you most if you fear them. You might even encounter strange aliens with pointy ears, wearing out-of-this world clothing and unconventional weapons. Every thing here induces fear—of the future events, uncertainty and insecurity.

Remember, human behaviour has been in the formation for thousands of years. En masse human behaviour is immutable. When people slip into Dark Zone they panic. They make irrational decisions. All this is caused by the fear of the unknown. "The only thing we have to fear is fear itself," said Franklin D. Roosevelt in a radio speech, during the dark days of depression. "Nothing is so much to be feared as fear," wrote the naturalist, Henry David Thoreau. Three centuries before a French essayist Michel de Montaigne wrote, "The thing of which I have most fear is fear."

According to King Solomon, human beings need to fear only God, but not anything else. He said, "fear God and obey his commands; there is no more than this. For God brings everything we do to judgement, and every secret, whether good or bad." Alexander Mac Laren says, "people of all ages fought their fears in one way or another, but the only thing that really conquers fear is faith in the Lord: "I will trust and not be afraid." "Only he who can say 'The lord is my strength' can say 'of whom shall I be afraid'?"

Whether you believe in God or not, you should not forget your belief in yourself. That's what gives you strength and power to face the frightening things in life. Be conscious of the frailties which are basic to human nature—fear of future uncertainty is one of them.

When fear advances logic backs away. "We are never prepared for what we expect," says James A Michner. This gives rise to feelings of anxiety. Learn to deal with it first; if it is realistic fear, be prepared to take necessary precautions.

House of Horrors

And there is the House of Horrors. It's a picture house that shows horror films. It is fitted with mirrors that generate illusions, delusions and confusing images. What appears is not real. The real things appear as unreal. The best horror movies are shown here. The best of Stephen King's stories can be enjoyed here. *The House of 1000 Corpses,* a horror film considered as one of the top 10 films of 2003, was opened at number seven. Such is the demand for horror movies. That only shows that there is a great number of people who love 'funny scare'. It's also a great fun observing people who get scared in the theatre. Sane people leave the threat in the theatre and take home the fun; and enjoy it every time they remember. Full of delightful funny scare, these films are made for the entertainment and amusement of the brave hearts. Enjoy the fun of imagination, albeit, of unreal threats. There is nothing to worry because they are not real anyway. Let us see what we can do with them in real life!

On the other hand some feeble-hearted people leave the fun in the theatre and take home the threats. Every time they remember they are driven mad. Life threatening experiences coupled with lack of self-confidence keeps their anxieties on the roll. Because of their weak hearts, they often suffer from phobias and nightmares. This in turn results in mental problems and psychosomatic illness.

House of Torture

It houses every imaginable gadget that is used to torture people: electric chairs, drills, shock producers, gas chambers, guns, daggers, hatchets etc. Every pain causing instrument is available before you name it. One graceful practice here is, no one is tortured without their consent. Even choice of the instruments of torture is left to the volunteers.

"Man's chief enemy is his own unruly nature and the dark forces pent up within him," says Earnest Jones. Brave hearts come here to act as machos to enjoy the pleasure of inflicting pain on others. Feeble hearts visit this place to enact the role of victims to enjoy the pleasures of torture. Endurance is one thing that is learnt here, the hard way—by experiencing excruciating pain. As William Barclay put it, "Endurance is not just the ability to bear a hard thing, but to turn it into glory".

The feeble-hearted who lack self-confidence, often experience sufferings. They carry their childhood memories of helpless frightening events. They feel they are the victims; they believe people in the world are out to victimise them. With pessimistic attitudes, they not only see but anticipate suffering everywhere. Pain is their lot, and suffering their fate. They anticipate, expect, and experience suffering in their lives.

None can control future

Our dreams and visions of future generate lots of hopes of bright future. When you project with future, hope appears on the horizon like a rainbow after the rain. The very sight of it is joyful. But the future is not without fears, as it gives rise to uncertainty, insecurity, and even nightmares. Thus, worrying about future is one of our great sources of unhappiness. When we spend time thinking about future, we are missing the happiness in the present.

Yes, we are "justified in looking into the future", as rightly said by Albert Einstein. But our thinking about future invariably invokes hopes and fears. Our worries about the uncertain future generates the wish to control it; but it is absolutely futile because no one knows the shape of things yet to come. That is why Nicole Kidman says "when you relinquish the desire to control future, you can have more happiness". Our challenge lies in implementing future plans and the wisdom in accepting whatever happens here and now.

Chapter 5

The Present: The Only True Reality

True happiness is to enjoy the present, without anxious dependence on future.

Lucius Annaeus Seneca (c.55 BC—AD 39)
Stoic philosopher

For all that has been, thanks,
For all that will be, yes.
Don't look back,
Don't dream about future either.
It will neither give you back the past
Nor will satisfy other dreams.
Your duty, your reward,
Your destiny are here and now.

Dag Hammarskjold (1905 – 61)
Swedish diplomat, Former Secretary General UN.
Nobel Prize for Peace 1961

The Present

"Past is really almost as much a work of imagination as the future," says Jessamyn West. "I have realized that the past and future are real illusions that they exist in the present which is what there is, and all there is," says Alan Watts. "It's the present moment that matters. The past and future are only succession of present moments, but we are always tempted to exaggerate their importance because they are gone, or because they are not yet come," says Wilfrid Lemoine.

Since the nature has cycles of its own, man is forced to adjust his living pattern accordingly. He works in the fields during the day and sleeps in the night. He sows in the rainy season and reaps the harvest when it is ripe. Even when he works in modern offices he follows a work schedule. He marks his steps in tune with the beats of the distant drummer. Our daily life follows a regular pattern; and we are often tired of the mundane routine work: the drudgery of the family chores, the requirements of the family, children's education, their settlement in life, comfort and security, health and financial problems and so many other matters in the society. We are not conscious of the finer moments in the present due to the humdrum of life on earth.

Besides we are flooded with lots of information that comes from newspapers, magazines, TV programmes, talk shows, and video cinemas. The *present* batters at us with such an incredible quantum of information that the pensive mind often retreats in to the past. In search of, if not wisdom, at least a peaceful meander into the by-lanes of our own experiences. Our mind is spending most of the time either in the *past* or *future*. As a result, we often run away from the discordant *present*.

Our mind oscillates back and forth in the stream of eternal time. In this process our *past* and *future* influence our *present*. Memories of our *past* experiences and our hopes and fears of *future* have profound impact on our *present* actions. Our wandering mind makes us recall the pleasant and unpleasant experiences; and guides us in seeking pleasure and happiness avoiding pain and sorrow. It has tremendous influence over our behaviour. It is serious about solving the problems we face everyday. But we are totally unaware of the movements of our mind.

Impact of the past on the present
Our mind stores all past experiences in our memory bank. It always brings back our memories whenever we want. Even otherwise, it always wanders in the *past* looking for all kinds of information relating

to *present* problems or issues, because it knows that life is a series of problems. The main job of our mind is to help solve our problems in life and make us happy. It supplies self-confidence, courage, determination to achieve and the skills we need to deal with the present problems. Our mind works to satisfy our needs, achieve life goals, and helps us enjoy what life offers. It also joins us in sharing our feelings of unhappiness when we encounter failures, setbacks, and disappointments. It helps us reminisce pleasurable and unpleasant experiences. In this way our past impacts on the present.

Pleasant experiences

Our mind does many lively wonders that help sustain our life. It usually visits our underground reservoir of aggregate memories of past events. In Memorial House it reviews our experience and revels in our successes and admires our achievements.

Wonders that sustain life

Sometimes it visits, the Hall of Fame to have a look at our achievements and delight in the honours bestowed upon us. It reminds our potential, strengths, abilities, aptitudes, interests, attitudes. "The greatest builder of confidence is your ability to do something, —almost any thing, well," said Gordon Dean. When we remember past successes we gain a lot of confidence in our capabilities. Mind builds in us the kind of confidence that says, "I can do it". "Self confidence is the first requisite to great undertakings," said Samuel Johnson. We look at ourselves with a sense of personal worth and pride. It boosts up our self-confidence, nurtures self-esteem and enhances self-reliance.

It frequently visits this place to take all the lessons of past successes into the present so that they can help solve the current problems. The experience gained in doing things successfully, is brought to light to explore its use in attempting more difficult tasks. The skills that are acquired are not only used but also improved further.

When it visits the Hall of Shame it invokes our conscience and persuades us not to indulge in shameful acts. One of Ashoka's edicts says,: "Verily, the slaughter, the death and deportation of men which took place in the course of the conquest of an unconquered country, are now considered deplorable by the beloved of the Gods." It is evident that his conscience was pricked, when his mind visited the Hall of Shame, after the terrible war of Kalinga. A visit to the Hall of Shame often helps us realise the immoral transgressions, omissions and commissions in our actions. After all what we do in the name of achievement should not ignore our moral obligations.

We must keep some souvenirs of our past, or how will we ever prove it is not a dream. These mementos will act as incentives for larger achievements in life. Our memories of the past successes will come to our rescue in everyday ordeals. They will reinforce our urge to succeed and do something worthwhile in life. They will act as spring boards for future success. Remember, our rich experience, self-confidence, the most valuable set of skills and talents, are virtually our diamonds in store. They are the assets we can fall back upon in times of need.

Blunders that harm life

Sometimes our *self* tries to dominate the *mind*. In the process, at times, we commit some *deadly blunders* that might harm our life and even cause death. Not knowing this, many people get trapped in their own pit, and continue to suffer throughout their lives. If we want to redeem ourselves from this agonising hell, we must know first what blunders we are capable of committing. And then allow our mind to continue the good work it is doing to help achieve whatever we want.

When our mind visits the Hall of Fame, we see all the things we have done successfully. When we compare our achievements with mediocre achievers, we may feel great. We may develop over-confidence, ignore logic, risk, and the need for interdependence, and start thinking no one can beat us. If you base your opinion of your self on achievements alone, you may develop superiority complex; you may be induced to brag about yourself. "'Don't talk about yourself, it will be done when you leave,' says Wilson Mizner. You know the proverb, 'Pride comes before disaster, and arrogance before fall.' You may even suffer from delusions of grandeur. If you indulge in such unrealistic thoughts, and you may even develop disorganized thinking, and end up in an asylum.

It may generate a sense of invincibility. Remember the story of Alexander's deification. Having won the known world of his times he thought he was no less than a living god. He insisted that his subjects should consider him as one of their gods. Many small states that came under his rule did accept. Even the reluctant state, Sparta complied ironically saying "since Alexander wishes to be god, let him be a god." Yes, it was possible for a powerful man to get away with it. But for people like you and me, such an attitude can create great problems.

When our mind visits the Hall of Shame we will discover that many great men have done some shameful things; and that we are not an exception. So we may think that whatever we have done is not such a bad thing. We may even imitate the great people and follow their foot steps in doing the wrong things. This is the blunder of shameless thinking.

Unpleasant experiences
Our mind continues to work with the purpose of finding avenues for our happiness, but we often encounter unhappiness. When we remember our mistakes and failures two things can happen. We may become depressed and develop inferiority complex or we may try to learn from them. We know this is going to help us in our future endeavours.

Wonders that sustain life
Sometimes our mind visits the Cemetery to express condolences for our dead failures. It ponders over our failures and lost opportunities. It takes us to the Kind Garden where it helps us to forgive ourselves and forget failures, mistakes, setbacks, disappointments in life. Pondering over our ignorance, it tries to teach what we can learn in the Kindergarten. It teaches the most unforgettable lessons from our past mistakes. It helps us learn that failures are our attempts to succeed. It helps us know our limitations, and teaches the things needed to achieve success. It imparts a lot of knowledge of realities of this world and teaches bitter truths of life

Remember, your *self* and your *mind* are perfectly aligned to restore your lost dignity. It considers your failures and lost opportunities gives new insights from unpleasant experiences. It broadens your perspective on the realities of life. It often gives new meaning to such experiences. Joan Mills says, "At odd moments, I relived losses, failures, occasions of despair—powerful reminders of our capacity to stumble, feel hurt, and go on. Once I had taken nothing from these experiences but pain. Now there was meaning. I added it to my store of recollected good."

Sometimes you can find opportunities in the crisis you face, and in the failures you encounter. "When it is dark enough men see stars" says Ralph Waldo Emerson. Henry Wadsworth Longfellow says, "The lowest ebb is the turn of the tide." Who knows this could be a turning point, a watershed of your life.

When people face defeat they have a chance to discover their weaknesses as well as strengths. Henry Ward Breacher says, "Defeat is a school in which truth always grows strong." Yes, you will know the truth about your capabilities when you encounter failures. But remember, defeat is only in your thinking. Jan Christian Smuts says, "A man is not defeated by his opponents but by himself." Instead of thinking that a failure is defeat, if you can consider it as your attempt to succeed, you will soon recoup your lost confidence. It has been said, that enemy bombing campaigns designed to affect the general morale and the will to fight rarely succeed; many times they bolster the very determination they are supposed to break. Your failures should serve as your enemy's bombing campaigns to bolster your determination to survive. Your failures should reinforce your determination to learn and succeed.

Don't be discouraged by occasional setbacks, consider them as your attempts to succeed. Try alternate ideas, go experiment and learn how the new idea works. Don't expect success in the first attempt. Keep working till you succeed. Think of the phoenix phenomenon. Like the bird that rose from ashes to life again, you must rise above failures to success. General George Patton once said, "Success is how high you bounce when you hit the bottom."

Every failure is a learning experience. We gain a lot of knowledge about ourselves. While we come to know our lack of skills and limitations, we may also discover the hidden potential in us. We not only learn from mistakes, failures, but also learn what is required to succeed in life.

Blunders that harm life

Let us consider the possible harm that could be done to us, when our *self* interferes with normal working of our *mind*. Sometimes while the mind is doing its duty, our *self* comes along with its negative feelings. Some of these dormant unconscious feelings are deadly in their effect. They can create great perils in our lives such as anxiety and depression. Happy feelings from Hall of Fame and unhappy feelings from Cemetery may induce manic-depressive-psychosis. When the mind visits the Cemetery we remember our failures, but we may refuse to take responsibility for them. Sometimes we may try to find a scapegoat, blaming people and things for our misfortune. We may feel sorry for the unintended mistakes. "Mishaps are like knives that either serve us or cut us as we grasp them by the blade or by handle," says James Russell Lowell. "If we cry over them they make us miserable; learn from them they help us in our achievements."

Sometimes we may pine over the lost opportunities. We may even get into sinking feelings for a long time. These feelings have serious repercussions long after the event is over. Their memory might trigger revival of the same old depressive thoughts. In view of our failures, it may question our capabilities. It may even nurture inferiority complex in us. But remember, "No one can make you feel inferior without your consent," as said by Elenor Roosvelt.

Don't ever think you are checkmated by fate. You must know that fate bows to him who defies it. What the fate destroys, the will rebuilds. Believe in yourself, but not the fate. Don't resign or compromise in life. Don't be unduly anxious, stop worrying and start working.

Impact of the future on the present

Our mind not only helps us in our day to day problems, but also helps us in realising our dreams. It always looks forward and dreams about our future. It helps us make future plans and achieve what we want. In this process it builds up a lot of hopes. When it foresees possible dangers, it takes reasonable precautions and makes elaborate plans to deal with threats. It brings back our thinking about future and impacts the present behaviour.

Pleasant experiences
Wonders that sustain life

Our mind takes us to Dreamland to help us dream, day-dream and fantasise. In the Creative Realm it helps us dream all the creative things we always wanted to do. "The promise that forever lingers in the air is the one that leads you to realise your dreams, says Bharat Savur. "So, feed, feel, and follow that promise. This is the bliss of the promise—a contemplative contentment in the now, yet a strong surging will to do more, evermore. For the promise is the spa of human spirit." Charles H Townes, a Nobel Prize winning scientist, says "And it's in this promise that we must live. For, the Promised Land is neither a destination nor a journey. It is the eternal, ever-fresh present continuous environment."

In the Futuristic Domain, our imagination is at work, always thinking about the sunny days ahead. We examine various scenarios and make future plans—short-term and long-term. We foresee future problems and look for solutions. We raise hopes, build aspirations and ambitions. We all act out our fantasies and dreams, make plans to achieve whatever goals we set out. Soon, we make our visions a reality in life.

Consider the remarkable achievements of the people who visited the Creative Realm. Their achievements not only gave happiness for themselves but also benefit the mankind.

It was here, Michaelangelo, one of the world's greatest sculptors, carved the most celebrated *Pieta* in marble. It was here, Leonardo da Vinci painted *Mona Lisa,* the world's most praised painting. Great masters like Botticelli, Raphael, Titian, Rubens, Remembrandt visited this place. Even Vincent van Gogh and Pablo Picasso were here.

Great musicians like Johann Sebastian Bach, Wolfgang Amadeus Mozart, Ludwig von Beethoven, Frederic Chopin, Richard Strauss and Anton Bruckner were here.

William Shakespeare was here all the time writing great dramas. It was here, Lewis Carroll wrote *Alice In Wonderland,* the most praised children's story book. Rabindranath Tagore wrote here, the Nobel Prize winning *Gitanjali*. Yes, Richard Bach wrote here *Jonathan and the Seagull* Robert Pirsig wrote here *Zen and the Motor cycle Maintenance*. Salman Rushdie has written here *Midnight's Children*. Isaac Asimov wrote all his science fiction novels right here. Greg Bear has written here *Eon* and *The Queen of Angels*. Paul Allen planned his *Science Fiction Experience* here.

Surely, J K Rowling visited this place and wrote five Harry Potter books- published in at least 55 languages –that have sold 192 million copies worldwide. Her imagination was so fantastic that people eagerly ordered for the copies of her fifth book *Harry Potter and the Order of Phoenix*, long before its release in 2003. A recent film by Peter Jackson was based on Rowling's book, *The Lord of the Rings: Two Towers,* that won the Oscar for best visual effects (2003). Again he produced *The Lord of the Rings: The Return of the King* based on JRR Tolkien's middle earth trilogy: *The Fellowship of the Rings, The Two Towers* and *The Return of the King*. It has won 11 Oscars including The Best Picture award. (2004). All that fantastic imagination is possible only at this place. These creative persons couldn't have produced such wonderful things without visiting Dreamland.

Copernicus discovered here the truth about the solar system. He found that the earth revolves around the sun. It was indeed a revolutionary idea for the world that believed that the earth is the centre of the universe. Isaac Newton, a mint master by profession, was busy all the time worrying about the problems of minting coins. Yet, in his spare time, he loved to visit Dreamland where he made stunning discoveries like the Law of Gravitation which explains the movement of heavenly bodies; and the three basic Laws of Motion. William Herschel, who made his living in England by music, was preoccupied most of the time with music lessons and concerts. He used to visit this place frequently in his leisure time. And what a surprise! He discovered the planet Uranus and its four moons (1871).

While engaged in a routine teaching job as a professor, Albert Einstein found time to visit this place and formulated his Theory of General Relativity which declares that gravity controls the behaviour of planets, stars, galaxies, and the universe itself. Stephen Hawking came up with his theory of Black Holes which create and emit particles that explode. It is an attempt to reconcile the contradictions of Einstein's Theory of General Relativity and Quantum mechanics. That is the magic of this Dreamland! Just imagine what this place can do for you. Visit it whenever you are free, discover yourself what wonders are in store for you.

"You may be tall or short, fat or lean. All of us have our limitations but there are no limits to what we can achieve. And to achieve something we all need a vision," says John Buchanan, the Australian cricket team coach who led the Aussies to win the World Cup in 2003. "I often observe children and I am interested in their dreams. Sadly when we all grow up our thoughts often turn negative and our dreams lose their possibility. The need is to have a strong vision and then set up a process by which that dream can be achieved."

And he dwelt upon the importance of planning. "We planned for this World Cup for the last three to four years. We began with the process of identifying the players who will last for this World Cup. And in the last twelve months, we got our combination. It also meant that we have to take tough decisions." He says, "if we are obsessed with the results we are likely to forget the process of creating the victory. If you are process driven rather than being result driven, the results are bound to follow."

A visit to Futuristic Domain made it possible to discuss the hopes and fears of future human beings on the earth. Visions of future of this planet prompted a great debate. The pessimists, the doom sayers are pointing out that the population will breed to the limit of breakdown—of food supplies, water, sanitation, and above all frustrated hope, despair, misery, and revolt below the decks. And, of course, the threat of nuclear war and the possibility of the destruction of the planet itself. On the other hand the optimists, the technology-fixers, point to the possibility of trouble-free prospects due to advancing knowledge and modern applications of technology. The risk of war can be offset by embarking, patiently, unswervingly, devotedly, on the concrete and cooperative task of peace.

Get the message from Napoleon Hill: "Cherish your visions and dreams as they are children of your soul; the blue prints of your achievements." Remember, that everything is within your resources. Don't allow your dreams to fade; push up your horizon till your dreams are realised. We the dreamers ultimately will become the achievers.

Blunders that harm life

When we indulge in dreams, we live most of the time in the world of fantasy. We may build castles in the air and live in ivory towers. We may remain great dreamers but poor doers. And our dreams may induce flights of reality. People who use drugs are the dreamers who love the illusions of reality in their fantasies. When their illusions lead to delusions, thoughts get disorganised and disoriented, they may end up as schizophrenics.

When the mind visits the Futuristic Domain we may visualise great future. But we may be engrossed in dreams, always planning without concrete actions. We may prefer to live on hopes without initiating any action. We may look up for luck and nothing else. When we prefer to live most of the time in *future*, we often forget the realities of life in the *present*.

Unpleasant experiences
Wonders that sustain life

Rabindranath Tagore reminds us what the poet of *Ishopanishat* says: "They enter the region of darkness who pursue the transitory. But they enter the region of still greater darkness who pursue the eternal. He who knows the transitory and the eternal combined together crosses the steps of death by the help of the transitory and reaches immortality by the help of the eternal." This was the thinking of the Vedic man who repeated the prayer: *Asatoma sadgamaya*—(Oh god), Help me pass through the unreal to the real; *Tamaso ma Jyotirgamaya*—Dispel the darkness and lead me into the light, *Mrityorma amritam gamaya*—Give me immortality from this mortal life (Brihadaaranyaka Upanishat). Modern man may get the subtle meaning that the courage to face darkness may lead to challenging encounters that prolong life.

When mind visits the Dark Zone, it helps us identify realistic fears. When it visits the House of Horrors it helps to discriminate realistic fears from the unrealistic ones. "A good scare is worth more to a man than good advice," says E W Howe. It prepares us to take precautionary measures to deal with realistic fears.

When the mind visits the House of Torture it helps us foresee realistic sufferings in life. It helps us see a crisis in advance and make contingent plans to deal with it. It builds up hope, faith, courage, endurance, and resilience.

Imaginary threats create havoc in people's lives. Brave hearts make necessary preparations to counter danger. When people entertain realistic fears, like fear of death, they prepare themselves to face the possible or expected events. If they foresee a crisis, they make contingency plans to deal with it. Individuals learn the martial arts like judo and karate for self-defence. They may develop weapons and build up armed forces to deal with external threats.

Fear of death is such a great threat, that made life insurance a billion dollar business today. Because of this fear, health is a serious concern for everybody. It helps us develop medicines, treatment methods, well-equipped hospitals. Health education, medical research, preventive medicine are our top priorities. Gyms and health resorts will never lose their charm.

Frightening experiences of psychological torture often toughen our psyche. Sufferings increase our determination to survive. "Storms make oaks take deeper root," said George Herbert. They build up endurance and resilience. Our endurance is one thing we should be proud of.

"Whatever it is you are most afraid of, is never as bad in reality as your imagination makes it seem before you encounter it. Whatever it is you are afraid of, never turn tail and run away but go towards it. You may be surprised how easily you can handle it," says Geoffery Moorehouse. Thoughts of realistic fears reinforce belief in yourself and your ability to deal with them. They generate hope and faith. "Hope is wishing for a thing to come true; faith is believing that it will come true," says Norman Vincent Peale.

The Greek word for hope is *elpizo*, which means, "to anticipate in confident expectation." It also means "trust". It has been said that man can live about forty days without food, about three days without water, and about eight minutes without air, and only one second without hope. Dr Viktor Frankl, an Austrian psychiatrist, observed in *Man's Search for Meaning* that a prisoner did not continue to live long after hope was lost. But even the slightest ray of *hope*, the rumour of better food, a whisper about escape helped some of the camp inmates to continue living even under systematic horror.

"Faith is the refusal to panic," says D Martin Lloyd Jones. Faith makes the outlook bright and the future glorious. Faith is dead to doubts, dumb to discouragement, and blind to impossibilities. Faith makes all things possible. When the end of the world is about to descend on us, only thing we can do is: hold breath and summon our faith and hope!

Blunders that harm life

Fear is the main theme of the Dark Zone. When we let the fear rule our mind the logic backs away; it induces phobias—unreasonable fears. The fear of darkness—nyctophobia may induce thanatophobia—fear of death. It may start a chain reaction of other fears. "Ignorance" Herman Melville once wrote "is the parent of fear." And that fear sometimes, spawns trigotry—closed-mindedness, myopia, xenophobia, and staggering forms of hostility toward people who look or sound different. Sometimes fear manifests itself in the segregation of our schools, neighbourhoods and churches. At other times it becomes a forceful, fiery hatred in which violent atrocities are perpetuated. "To hate and fear is to be psychologically ill; it is in fact, the consuming illness of our time," says H A Overstreet.

Fear and threats are the key weapons people wield in real life to get things they want. For example, we have dictators who use it liberally to control people. There are suicide bombers who threaten to blow up if their demands are not met. Spouses threaten to seek divorce. Teachers threaten to punish students. Employees threaten to strike work. Nuke threat is the favourite of rogue countries. Look at the penal provisions in our laws; virtually a system of threats to force us behave.

When the mind visits the Dark Zone, some brave hearts find pleasure in teasing the feeble-hearted. They indulge in wild ragging and violent jokes. Scaring the gullible and the vulnerable is their pastime. They derive sadistic pleasure when someone gets scared. Frightening masks, deadly weapons, and all other scary material is a billion dollar business these days. Even the innocent children are given toy guns to play the make-believe games and enjoy the scary fun; this may induce them to play with real weapons when they grow up. This diabolic fun takes a vicious form in real life, resulting in deplorable violence on innocent victims.

Have you noticed the recent wild new advertisements. Sometimes we see brash and wildly inventive advertisements, with a neo-slapstick approach. They make unvarnished use of cartoonish violence for laughs. The humour is pitched at a rowdy, generation Y sensibility. We have a generation that equates political incorrectness with a release from constraint. Violence becomes a source of comedy for this generation because they know violence will be shocking to their parents, teachers or other authority figures. What is funny for them is what trounces authority, so advertisers try to tap the youth demographic by taking that attitude toward political correctness, saying in effect, we are no more constrained by middle-class values than you are. Why not allow good sense to prevail? Purpose of humour is not to hurt but to relieve us from hurt feelings.

Some people who visit House of Torture leave the fun there and take home the threats. Everytime they remember they are driven mad. The frightening future may induce unreasonable fears in the feeble hearts. They are easily frightened of the imagined consequences. Poor self-image and lack of self-confidence may not provide the courage to deal with any threats to life. They suffer even before any event occurs. They cry today for woes of tomorrow. They may suffer from nightmares and develop anxiety syndromes and bouts of depression. This is how our dreams of frightening future affects the present.

Kristin von Kreisler, a dream researcher, tells that even "Stephen King, author of nightmare–inducing horror novels, has a recurring nightmare of his own: He's working in a hot, cramped room and a mad woman is hiding behind the attic door, brandishing a scalpel. If he doesn't finish his work, she will burst through the door. And she does." Fear of the unknown may induce unmanageable stress; and in the long run may result in psychosomatic problems.

Consider this strange phenomenon of the effect preceding the cause. Take for example, anxieties about the impending doom. In the passage of time the frightening event is far away in the distant future, yet human beings feel for the consequences right now. Why should the effect precede the cause? What a disconcerting phenomenon?

Examine your unrealistic fears to address, tensions to ease, anxieties to pacify. Be prepared to face anticipated or unexpected events, make contingent plans. Remember, if you can control risk elements, you can take calculated risk. Learn to control what you can and manage what you can not. Seek diversion, spend sometime in leisure activities and look for relaxed moments. Moshe Waldoks says, "A sense of humour can help you overlook the unattractive, tolerate the unpleasant, cope with unexpected, and smile through the unbearable."

Don't misuse gifts of imagination. Don't imagine unfortunate events with negative consequences. Don't invent crisis or entertain thoughts of disaster; don't cry before the event occurs. Remember, if you worry now for the events yet to happen, it will cause anxiety and suffering. Don't worry about tomorrow, the sun will definitely rise to cheer you up. Think about the current problems; divert your mind to the *present*. That is where you are now living, that is when you can find happiness.

Accept the joy in the eternal now

"You can not step twice into the same river; for other waters are continually flowing on," said Greek philosopher Heraclitus. "In rivers, the water that you touch is the last of what has passed and the first of that which comes: so with present time," said Leonardo da Vinci. You cannot experience the present moment once again, because by the time you look again, new moments will have flown into the stream of time replacing the moment you have just seen.

John F Kennedy knew the importance of concentrating in the present moment. Robert Saudek, who conferred with him at the

White House while producing the late president's book *Profiles in Courage,* for television, later told friends, "He made you think he had nothing else to do except ask you questions and listen—to your answers. You knew that for the time being he had blotted out his past and future. More than anyone else I have ever met, president Kennedy understood the importance of *now*." Note the words: "*he had blotted out his past and future*" and "*now*". John F Kennedy was famous for the incisive questions he asked and the way he listened. That means, all concentration right *now* to understand and grasp what the *present* moment has to offer.

He understood the fact that if we don't pay attention to the present moment, we miss it forever. When we indulge in remembering past events, we are missing what is happening in the present. When we get lost in our day-dreams and fantasies, we also lose our present. Unless we block our past and future, we cannot experience the *present* moment.

You can concentrate in the present moment if you can stop the pendulum of your mind for a while; forget thinking about your past or planning for future. Now you are there in the *present* moment, which we call *now*. If you miss this *moment* of infinity you miss it for ever. John Boslough tells us, "Stephen Hawking spends most of his time thinking about the very early universe: the first trillionth second or so after big bang." Note the words *the first trillionth second!* Does it constitute what we call a *moment* –a very brief period of time? Yes, it is. The ephemera counts only moments, not hours. Butterflies count moments but not months, and yet they have time enough. Every moment has the potential to offer a few wonders of this world.

"The only true reality is the present," says Wayne Amos, "The past is gone and the future is not yet. It's the present moment that matters." He describes the joys and pleasures of experiencing the present moment, we call *now,* in his article "Eternity's Sunrise" (*Reader's Digest,* April 1965).

"The leaves rustled in the breeze" says Amos. "A bird called its notes so clear they seemed to split the air. I forgot my story and listened to the leaves and the bird and felt the same inexplicable happiness I had felt a life time ago in the same farm. I was in the scene, part of it... I was *there*.... The moon was *there*. Oh, it was hopeless trying to put into words." He says that there was a secret in that magic moment.

"No one can explain it" said Riley, his friend. "I have found hints in many of the books I've read. But first I felt it just as you did. And so did the men who tried to write about it. They felt it independently, separated by oceans and centuries; yet, they all shared the same experience... If I had to put it into one sentence.. I would say, 'Full consciousness brings joy.' One of the mysteries is that the universe contains innate joy. Once you fully open your senses to anything—a sunset, a water fall, a stone, a blade of grass—the joy comes. But to open the senses to become really conscious, you have to drop out the future and the past and remain for a time on what T S Eliot, in his poem 'Burnt Norton,' called "the still point of the turning world," the present.

"That long-ago night was beautiful to you because of the unusual circumstances. Waking up at midnight in a haystack turned you upside down. You stopped planning into the future and thinking into past. You were *there* in the now.

"Children have these moments frequently. But they grow up and lose the capacity. Yet with dim memory of the ecstasy and hope for more, they pursue this hope for the rest of their lives, forever grasping and forever analysing. They're on a journey which has no destination except death. For this reason most men do actually live 'lives of quite desperation.'"

"Schopenhaur said most men are 'lumbermen.' They walk through a beautiful forest always thinking: 'What can this tree do for me? How many cubic feet of timber will it produce? Last year I netted so much; this year I must do better. They are always there in the past or future. They are always *becoming*, they never *are*.

"Then through the forest comes the artist, though perhaps he never painted a picture. He stops before a tree, and because he asks nothing of the tree he really sees it. He is not planning the future; for the moment he has concern for himself. The self drops out. The time stops. He is there in the present. He sees the tree with full consciousness. It is beautiful. Joy steps in unasked.

"It is not important how you explain this; It is the feeling, the experience that counts. Some people believe that everything in the universe—a field of wheat swaying in the wind, a mountain a cloud, the first snowfall of the winter—has a being, an intelligent soul of its own. When we think of things in this way it is easier to love them, and love is the prime ingredient of these experiences. But our love must not be possessive. William Blake put it perfectly when he said, 'He who bends to himself a joy doth the winged life destroy; but he who kisses the joy as it flies lives in Eternity's sunrise'.

"Martin Buber says we can learn to love the world–things, animals people, stars—as *Thou*. And that when we do love them as Thou, they always respond. This is probably the greatest thrill of all—the response of joy to joy.

"I believe most men can have their glimpses of the eternal, their timeless moments, almost any time they choose. Many of our little practical tasks –say we are hoeing the garden, picking fruit or trimming a hedge—require only a hundredth part of our consciousness. We use the other 99 parts day-dreaming of tomorrow or yesterday. If we can watch the moments of hands, the trembling of leaf, feel the sun on the skin, the breeze in our hair and eliminate quickly the constant intrusions of thoughts of past and future, if we can successfully do this, for even ten seconds, the joy will come. The eyes will shine with a new light, and if a stranger passes during one of these moments and you exchange a glance, the chances are that he, too, will share in the mystery.

"In the silence that followed I heard, to the exclusion of all other perceptions, the musical call of the lark. There was strength in the loud, brief song and flute like delicacy, peaceful, plaintive; and, overall, there was a joyous acceptance of the eternal now, astride the centuries and millenniums." Complete immersion in the "now"—the present moment, is necessary to enjoy what the nature offers—eternal joy.

Let us spend a little more time, on this subject, 'here and now,' because that is what we have been missing in our lives. We often learn a lot of things when we hear other's experiences and reflect. It often helps us to recall similar experiences in our lives; and look for exciting moments hereafter. Jean Bell Mosley's wrote an article "Take

It From the Here and Now" *(Reader's Digest,* Sept 1968). Let us listen to her encounters with 'here and now' and her "born again" experiences—her baptism in the joyful moments of the world.

"My garden was the apple orchard. To the west stretched the corn field. Through my slatted front windows I could look down to the river and across and beyond, up to the foot hills that folded peacefully into each other. In spring, violets nodded near my triangular dwelling, to be replaced in summer by meadow-sweet and later on, the feathery plumes of the golden rod. Butterflies came and went in a gorgeous array, and sometimes bees, drunk with nectar, reeled in and out.

On the precious morning I was "born," there hovered close to the earth a mingled scent of wild honeysuckle and new-mown hay; the sky was incredibly blue and I was lying on my back under elderberry ceiling, watching a jay that had come to dine on the ripe berries.

We stared at each other. Suddenly I no longer seem to be a separate entity. When the summer breeze ruffled the jay's feathers I could feel their exquisite softness. When the jay squashed a berry in its beak, I could taste the sweet purple goodness. I don't know how to describe it except to say that I was somehow *at one* with the bush, the breeze that stirred the bush, the grass, the sun, the trees, all things everywhere.

It was the first real intensification of life I had known. I was *present*—at home with all things and, as young as I was, I somehow knew that this state was ineffably sweet, infinitely desirable. I had the indescribable sensation of everything moving along in a mysterious, mystical pattern of which I was part. Perhaps only once in a life-time to have this glimpse of cosmic harmony, the peep at life as it is surely meant to be.

Now, many years later, I often wake up of a morning and whisper a soft "Present" to some unspoken roll call. This is not the same as answering to indicate physical presence. It is a marshalling of all my senses to stand on tiptoe, to see and hear and smell and touch, to be keenly alive, to cry out with silent joy that "I am here." It is to give whatever factors were present on that "birthday" free REIN.

When summer rain creeps slowly on the parched cornfield and the spattered dust seem to spring up to meet it, I rush out to stand among the stately stalks, look up at the sky, sniff the pollen, feel the wetness on my face. And my whispered "present" mingles with the gentle patter of rain on the thirsty leaves.

Wherever I am, there I want to *be*. When the rabbits play in the midnight in the garden, I want to wake up, rest my head on the windowsill to be *present*. When a procession comes marching down the street, drums rolling, batons twirling, flags waving, I want to touch elbows with the crowd, exchange greetings and, to myself say, "Present." When the little one next door invites me to "Come and see what slept in the hollyhock blossom last night," let me go! And when there is sorrow, let me feel that, too. When senses are dulled, one passes through life without ever having been *present*.

Tonight when twilight falls, filling the low spaces with blue shadows and bringing into view the stars and lights from other houses, look up at the fading remnants of the day; Concentrate for a moment on all that you see, then all that you hear and smell and feel, one sense at a time. Say, "Present." Perhaps, for one exquisite moment may be."

That's it. The message of "here and now" is clear: "Concentrate on all that you see, hear, smell and feel. For one exquisite moment, you may sense the meaning of life!"

Remember happiness is in the *present* but not in the distant future. Rabindranath Tagore quotes in his book *Personality*, a poem from *Ishopanishat*. The poet sings, that "The earth is His joy," and everything here is joyful. Tagore himself wrote the following poem *Joy*.

> And Joy is Everywhere;
> It is in the Earth's green covering of grass;
> In the blue serenity of the Sky;
> In the reckless exuberance of the Spring;
> In the severe abstinence of the gray Winter;
> In the Living flesh that animates our bodily frame;

In the perfect poise of the Human figure, noble and upright;
In Living;
In the exercise of all our powers;
In the acquisition of our knowledge;
In fighting evil.
Joy is there Everywhere.

Yes, as the poet says there is a great abundance of joy everywhere in the world. There is innate joy in the universe. It is beyond the dimensions of space and time. It can be found everywhere at any time by anybody. Every moment has the potential to offer plentiful joy. The reality of joy is in the perception of our mind. "Without the perception of beauty the wings never spread, the mind lives in shadow, the heart fails," says Pearl S Buck. All of us are endowed with the ability to perceive beauty and joy in life. It is our perception that makes us happy.

Finally our *mind* seems to convey a thoughtful message: Our domain is the present. Let us not allow ourselves drifting into the past, nor do we avoid realities of the moment by lingering in the future. We know, we can not change the past, but we can ruin the present if we are not careful. So, let us not squander precious little life-time feeling sorry for the past that never returns nor worrying about the future that is uncertain and live a joyful life, as long as we live!

Gautama Buddha preached long ago: "The secret of health both for mind and body is not to mourn for the past, not to worry about future nor to anticipate trouble, but to live the present moment wisely and earnestly." Psychotherapist Wayne Dyer, says "Present moment living, getting in touch with your 'now' is at the heart of effective living. When you think about it, there is really no other moment you can live. Now is all there is and the future is another moment when it arrives. One thing is certain, you can not live it until it does appear." So, be determined to live in the present and try to enjoy every moment of your life!.

Let us close this chapter with an ancient Sanskrit poem from Kalidas's

Ritusamhara
> Listen to the exhortation of Dawn!
> Look to this Day!
> For it is life, the very Life of Life.
> In its brief course lie all the
> Verities and Realities of your existence.
> The Bliss of growth,
> The Glory of action,
> The Splendour and Beauty;
> For yesterday is but a dream,
> And tomorrow is only a vision:
> But today well-lived makes,
> Every yesterday a Dream of Happiness,
> And every tomorrow a Vision of Hope.
> Look well therefore for this Day!
> Such is the salutation of Dawn!

Chapter 6

Precious Gifts of Life : Unwrap Joy

The life of ours has been filled with gifts of the divine giver.
Rabindranath Tagore (1861 – 1941)
Indian poet, Nobel Prize for literature 1913.
The giver of life gave it for happiness, not for wretchedness.
Thomas Jefferson (1743 – 1826)
Former US President

Let me tell you a pathetic story of the hungry folks of Palikhan (Chattisgarh, India), who are living a life of poverty above an abundance of mineral wealth. Their story was in the news recently (*The Hindu Business Line*, March 10, 2003).

The diamonds first appeared a decade ago, washed out of the soil by the monsoon rains and collected by the local people for sale into the illegal trade. Now the government of Chattisgarh is trying to create some order and has already fenced off many areas.

According to a government report the diamond mines in the state could turn out to be among the top 22 in the world. "Chattisgarh is nestling atop the world's largest Kimberlite area," it says. Mangaldas, a watchman guarding the fenced land, says "We lead a lavish life here. We sleep on diamonds. We walk on diamonds" Barnuram, a wizened old man with a walking stick, says he found a diamond in his field about 10 years ago. "My son was preparing the soil for planting and he happened to see a stone and he picked it up. He said to me "This looks like a different stone. What shall we do with it?" So Barnuram took it to a village nearby where, he says, a shopkeeper took one look at it and without hesitating exchanged it for Rs. 3,000 and five kg of rice. "He fed me, gave me tea and kept the stone. I had no idea what the actual value of that stone was?" And he says "I am hoping companies will come here and dig for diamonds. That will help us to become rich. Because until now we don't have enough to eat." Since then his 2.2 acres of land was fenced off and soil samples were taken.

Diamonds are there buried in the fields. When they are mined out by companies, they will reap the profits. Owners of the diamond fields will also be benefited. The story of mankind is no different from the story of the hunger stricken folks of Palikhan. Like them, we all have diamonds buried in our minds. Like them, we will also go hungry to bed as long as we don't exploit our own diamond resources. Sometimes the hunger is biological, but most of the time it is a psychological one. It is the hunger for happiness. 'So near and so far' is the story of the elusive happiness.

Poor Barnuram has asked this question: *"I had no idea what the actual value of that stone was."* But it is the question that should be asked by everyone of us. Surprisingly, we human beings have plenty of diamond fields in our minds, the worth of which no one can estimate. Everyone of us is presented with gifts of several diamond fields on the very first birthday, so that all of us can enjoy the benefits throughout our lives. These gifts are intangible but they can help you get many material things as well as intangible things like joy and happiness. In other words, you are born with gifts that can bring you happiness. That implies, you are born to be happy. Every one of us can enjoy life if only we endeavour to exploit our diamond-resources and derive the benefits. The choice is left to us.

The gifts of life for your happiness

"Men are capable of greater things than they can perform. They are sent into this world with bills of credit and seldom draw to their full extent", says Horace Walpole. Do you know that you have received invaluable gifts of *navaratnas* on your very first birthday? They are so enduring that they will stay with you, as long as you live. And of course, they leave this world along with you. In point of fact, they live and die for you. That is their commitment. They live to serve you, help you achieve anything you want. They feel happy, when you get what you want to satisfy your needs. Whenever your goals are achieved, they celebrate the occasion. Whenever you feel happy, they will also enjoy the moments of your happiness. They live and die to make your life happy. That is their mission.

Your gifts of life are inexhaustible resources; they are the great gifts of faculties and energies that can make things happen in your life-time. We have every right to use this inherited wealth –to do things we want to do, and make ourselves happy. In fact happiness is our birth right. Be it right to wealth or right to happiness, benefits will accrue only when the right is exercised. It requires inner desire and effort on our part. How we make use of them is left to our choice. If you don't make use of your life's gifts and still say "I am unhappy," its like 'sleeping on diamonds and going hungry to bed.' Then, there is no difference between you and the hungry folks of Palikhan. Would you like to know your gifts?

Chapter 7
Gift of Unique Body and Wonderful Self

Every man is a builder of a Temple called his body, nor can he get off hammering the marble instead.

Henry David Thoreau (1817 – 62)
American naturalist, Practical philosopher

Self-reverence, self-knowledge, self-control, These three alone lead life to sovereign power.

Lord Alfred Tennyson (1809 – 92)
English Poet Laureate

Awareness of body
"One fine moment in childhood, you must have suddenly realised that you have a body of your own. And people are calling you by a name that identifies you. It implied a whole series of circumstances. In the first place there is your family, a number of brothers and sisters, cousins and relatives, and a whole fabric of daily life. Sooner or later you will realise that "—you can't get out of it now, not for a long time: you will have to go through with being a child, and growing up, and getting old, before you quit of this mad prank." Richard Hughes puts these words in the mouth of Emily, in his novel *A high wind in Jamaica*. They are indeed true of every human being.

We have been told that the earth is the only place in the universe where life exists. That the human beings, the highly evolved life forms, are unique in this universe. You are one among them with your own unique identity: a unique being among the unique species. There is no person like you in the entire world. That makes you special! "Many of the world's great minds believed that our best energies surface only if we love ourselves and rejoice in our uniqueness," says Dov Peretz Elkins.

When we think of life we always think about our bodies. "Body is the name of a stream of matter, continuously changing," said Swami Vivekananda. From birth to death, human body undergoes gradual change. Man learns to make continual adjustment throughout his life. His experience covers all the stages of life: infancy, childhood, adulthood, middle age, and senility. The knowledge he gains from experience guides his daily life and his plans for future.

Your responsibility for your body

According to the Gita, our body is a vehicle for achieving things in life; and hence our responsibility to take care of it. In this respect listen to the advice of Will Durant : "My first request to you is: Be healthy. It is within your will. Barring inherited or childhood ailments, sickness is a crime: it means that you have done something physiologically foolish, and the nature is being hard put to repair your mistake.

Our bodies are what we eat, plus what our ancestors ate. Don't let restaurants lure you; they will burden your flesh in proportion as they lighten your purse. Perhaps one of the cardinal errors of our time and land is that we continue in a sedentary life with the diet that served to provide muscle and heat. The hospitals are littered with people who have allowed an excess of imports over exports to disturb their internal economy.

And exercise! Nature, intended thought to be a guide to action, not a substitute for it; thought unbalanced by action is unnatural. Do some physical work for at least an hour every day."

Self-awareness

When you recognise your body, with unique features of its own, you identify yourself with your body and say, "I have a body of my own". Who is saying this? Probably you will say, "myself." When we use the words 'myself', 'yourself' and 'ourselves' what do we really mean by the word self? It is a bit difficult to define, but one thing is clear. We imply that this thing called *self* is independent from the *body*. That's how awareness of self begins. Most of the awareness of our self is rather a gradual awakening.

Discover yourself

Many of the world's greatest minds have believed that our best energies surface only if we love ourselves and rejoice in our uniqueness. Wise men over the centuries have believed that the key to success as a person is self-knowledge. We still pay lip service to the ancient counsel "Know thyself"; you can't know anybody else in the same way. "Indeed, as I have learnt, it is only when alone that one can really make acquaintance with oneself," says Philip Wylie. "Whatever it is that you recognise—heart, spirit and imagination, quite free from outside stimulus. And knowledge of that self is, in a sense, all the actual knowledge you can ever have; the rest is in books or other people's heads." "Truth shall make you free, but first it shall make you miserable," says psychotherapist Carl R Rogers. Whatever it is find the truth about yourself. "If we could recover both the appetite for being alone and its product, self-awareness, we would again produce dreaming doers," says Wylie. "We need such people as never before: *thinkers* who can face the titanic problems peculiar to our time."

You have to find out who you are all by yourself. 'The attainment of this goal may sound easy but, in fact, most of us cover up who we really are,' say Psychoanalysts Mildred Newman and Bernard Berkowitz in an article "You Can Take Care of Your Life." "Here are some questions designed to help you. Deal with them frankly, and treat yourself with kindness and respect. Don't put yourself down if the emerging picture is not to your liking. There were probably good reasons why you turned that way. Respect the life you have been living even though you may want to change it."

The ideal surroundings for study of oneself is some untouched place outdoors, which, in spite of man's exploitation of nature, still offers relatively secluded spots for meditation. But solitude can be created in the mind whenever a person can spend time alone. With a little practice even a man in a crowd can be alone. As Shakespeare said, "Who can say more than this rich praise, that you alone are you."

What is important in your life?
What excites you? When was the last time you really felt stirred by something? How about last half-dozen times before that? The answers can provide some powerful clues to your real identity. If you respond that you rarely feel excited, then you will have to dig to find out.

How do you spend your free time?
Is there a special pastime that truly holds your interest? If so, you may have the thread with which to unravel the mystery of yourself. But if you spend your free time sleeping, daydreaming or watching television, that's a pretty good sign that you are reading something that can change you.

How do you feel about non-leisure time?
What things about work or school do you like? Finding something interesting and worthwhile in whatever you do is a measure of your creativity and adaptability. If you can surrender yourself to the simple pleasure of a job well done, even if the work is not your choosing, you already have the basis for happiness and success.

On the other hand, if the mandatory chores of life are always unpleasant to you, you have created a double burden. There are always difficult or boring things that have to be done. If you concentrate only on the resentment you feel, you allow yourself no chance to find a means to make the job easier, quicker or more pleasant.

What if all the possibilities are open to you?
If you were left an inheritance by a rich uncle, what's the first thing you do? This question can be a fun because it helps make your fantasies conscious. Is there one special fantasy that you return to over and over? What do you think of regularly just before you fall asleep?

Can you face the facts?
One of our few comforts is that we of this earth are only human—there are few saints among us. Can you accept the fact that some of

the things you've been telling yourself may not be true, that you have made mistakes? Facing the mistakes and misconceptions of your life does not mean emphasising or exaggerating them. It is simply taking the bitter with the better.

Are you willing to change?
An artist occasionally steps back from his work to gain perspective. Similarly, a creative person will "step back" from time to time and take stock of himself to see what might need reshaping. Some things, obviously, are inherited and unchangeable. But those you have acquired by learning and imitation are not immutable—your walking, talking, facial expressions, your thinking, and believing. Indeed it is your right, if not your obligation, to change yourself exactly as *you* see fits.

Can you tune into your self?
Like many others, you may think that the only important things are those you've heard or read somewhere else, or that listening to your own thoughts is self-indulgent. If so you are cheating yourself. Your own thoughts and ideas can lead you to the most important moments in your life.

Be sensitive to your negative feelings as well as your positive ones. If you stand your ground and face difficult feeling—such as anxiety or depression—it has a way of shrinking to manageable size. In fact, anxiety can be a signal that new adventures, or new possibilities, lie ahead.

Do you know who you are?
Your sense of self —call it self-respect, self-esteem, being your own best friend—is the backbone of the move towards taking charge of your self. Define yourself, describe what makes you, *you*. Then, when you know better who you are and what you stand for, don't let anything or anyone persuade you to go against yourself.

"One final word of encouragement," say Newman and Berkowitz. "Once you get on your own side, once you decide to act in your own behalf, you will begin to see possibilities and potentials you never knew existed (Sounds like magic. We have seen it happen over and over). Having learnt to deal with your anxiety and doubts, you will be free to face new challenges. And you will find courage to use the strength and creativity you barely suspected you had."

Recently, psychologists at McGill University found that "People's feelings of insecurity are largely based on worries about whether they will be liked, accepted and valued by their peers and significant others". Psychiatrist David Burns says, "No matter what you are like —whether you're rich or poor, insecure or outgoing, brilliant or average, attractive or plain—some people will like you and others couldn't care less. *Nobody* gets accepted by everyone. But if you accept yourself, then far more people will be attracted to you."

Ten commandments of self-confidence

"You must carve out a strong self-image before you plan to achieve anything in life," says Maxwell Maltz, the psycho-cybernetics guru. A strong self-image builds up self-confidence. He insists that self confidence is "a vital factor in the life of any human being who strives for goals and successes and satisfaction." Let us consider his ten commandments for improving self-image and self-confidence.

C : Concentrate on a strong self-image.

O : Offer it full partnership in life.

N : Never let it disappear; you must work to reinforce your sense of self.

F : Fulfill yourself with your self-image.

I : Infuse your self-image with compassion when you meet setbacks.

D : Develop it everyday; only your true sense of self can make you strong.

E : Elevate your self with your self-image so that you need not fear.

N : Nourish it; don't let a false sense of selflessness convince you that it is not basic to your happiness.

C : Create a climate in which it can grow; spend sometime everyday thinking, with humility, about yourself and the world.

E : Enjoy it; continually reactivate the success instincts, the success mechanism, within you.

You must have confidence in your self to achieve anything in life. Samuel Johnson wrote, "Self-confidence is the first requisite for great undertakings." Remember confidence borne out of your successful experiences is the real confidence. Reinforce your self-image by remembering the pleasant feelings associated with your achievements. Build the edifice of your self-confidence on the bricks of your past successes. Your need to succeed will make you come alive with more confidence. Strong beliefs turn your thoughts into reality. If a person believes something to be true then he will act out that belief in the same manner. That is what psychologists call self-fulfilling prophecy. Napoleon Bonaparte graduated 42 in a class of 56 at military school. But, he became a great conqueror. Imagine his level of self-confidence and self-esteem!

You can redesign your personality

In an article "Three Steps to Self-confidence", Ponchitta Pierce explains Dorothy Sarnoff's approach to help the uncertain to "redesign" their personalities. She says that every person has positive traits. One must "take those strong qualities and put them into the person whose future is at stake—you." In Speech dynamics course she helps people to be more confident. "It's taking the best of yourself, and making it better."

Sarnoff's unusual ability to help people stems from a life filled with its own trials. At the age of seven, she considered herself the ugliest child in her neighbourhood and was painfully shy. Fortunately a teacher was able to help her. "She kept telling me that I could do things," Sarnoff says. "And because she told me that I could, I did."

She observed that people are generally encouraged to look better; but "what good is that when they open their mouths?" She aims "at making people more appealing to *both* the ear and the eye." She helped people how to look better with appropriate dress; and more importantly, how to impress people with their speech. According to Sarnoff there are three basic keys to redesigning one's personality :

Evaluate yourself

You must be as conscious about your positive side as you are about the negative. Look deep inside yourself and find things you like. Are you imaginative, innovative, compassionate, patient? Acknowledging your good points raises your self-esteem right away. If you find that you have some irritating traits write them down as a first step towards eliminating them. Awareness is the first step in correcting oneself.

To know how others see you, place a mirror near your telephone. How do you look when you speak? Are your eyes alive? Are you sending out negative signals? If so, change them.

Make yourself interesting

When you speak, your voice is important. Wispy voice indicates lack of self-confidence. Listen to your voice on a tape recorder. Is it nasal, high, nagging, apathetic, shrill, whining? Do you speak chop-stock phrases? The body is "sound sensitive" and such unappealing verbal mannerisms can turn a listener off. Smooth and mellow tone can add warmth to your personality.

One way to make yourself interesting is to take in enough "food" for conversation and to be well-informed on many subjects. Skim through current magazines and newspapers, listen to the latest news. Visit museums, plays, cultural activities. Use more imagination, a larger vocabulary, more colourful descriptions. Learn to communicate your feelings. If you are shy, learn to ask a 'stimulating question'. Be a good listener and know when to respond.

Be pleasantly assertive

If you want to say "no," say it without annoying people. Keep your voice warm, and the face smiling. Learn to resist peer pressure by saying no gracefully. Being pleasantly assertive also means knowing how to criticise without tearing down. Begin by acknowledging few good points, saying "That's a good idea. But do you think you must go at it this way? In this "inverse approach," your ideas come across as constructive suggestions, not as slap-downs.

Don't forget your posture. "Sitting tall and erect, or standing straight helps you look more confident and alert in a conversation".

Whether you're asking your boss for a raise, or making a speech, or just talking to friends "psych" yourself constantly. The minute you enter a room with such a mission, say to yourself "I care I know I am coming across well." If you tell yourself often enough you'll soon have solid reason to believe it.

The awesome power to be yourself

"The concept that we ought to know and be ourselves goes back to the first time a human being wondered, *Who am I?*" says Ardis Whitman. "Socrates taught that to "know thyself" is the basis of all knowledge; Shakespeare wrote, "To thine own self be true, thou canst not be then be false to any man." Like all the great ideas, the concept rises and falls with the tide of history.

By following "be thyself" philosophy, people like Socrates, St. Francis of Assissi, Mohandas Karamchand Gandhi derived uncanny power. Imagine changing a community just by being oneself. "*That is power*," says Whitman. "They all spoke and acted themselves, resolutely standing up for what they believed. They had the inner purity of people true to their ideals." Always, we seem to be asking, "How can I make my life count for something?"

Authenticity makes each person's life count by restoring *power* to the individual. To be oneself is a natural, human and universal power, which brings with it a cornucopia of blessings. Authentic people have *A sense of direction*; they recognise the direction in which their lives are meant to go. The authentic person has *Self-generated energy*.

He does not dissipate energy in self-contradictions. His self-honesty reduces internal conflicts, and he feels alive and exhilarated. His energy is turned on by doing what matters to him. He has *the power of example*. Just by being himself, he makes a statement about what is to be done. He mobilises the energies of others, by inspiring them. He has *the power of self-love*. A person who respects and values himself is much more likely to be able to do the same for others. No energies are wasted in protecting a shaky ego. No one can summon *the power of the spirit* just by wanting to. But it seems to come often to those most centered on deep self where discovery begins.

"Striving for authenticity is not easy" says Whitman. "It's a life time endeavour, and nobody ever makes it all the way. It is a becoming rather than ending, something we learn day by day." Here are some ways to begin:

Pay attention to what is going on in your life, inwardly and outwardly
Keep a diary and see how you change over time and discover what muffled longings are being expressed. Few of us are so monolithic that we don't harbour conflicts within ourselves. Admit them. Listen to the dialogue within and record it in your diary.

Accept the idea that nothing is wrong with being different from other people
The truth is, all of us are different, and we are meant to be. "Each one of us," wrote philosopher Paul Weiss, "is a unique being confronting the rest of the world in a unique fashion." Seek out your deepest convictions and stand by them, live by them.

Spend time with yourself
Solitude is at the heart of self-knowledge, because it is when we are alone that we learn to distinguish between the false and the true, the trivial and the important. "Solitude" said Nietze, "makes us tougher towards ourselves and tender towards others."

"As with splitting of atom, the opening of self gives us access to a hidden power," says Whitman. "Authenticity is a sensitising and blessed power. It comes with a feeling at home with oneself, and therefore at home in the universe. It is the greatest power in the world—the power to be ourselves."

"I was anxious to be what someone else wanted me to be" said Elizabeth Coatsworth. "Now I have given up that struggle. I am what I am." That's the way the authentic people express themselves; they realise that they derive awesome power by being themselves.

Cultivate your own character
"It is character that pays everywhere," says Swami Vivekananda "Upon ages of struggle a character is built. Character is repeated habits, and the repeated habits alone can reform character." Thiruvalluvar says, "What is done with spotless mind is virtue. All else is a vain show. That conduct is virtue which is free from these four things: malice, desire, anger, and bitter speech. That pleasure only which flows from virtue is pleasure; all else is not pleasure, and it is without praise.

Virtue will confer heaven and wealth; what source of happiness can man possess? Let self-control be guarded as treasure. There is no greater source of good for man than that."

"We have put too much stress on intellect, too little on character," says Will Durant. "Character comes second only to health. The greatest task assumed by schools is to transform egos into gentlemen. A gentlemen …is a person continually considerate.

Speak no evil of anyone; every unkind word will sooner or later fly back into your face and make you stumble in the race of life. To speak ill of others is a dishonest way of praising ourselves. If you can't say good or encouraging things, say nothing. Nothing is often a good thing to do and always a clever thing to say."

"All of us are experts at practising virtue at a distance," warns Theodore Hesbergh. Unless we put our character first, we cannot claim to be authentic in our lives. Our own virtues and character speak about ourselves more than words and deeds!

Chapter 8

Gift of Marvellous Brain and Fantastic Memory

Compared to me other wonders of the universe pale into insignificance.
Human Brain
In J D Ratcliff's "I am John's brain."
Reader's Digest June 1974

A memory may be a paradise from which we can not be driven, it may also be a hell from which we can not escape.
John Lancaster Spalding (1840 – 1916)
Archbishop of Scintopolis

We cannot be aware of our existence without our mind; but our mind cannot function without brain, a vital organ of the body. It accounts for all our thinking, knowledge, memory, actions, and feelings. It is not part of you; in fact, you are your brain—the mind in your brain, your personality, your reactions, your mental capacity. You think you hear with your ears, taste with your tongue, feel with your fingers. But the truth is, all these things happen inside your brain. Your brain tells you, when you are ill, when you are hungry. It governs your sex urge, your moods, and everything. Little wonder the Oxford University professor Colin Blakemore in *The Mind Machine,* describes human brain as "the most complex piece of machinery in the universe." It is indeed the greatest gift you are born with.

Human beings are the highly evolved species in the world. The main reason is the evolution of the most complex human brain. There is no parallel to it among all the living beings in the world. Our knowledge about human brain is incomplete. Scientists are still in the process of unravelling its secrets. But each time the neurosurgeon lifts his scalpel to enter that still-mysterious world of human brain— an organ like any other, except that it produces thought—he challenges the limits of his knowledge. Medical reporters, Jon Franklin and Alan Doelp say that a journey into this universe is as fantastic as a voyage into outer space, just as promising for the future—and every bit perilous. Ronald Kotulak, summarises in *Inside Brain*, the incredible pace of brain research in the past decade. Jeri Janowsky, a neuropsychologist says, "Anything you learned two years ago is old information—Neuroscience .....is exploding." Yet, this writer ventured to collect the available information on the Internet and other resources to provide substance for our purpose here.

You are the owner of the most powerful computer in the world
It is not bigger than a large grape fruit. It is much smaller than the heart of a lettuce. You could hold it easily in one hand. It generally weighs under three pounds (1,500 gm). Yet it is thousand times more powerful than the most powerful computer in the world today. And it is all yours: the brain that you and other humans have is so unique.

A fruit fly has 100,000 active brain cells. A mouse has 5 million, a monkey 10 billion. You have had 100 billion since birth. And from the very earliest days of life those cells form new learning connections or synopses, at an incredible rate of 3 billion a second. Those connections are the key to brain power.

By comparison, in the first three days of 1997 space journey over the surface of Mars, millions of users made 200 million Internet "hits" to follow progress. Yet your brain can make 15 times as many new connections in a second as all the Internet users made in three days. No one is using more than a fraction of that amazing ability. And everyday, scientists are learning more about how to improve the process.

Let us listen to what Tony Buzan, a psychologist and memory expert says: "Your brain is made of a trillion brain cells. Each cell is like most phenomenally complex little octopus. It has a centre and many branches and each branch has many connecting points. Each one of those billions of brain cells is many times more powerful and sophisticated than most of the computers around the planet today. Each one of these cells connects, embraces, hundreds and thousands to tens of thousands of others. And they shuttle information back and forward. It has been called the enchanted loom, the most astoundingly complex, beautiful thing in existence. And each person has one." This is to remind you that your brain is more powerful than you think it is!

Of these trillion cells, about one tenth consists of active neurons or nerve cells. Each one is capable of making up to 20,000 different connections with other cells. Professor Robert Ornstein of Stanford University says, in *The Amazing Brain*, "the possible number of connections is probably bigger than the number of atoms in the universe." Doubt it? Then consider what happens if you took only ten everyday items –like the first things you did in the morning – and combine them in every possible sequence. The result would be 3,628,800 different combinations. Take 11 items, connect them, and the number of possible combinations is 39,916,800! So now try combining 100 billion cells in every possible way—when each one can make up to 20,000 different connections—and you get some idea of the creative capacity of your own brain.

And how do you make the most of its great ability? Buzan says, "you make the most of your mind by first studying what it is. The first thing you do is find out what it is made of and how it works. How does memory work? How does concentration work. How does creative thinking process work? So you literally start to examine and explore yourself." Start that exploration and you will come up with some surprises.

You have four brains in one

First, you have got four brains in one—on three different levels, from top to brain stem, and the fourth tucked in behind. Next your brain has two sides. Each controls different functions, and processes information in different ways. These sides are linked by an amazing electric and chemical relay-system that itself has 300 million operation of nerve cells. This shuttles information around instantly like a multinational automatic telephone exchange.

We also now believe that each of us has many different "intelligent centres" in the brain. But very few of us develop more than a small part of that talent ability.

Your brain also works on at least four different electrical wave-imprinting new memories; it is essential for retrieving old ones. When it is dried up, Alzheimer's disease results. The storage of acetylcholine first robs Alzheimer's patients of their short-time memory and eventually their long time memory as well.

The body and mind as one

Fortunately neuroscientists are regularly making important discoveries that will have enormous effect on learning, memory, health and our ability to stay mentally active throughout our life.

Recent research also confirms ancient religious beliefs that the body and mind act effectively as one. Here professor Candace Pert's findings are particularly important. She first came to prominence in the early 1970's for her discovery of the brain's opiate reception. She describes receptors as sensing molecules—as microscopic molecular scanners. Now her continuing research has revealed "the molecular basis of emotions": the tiny peptides that lock into the mind's receptors. But the resulting molecules of emotion are not confined to the brain. They "run every system in our body." And "the peptides are the sheet music containing notes, phrases, and rhythms that allow the orchestra—your body—to play as an integral entity." These memories—so vital for learning—are stored in all parts of the body. And whatever new information enters the body —through sight, sound, taste, touch, or smell—memory traces are stored not only in the brain, but in the body as well. In this way, she says, the body is "the unconscious mind." And the mind and body work as one for filtering, storing, learning and remembering key elements of learning.

Memory : the brain's wonderful filing system

"Memory is the diary we all carry about with us," said Oscar Wild. "A man's real possession is his memory". "In nothing else he is rich, in nothing else is he poor," reminds Alexander Smith. Joan Mills, says "Our memory is 'a wonderful whirligig time machine, that takes you into our past as and when we wish. Memory is so much more than words and images, more than skills and arithmetic and good behaviour kept handy. Every cell in us seems to collect its own souvenirs of our experience. Mouths remember kisses, fingers hold memories of fire. A mother's ribs have perfect recall of the upward thrust of the unborn baby's fist. The retentive ear hears the closing of the door, a phrase of song—and away fall the years. At odd moments, I relived losses, failures, occasions of despair—powerful reminders of our capacity to stumble, feel hurt, and go on. Once I had taken nothing from these experiences but pain. Now there was meaning. I added it to my store of recollected good. Life will inform me I decided, it always does." We must all sing, "Thanks for the Memory" along with Bob Hope, the American Comedian.

"You never realise what a good memory you have until you try to forget something," says Franklin Jones. "Actually, you have a prodigious memory," says John Frazier. "In a few cubic centimeters your brain stores more information than can be stored in a large computer. Furthermore, it can do things that would baffle any modern computer: remembers how burning leaves smell, or how strawberries and cream taste. One researcher calculates the brain's storage capacity at a thousand billion pieces of information."

Yet, most of us worry about our forgetfulness. Perhaps you go into a room and forget what you came for, go blank on names, mislay things. Or there may be something on the tip of the tongue, but you can't get it off. Don't fret. You are perfectly normal. Gordon Bower of Stanford University says, "It is the nature of the mind to forget—and the nature of man to worry about forgetfulness."

"In man's memory nature has created a truly remarkable storage system, one that puts microfilm to shame. This system contains enormous number of "memory traces," individual bits of information which represents past as definitely as cuneiform markings on clay tablets."

Memory is an awesome process that has long fascinated inquiring minds. Only recently, however, has there been a concentrated effort to define, measure and work out its mechanics. Neurologists, psychologists, molecular biologists, biochemists have been exploring this phenomenon.

Our brain is the storehouse of memories of our experiences. "Experience stirs up things inside our heads, barrages of brief electrical impulses flash along nerve fibres running from sense organs to brain," says John Pfeiffer. "Images, sounds, odours, all the things we note in the outside world, are represented by coded patterns of impulses—living "sparks" each lasting only a few thousandth of a second. These are transient signals. Yet somehow certain selected patterns of information are fixed—frozen in flight as it were—and transformed into permanent records among intricate nerve cell network. They are filed away systematically and with amazing compactness for future reference. A good deal of what we remember seems to be filed away in some sort of time sequence, like the frames in a strip of microfilm. When resurrected the film runs forward, never backward, at time's own unchanged pace".

The mechanism of memory is not confined to cortex. Brain wave studies show that the electrical activity of the cortical "limbic" structures—centres located round the inner borders between the cerebral hemispheres—changes during learning. When these deeper parts are damaged, the brain is incapable of forming new permanent memory traces, while old memories are still stored intact. That is, the person does not forget anything; he simply fails to register what happens.

Scientists are still wondering whether it has unlimited storage space or must be continuously culled to make room for new information. They don't even know exactly where in the brain memories are stored. Research studies suggest that while short-term memory is electrical, long-term memory is chemical. They have elaborate computer models to simulate "episodic memory"(used to recall a single event, such as a name face or date) and "semantic memory" (used to recall entire information systems, such as language, mathematics or how to drive a car).

Scientists have diagrammed the distinctions between long-term memory" and "short-term memory." "Long-term memory is a consummate wonder," says Frazier. "Once a bit of information gets in, it is apparently there for life." All our experiences are stored in the long-term memory probably for life. You may not be conscious of all the things tucked away in the marvellous filing system of your brain. Short-term memory is severely limited. You can hold a seven digit telephone number, but not three or four. And the chances are if you get an engaged signal, you will have to look up the number again. As you read this, you store the words in the short-term memory; at the end of the sentence you extract meaning and discard the words. Short-term memory may last only for a few seconds. But if a short-term item is encountered often enough – the name of your neighbour, for instance—it will be moved into permanent storage in long-term memory. A meaningful situation, a reliable reference point, assists in the transfer. Studies reveal that this transfer is achieved through a chemical process. And our memory is chemically stored.

The most striking feature is the brain's back-up system. It stores each memory in various places. Consequently the sight of an apple tree or the sound of a brook could trigger the same memory of a special spot in the country. Thus, it is possible for anyone to have part of brain destroyed and still manage quite nicely. You may have difficulty in retrieving your memory but it is there. We are unconscious of the vast amount of information we have stored, but under special conditions, it can be retrieved. Hypnosis enabled a brick layer to recall exactly an unusual pattern in a wall he had laid 40 years ago. A middle-aged man described his first class room in minute detail.

Dr Wilder Penfield, a Canadian brain surgeon, in the process of surgical treatment, found where some records of memory are stored in the brain. With low voltage pointer he touched various points in patients' brains. The tickle of electricity activated storage areas and brought back events long forgotten. A woman heard Christmas carols in a church in Holland she had attended as a child; another relived the birth of her child 20 years before. A tickle of electricity in one place one might "see" a long forgotten primary school teacher. Stimulated in other places, he might hear a train whistle or recitation of a nursery rhyme he couldn't have recalled a few hours earlier. Amazing!

Gift of Marvellous Brain and Fantastic Memory 81

Our brain is like an old attic containing mementos of a life-time. You may not be aware of what is in the attic, but it is there. If the memory is stored chemically or otherwise, how is it retrieved? The mysterious electrical activity of the brain (brain waves) may play a role in activating memory, just as Dr Penfield's electrical probe did. A few rare individuals can look at something and have total recall of minute details. Toscanini was reputedly able to study a symphony score and file it away in his memory, perfect to the last note. The Shass Pollaks, a group of Jewish memory experts memorized 12 volumes of the Babylonian Talmud perfectly. A friend of mine, Kunal Kumar Chattopadyay, a Chief General Manager of State Bank of India, can recite the Gita in one stretch. Human memory is like a muscle; it must be exercised to retain its tone.

"The harvest of old age is the memory and rich store of blessings laid up earlier in life," said Cicero. But unfortunately memory loss is one of the main worries—and irritations—of aging. "Of course, some forgetting may be useful, to help ease the pain of growing old," says Roy Rowan. "Or it may simply keep the human memory blank from getting overloaded. Nobody knows. In any case, even the sharp-etched memories can prove to be mercurial. Sometimes they just vanish." Psychologist Fergus Craik of University of Toronto says, "Perhaps the best advice is to keep mentally active by reading, observing and learning. The brain responds to exercise. Memory decline is far less in the intelligent and mentally active persons than others."

While no definitive general explanation of memory has come from all the scientific experiments, several new insights have been gleaned. Roy Rowan lists them as follows:

- Biologically, it seems that age has less to do with memory impairment than previously suspected. However, as more knowledge is acquired, there may be more interference, between competing new and old memories.
- Memory impotence feeds on fear of failure. Don't panic. Frequently a less direct attack on the elusive name or number will produce the answer.
- Mild stress can improve memory by forcing the body to produce chemical brain stimulants. Too much stress may

produce "final examination syndrome," a disruption of cognitive processes. Individuals usually have their optimum levels of stress.

- Some apparent loss of memory may simply be the effect of an environmental change—for example, the out-of-context bewilderment that causes you not to recognise your own doctor, when you unexpectedly run into him at the airport.

Scientists breakdown memory process into three phases: registration, consolidation, and retrieval. In phase no. 1 paying attention is obviously essential for acquiring new information. "But you have to do more than just experience an event to remember it," says Thomas Landauer, a psychologist at Bell laboratories in Murray Hill, USA. "You have to do some kind of work on it." Repeating the same fact over and over immediately upon receipt, is futile, he believes, except for short periods. For example, repetition will help one to remember the telephone number long enough to dial it, but not much longer.

For permanent retention, Landauer recommends what he calls "spacing of practice"—allowing an interval between rehearsals. With each practice, he claims, you are in fact creating a new memory, which may be stored in a different place.

For recall of lists, Landauer recommends categorising; for example, housewives out for shopping should think of vegetables, meats and dairy products separately. Numerous memory systems have been devised in recent years that provide links to help forgetful individuals. Some use mnemonic devices—named after Mnemosyne, the goddess of memory, to improve their memory. As Randy Rodman said, "Mastery lies only in practice, over and over and again and again." All rely on association—linking the thing you are trying to remember to some thing you already know. For older people who fear memory loss, researchers have good news. The human brain remains plastic and capable of learning until late in life—provided the person remains sufficiently challenged. According to Dr Arnold Sceibel of the Brain Research Institute at the University of California at Los Angeles, learning new skills such as a foreign language or a musical instrument, or accepting new community responsibilities, will slow the retired person's memory deterioration.

"The formation and storage of memory traces are infinitely complex phenomena; the mechanism of recall or retrieval is even more mysterious," says Pfeiffer. "Try to imagine what takes place in your brain when some one asks you a question like, Have you read *The Improbable Marquis* ?" or "Do you know Ronald James?" You will respond with in a few seconds and probably correctly. Yet to perform this feat you have somehow searched through memory files containing records of thousands of titles and names.

Life being a series of problems and solutions, we cannot survive without drawing from our inner resources. We recall our learning experiences from the past, use them and apply them in handling problems here and now. Memories of past experiences bring renewal, confidence and hope in our lives. That is where our mind comes to our rescue releasing great energies to uphold us all through the trials of our lives.

Your brain has great untapped potential

Your brain's come back powers are mighty. Its story is by no means over. If your brain's accomplishments to date loom large—Speech memory, reasoning, and all other wonders—they may be as nothing compared to what lies ahead. Remember that your brain's resources have been barely tapped. Its potential is enormous. For men a few hundred thousand years in the future, present human brain may seem quite as primitive as Neanderthal man's brain seems today.

"Your mind is your most exciting asset," says Michael Drury. "The ugliest men and women can be attractive because of their minds. Your mind is one thing that never grows old. Its resilience is astounding. It can remain dormant for decades and still spring forth like the morning." The very purpose of this chapter is to drive home this point. Since we do not know what potential is hidden inside us, we often tend to underestimate ourselves. We have to realise that all of us have untapped potential of great talents and energies. It is high time we realize this. Richard Bach says that any one can achieve any thing in this world. "Trick is," one should stop seeing oneself "as trapped inside a limited body." "Everything that limits us we have to put aside" We must try, "to overcome our limitations." If we can see unlimited potential in us, we will be able to achieve great things in our lives.

Chapter 9

Great Gifts of Knowing, Thinking and Learning

The gift of knowledge is the greatest gift in the world.
Swami Vivekananda (1863 – 1902)
Indian monk

*Reason's biological function is to preserve and protect life and postpone its extinction as long as possible. Thinking and acting are not contradictory in nature; they are, rather, the foremost features of man's nature. The most appropriate description of man as differentiated from non-human being is a being **purposively** struggling against the forces adverse to his life.*
Ludwig Elder Von Mises (1881 – 1973)
Austrian economist

"Ignorance is the night of the mind, but without moon and the stars," said Confucius, a Chinese philosopher. "Men of all classes are profoundly ignorant that they are ignorant," pointed out Socrates, a Greek philosopher. "The door step to the temple of wisdom is the knowledge of ignorance," says Charles Haddon Spurgeon.

"Knowledge is the greatest gift in the world", said Swami Vivekananda. "Knowledge is not something to be packed away in some corner of our brain, but what enters our being, colours and emotion, haunts our soul, and is as close to us as life itself," said Dr Sarvepalli Radha Krishnan, an Indian philosopher.

"Knowledge is the child of experience," said Leonardo da Vinci. Our experience is the result of interplay of our senses and the brain. Sensations brought in by our senses are interpreted by our mind in a meaningful way. Sensations when recognized and given a meaningfuls label, become our perceptions. What we see is what we get, and therefore the world we see is a subjective perception. Perception is our only real knowledge. When we go beyond what is given by senses, and derive some more meaning we call it cognition and understanding. That is the beginning of our knowledge and wisdom.

King Solomon's proverbs say : "I am wisdom, I bestow shrewdness and show the way to knowledge and prudence. In my hands are riches and honour, boundless wealth and rewards of virtue". "Happy he who has found wisdom, and the man who has acquired understanding, Long life is in her right hand, and in the left hand riches and honour".

As apostle Paul said, "our knowledge is partial" because at no point in time the information brought by our senses is complete. But our marvellous brain interprets it and makes meaning out of the available information. That is why the more we know the more wise we become.

"A man is but a product of his thoughts, what he thinks, that he becomes", said Mahatma Gandhi. Will Durant says, "Nature intended thought to be guide to your action, not substitute for it. Thought unbalanced by action is unnatural." Earnest Dimnet says, "The more a man thinks, the better adapted he becomes to thinking, and education is nothing if it is not methodical of the habit of thinking".

Judgment and evaluation are by-products of our thinking aided by our reasoning. Our judgement tells us what is right and what is wrong, what is good and what is bad. It discriminates the beautiful from the ugly. In every problematic situation our evaluative faculties help us judge the probability of success, the incentive value, and the strength of our need before taking any action.

Our language is full of evaluative adjectives. Our attitudes are, in fact, our evaluative statements. David Kretch and R S Crutchfield defined attitude as "a relatively enduring disposition to evaluate a social object or issue positively or negatively". Clement Stone says "there is little difference in people but that little difference makes big difference. The little difference is attitude. The big difference is whether it is positive or negative". Psychologist William James says, "the greatest discovery of my generation is that human beings can alter their lives by altering their attitudes".

Observing and learning increase our knowledge and understanding. Observatories have helped us in understanding the movement of stars and planets. Observation of various phenomena in scientific laboratories have contributed to our knowledge about the things around. The faculty of learning is unique to human beings. Animals learn by conditioning, while knowledge comes to human being more by cognitive learning and understanding. Learning brings permanent change in our behaviour. Schools, colleges, universities and other centres of learning increase our knowledge and understanding of the world.

The subconscious mind

Our knowledge of the mind is incomplete. More so we are not aware of the subconscious mind. Its main focus is to make our regular behaviour as automatic as possible so that our awareness is free to focus on new information. Its dynamics are linked to the psychosomatic and autonomic nervous systems. It profoundly influences our lives with its continuous stream of instructions and imperatives to cope with what is expected. It is the storehouse of everything we have learnt in our lives. It is more than a memory bank. It has its own objectives related to psychological and physical matrix of the individual, primarily linked to the survival. Unless properly instructed, it will tend to protect the integrity of its old learnt purposes against any new purposes. In short, we are highly unlikely to achieve our objectives unless we enlist the help of our unconscious mind. We have to teach our mind to accept change.

Your ideas are your assets

Ideas are products of the mind. "An idea can turn out to be dust or magic depending on the talent it rubs against", says William Bernbach. That is why, as some one said, "bring ideas in and entertain them royally, for one of them may be king". "A man with a new idea is a crank until the idea succeeds," said Mark Twain. Yes, people may laugh at your ideas, because they may appear, when first conceived, as ridiculous and wayward. Simply ignore those people, and continue to work on your ideas until you succeed. Your ideas, can become successful, if you believe in yourself, your ideas and your success. Very few ideas become successful in the first attempt; failures and setbacks are very common while trying new ideas. Cherish your ideas as they are indeed your treasures worth emulating. Pursue them with determination and perseverance. Who knows your future may depend on them?.

Release the breaks on your brain

Michael Drury says, "Most people are brighter than they think—on two levels: brighter than they suppose themselves to be, and brighter than they habitually allow themselves to function." We do not know why this is so, but one reason may be that disclaiming brain has a democratic sound. Another reason is that people slide into disparaging their minds without realising it. Pretty soon they are persuaded.

If you are determined to scuttle your brain, Drury tells ten ways to do it:

Whatever the idea decide that you haven't got time

People who have time make it out of the same number of hours a day allotted to everyone else. Learn to do small bits of work whenever you get a few moments of time, rather than waiting for unlimited time.

Make judgements of your ideas

Every mind generates ideas all day long, because life, by definition, is a series of problems and solutions. Some ideas are merely operational: whether to have omelette for breakfast or go to Rome for a holiday. Others have potential for growth and control: may be you want a degree, or a new job, or to study law, piano, golf.

At once arguments, set in. It will never work. You've no ear for music; you've never been good at sports; your family will disapprove; above all it's a bit late in the day to make changes. There is nothing wrong in weighing pros and cons, but give an idea a chance to grow;

cultivate it; get some facts. You don't trample all over a seedling and then wonder why it died.

Never give your mind anything to chew on
Nobody stops eating at the age of 20, but starved imaginations are commonplace.

If you never read a book, ask questions or travel, no wonder your intellect is undernourished. One of the simplest remedies for this is to take out of the library a book that you are fairly sure you either won't like or won't understand, and read it all the way through. The other side of the coin—equally dangerous as using your brain—is to become a perpetual student, forever taking courses, in the delusion that one day you will know enough to begin to think on your own. Storing up information in an intellectual silo without ever using it will cause fermentation, nothing more. Both ways—starving or stuffing your mind—are delaying tactics, ways to avoid thinking.

Hide your talent under a bushel
Architect Frank Lloyd Wright once said, between arrogance and false modesty he would take arrogance anyday. Arrogance at least accomplishes something. If you really want to stifle your mind, smother it with statements like, "It's nothing; anybody can do it; it's just common sense."

Do something else instead
If you want to try something alarming, sit down with the intention of thinking about something for 10 minutes—a decision that's been facing you, a report you have to make, even such a mundane thing as planning menus for a week. In 30 seconds you will have discovered a job requiring your urgent attention. The task is legitimate and not exactly mindless, which is why it effectively blocks your mental exercise. Nobody can think of two things at once. Tomorrow will do for using your mind, and tomorrow and tomorrow.

Expect instant claim
Drury once interviewed Paul Newman after he was hailed as overnight success in a Broadway show. He laughed hollowly at the term. "Oh, sure," he said. "'Overnight' after ten years in plays that folded and

touring companies where you were lucky to get the bus fare for the next town."

Two things easily defeat the would be thinker: anger at unresponsive public, and fear that somebody else will make the money. The councillor who suggests a fund raising scheme that is voted down, and announces that he won't waste his energies on a new plan, is undermining his own intelligence. A man, Drury knows had a fresh idea for a new local business, but dropped it when the man willing to finance it wanted half the profits.

Foist half-formed ideas on somebody else
To suppose that other people never have ideas and that all one has to do is to waft his brain storms out to dazzled menials waiting for something to work on is sheer ego-patting. Ideas are cheap; any mind sprouts them like mushrooms, unless it is trained out of doing so.

Don't be specific
Unfocused thinking is aimless, a first cousin to daydreaming. Drury admires handicrafts of all kinds, but it took him 30 years to discover that admiration and even faint talent were not production. He couldn't weave, and do wood-work and make pottery, and at the same time devote his energies to his own work. Nobody can do everything. When he accepted that, he felt much lighter and free to think about the things that really were his business.

Assume that everything has already been thought of
An editor, Drury worked for used to say, "Nothing has been done our way till we do it." Twenty years ago, a friend of his with three children tried to interest somebody in pre-packaging baby food in throw-away containers. After months of research with Department of Agriculture, milk companies and chemists, she concluded that her modest brain was no match for the experts. The idea has been discarded as unworkable. Today the product is on the department store shelves.

Suppose that thinking is cold and not human
Watch a child who has just learned to read, and you will know how false that is. Your mind is your most exciting asset. The ugliest men

and women can be attractive because of their minds. Your mind is one thing that never grows old. Its resilience is astounding. It can be dormant for decades and still spring forth like the morning.

Drury has given ten tested ways to keep this from happening. If you fail to follow them you will find out what has been said in the beginning is true: You are brighter than you think.

Structure of intellect

According to J P Guilford our mental structure is composed of two major categories of factors: memory and thinking. Thinking may be subdivided into three areas: cognition, evaluation, and production. Further the productive thinking abilities may be subdivided into convergent thinking abilities and divergent thinking abilities. Intelligence generally includes the convergent thinking abilities; while creativity includes divergent thinking abilities. After three decades of research into the nature of human intelligence and mental abilities Guilford proposed his three dimensional model of "the structure of intellect." This model presupposes the existence of 120 measurable human abilities each definable in terms of specific content, operation and product. Guilford was able to operationally specify more than half of them. For our purpose here we shall consider in general, what we call intelligence (the convergent abilities) and creativity (divergent thinking abilities).

Convergent thinking : intelligence and problem-solving

"Genius," said Dr Edward de Bono psychologist and professor at Cambridge University, "lies in solving the problems of everyday life—and everyone can get better at it." He assembled a set of simple skills for improving thinking. Morton Hunt tells about them briefly:

Plus, Minus, Interesting (PMI)

The crucial step in better thinking is to *see* things without limiting your vision. Try this experiment: Look around the room for red objects. (Don't read on until you've done so). Now close your eyes and ask yourself how many green objects are there. Look again. Surprised? It was your focused attention on red that kept you from noticing things of another colour.

It's the same with an idea. When most of us first hear a new idea or a new solution to a problem, we react instinctively by either liking it or disliking it. Then we use our intelligence to defend that view point. An easy way to escape this trap is to do the PMI. De Bono illustrates the technique with this example: in a discussion about design of public buses, someone suggests taking out all the seats. What is your reaction? Why?

Whatever you said, take another look at the matter, this time using PMI. Spend three minutes writing down every good point you can make about this idea, every bad point, and every point that is neither good or bad but simply interesting. Most people are surprised to find that they generate eight or ten Pluses, as many Minuses, and a handful of Interestings. The aim of doing PMI is to achieve *broad-mindedness* in our thinking, rather than remaining the obedient servant of our own prejudices. To put it another way:

The PMI is an attention expander; it prevents us from seeing only red.

Considering all factors (CAF)

This tool is a conscious effort to make sure you've thought of everything that might be relevant in making a decision. Suppose you are thinking about buying a new house. Do a CAF to be sure you ask all the right questions. While obvious issues such as size, cost and layout are bound to come to your mind, without deliberate effort to list every relevant factor, you might overlook others. How good is TV reception? Is there a local leash law? Can the pipes be drained quickly in case of a power failure in freezing weather?

Consequences and Sequel(C&S)

While PMI and CAF open all sorts of possibilities, C&S helps us to judge which are the best. One of the traits that makes us different from animals is our ability to imagine the outcome of our actions. But we can greatly improve this ability by learning to use it in a systematic way. The De Bono technique is to imagine the probable outcome of a decision in four distances in future: immediate, short-term (1 to 5 years), medium-term (5 to 25 years), and long-term (over 25 years).

In his course De Bono asks such questions as, "What if the world runs out of oil?" Or "What if a new electronic robot replaces human labour in factories?" Students are astonished to see how their predictions of immediate and short-term effects lead them on to perceive long-term possibilities. Soon they acquire enough skill to apply the method to decisions in their own lives.

Aims, Goals, Objectives (AGO)
An often unused tool of better thinking is the practice of making a list of all your reasons for doing a particular thing. Most of us assume we know what our goals are, but often we have hidden or unconsidered goals that get in our way. The pursuit of one goal may keep us away from reaching the other.

Defining our goals can lead to creative solutions to our problems. De Bono tells of a grand mother trying to knit while her yarn was being tangled by the family toddler. Exasperated she put him in his playpen, but he howled so loudly that she had to take him out. Then she realised that her goal wasn't to pen the child, but to separate him from the yarn. So she solved the problem by leaving him out—and climbing into the playpen herself!

First Important Priorities (FIP)
This step helps you to evaluate and to choose among the many possibilities you thought up by means of other tools. De Bono and his colleague, Michael de Saint Arnaud, give this example:

Suppose someone wants to borrow money from you. Consider all the factors and choose the three most important. The top priority might be, "When it will be returned?" followed by "Can you trust the borrower?" In the case of parent lending money to a daughter, the top priority might be, "What does she wants for?" Too many of us make gut-level basis; we do what *feels* most important—but the feeling is no substitute for thinking.

Alternatives, Possibilities, Choices (APC)
Even after using the preceding tools of thought, you may not have found a satisfactory solution to your problem. The key to finding alternative is to look for possibilities outside your usual thinking

patterns. Edison, in searching for a light-bulb filament, tried thousands of unlikely materials, including cork, fishing line and tar, before succeeding with a strip of carbonised cardboard.

Learn to think "wild." Let yourself imagine all kinds of possibilities, including those you would ordinarily consider impracticable or ridiculous. Permit your mind to float free and take out what it offers. Use good sense and judgement only later to weed out what's impossible.

There are number of ways to search for creative alternatives. One is exact opposite of what normally comes to mind. Another is to check your assumptions; may be you have not found a good alternative because you've unnecessarily limited your search. The classic six-match problem is a case in point. Lay six matches on a table. Arrange them to make four equal-sided triangles. If you don't know the answer, you will probably decide there's no way to make more than two triangles with six matches. But who said you have to solve the problem in two dimensions? If you ask yourself the question, the solution suddenly becomes obvious: You can make a tetrahedron (a four-sided pyramid), each face of which is equal-sided triangle.

Other Point of View (OPV)

Often the problems involve a conflict with someone such as your spouse, boss or neighbour. You will be better able to find a solution if you try to see the situation from other person's viewpoint. To see how OPV can help your thinking, write down whatever views the other person is likely to have about our disagreement. Not only are you sure to produce thoughts that surprise you, but you may well see solutions to the problem.

Divergent thinking: imagination and creativity

Creativity is an area even angels feared to tread. JP Guilford isolated abilities that constitute creative aptitude. He says that "originality" is essential for creativity. Besides there are other facilitating abilities : Ideational fluency, Associational fluency, Word fluency, Expressional fluency, Adaptive flexibility, Spontaneous flexibility, Sensitivity to problems, Redefinition and Elaboration.

"The human race is governed by its imagination." observed Napoleon Bonaparte. "To achieve the marvellous, it is precisely the unthinkable that must be thought" said Tom Robbins. Creative imagination of human beings led to innumerable discoveries, inventions, and innovations. All the scientific progress that we see today is the result of the genius of human mind and its creative faculties. More than ever the need for creativity is of utmost importance today.

"In a time when knowledge, constructive and destructive is advancing by the most incredible leaps and bounds into a fantastic atomic age, genuinely creative adaptation seems to represent the only possibility that man can keep abreast of kaleidoscopic change in the world," says Carl R Rogers, one of the eminent scientists of our times. "With scientific discovery and invention proceeding, we are told, at a geometric rate of progression, a generally passive culture bound people cannot cope with the multiplying issues and problems. Unless individuals, groups, and nations can imagine, construct, and creatively revise new ways of relating to these complex changes, lights will go out. Unless man can make new and original adaptations to his environment, as rapidly as his science can change the environment, our culture will perish. Not only individual adjustment and group tensions, but international annihilation will be the price we pay for the lack of creativity. Consequently it would seem to me that investigations of the process of creativity, conditions under which the process occurs, and the way in which it may be facilitated are of utmost importance. I maintain that there is a desperate need for creative behaviour of creative individuals." Such is the concern, for the need for creativity in the world today.

Unlock your own creativity

"Discovery consists of seeing what everybody has seen and thinking what no body has thought," said the Nobel Prize winning physician Albert Szent-Gyorgyi. How do we start thinking about what nobody has thought?. "Usually it takes a whack on the head, like Sir Isaac Newton supposedly had when an apple striking his skull awakened him to the laws of gravity," explains Roger Von Oech. "Whacks can range from something as major as losing a job to as trivial as wanting an unusual dish for a dinner party. We're more likely to respond creatively—which is to say, think of a new idea—if we've already been chipping away at the mental locks that close our minds."

What are these locks? Von Oech explains, "for the most part they are our uncritical acceptance of seven common statements."

"Find the right answer."
Almost from the first day of the school, we're taught that there's one right answer to every problem. But many important issues are open-ended. Take the question "What do I do now I've lost my job? The obvious right answer is: "Look for another job." There is also a second right answer: "Go to school and learn a new trade." Or a third: "Start your own business." The act of looking for a second answer will often produce the new idea you need. As French philosopher Emile Chartier said, "Nothing is more dangerous than an idea when it is the only one you have." Think as many alternative answers as you can.

"That's not logical."
Hard logical thinking can be death to a new idea because it eliminates alternatives that seem contradictory. New ideas germinate faster in the loose soil of soft thinking, which finds similarities and connections among different things or situations. In his workshops Von Oech asks people to create metaphors. A manager had been thinking logically about what was wrong with his company, but couldn't get a grip on it until he came up with this metaphor: "Our company is a galley ship without a drummer. We've got some people rowing at the fullest, some at one-half beat, and some dead beats." This man made himself the missing "drummer," with the result that the operation smoothed out.

"Follow the rules."
To get an idea you often have to break rules that makes no sense. Nolan Bushnel, the founder of Atari Inc., and inventor of the first video game, is a dedicated rule breaker.

Once he was making coin-operated games for fun. For a long time he followed the rule that the playing field had to be 66 cm wide. Only when he threw away that rule and made the field 76 cm was he able to increase the game possibilities.

"Be practical."

To grow, ideas initially need the wide realm of the possible, rather than the narrow path of the practical. You can enter the realm by asking, "What if." An engineer in a chemical company startled his colleagues by asking, "What if we put gun powder in our house paint?" When it starts peeling in a few years, we might put a match to it and blow it off?" The house might blow up with such a paint, but this engineer was talking to "idea" men who brushed aside the impracticality and started thinking. Eventually they came up with the idea of an additive that could later be activated and cause the paint to be easily stripped off the walls. The company is now developing the process.

"Don't be foolish."

Humour can show us the ambiguity of situations, revealing a second, and often startling answer. Being foolish is a form of play. If necessity is mother of invention, play is its father. When faced with a problem, let yourself play, risk being foolish. And write down the ideas that then come to you.

"That's not my area."

Fresh ideas almost invariably come from outside the area of specialisation. Creative people have to be generalists, interested in everything and aware that what they learn in one field might prove useful in another. We're all generalists at home—chefs, decorators, teachers, gardeners, handymen—and home is where to start being creative.

The average homemaker is confronted daily with more creative opportunities than the middle manager in a company sees in a month. Look for ideas from diverse fields.

"I'm not creative."

Most of us entertain the idea that creativity is only for artists and inventors. And when we criticise ourselves as not being creative, we set in motion a self-fulfilling prophecy. A person who thinks he's not creative in his everyday life won't try a creative solution to important problem. Self-esteem is essential to creativity because any new idea makes you a pioneer. Once you put an idea into action, you're out there alone taking risks of failure and ridicule.

As management consultant Roy Blitzer said, "the only person who *likes* change is a wet baby." Von Oech says, "But we need change—the type of change that come only through the creative thinking of all the people, not just the geniuses".

Realise your creative potential

"A soul without imagination is what an observatory would be without a telescope," said Henry Ward Beacher. And without a telescope you will miss all the wonders of the starry universe. Imagine what you will miss in your life without imagination and creative ideas.

"The heart of all new ideas lies in the borrowing, adding, combining, or modifying the old ones, says Michael Le Boeuf. "Do it by accident people call you lucky. Do it by design they call you creative. All of us have the ability to create ideas almost at will. The problem is to understand and utilise the processes that allow us to do it most efficiently and effectively."

Think of your creative abilities as your mental muscle. To get the most from this muscle, you must exercise it, strengthen it, and visualise its capacity to work for you. It is generally agreed that the act of developing new idea involves some five steps.

First insight

You have a problem you want to solve or an activity you want to do—you want a better job, the house needs decorating, your company produces a waste material you would like to turn into a profitable by-product. All these are examples of first insight.

Preparation

Now you investigate all the possible ways in which this germinal idea can be developed. Get as much information about the subject, read, take notes, talk to others ask questions, collect information. Be receptive to your own senses. Picasso once remarked, "The artist is a receptacle for emotions that come from all over the place; from the sky, from the earth, from a scrap of paper, from a passing shape, from a spiders web. These ideas form a spring board for launching our own imaginations".

Incubation

Now let your subconscious take over. Take a walk, take a nap, take a bath, work on another project or hobby, sleep on it. As Edna Ferber once noted, "A story must simmer in its own juice for months or even years before it's ready to serve."

Illumination

This is the climax of the creative process. An insight pops into the mind, and suddenly everything falls into place. Charles Darwin gathered information for his theory of evolution. Then one day when he was riding in his carriage, it all came together. "I remember," Darwin wrote, "the very spot in the road when to my joy the solution occurred to me." Illumination is the most exciting and joyous phase of creative process.

Verification

Yet for all its wondrous insights, illumination can be terribly unreliable. Intellect and judgement are brought into play, and your hunches and inspirations are logically confirmed or denied. You back off and look at your ideas as objectively as possible. You solicit the opinions of others. You revise your good ideas to make them better and often come up with new and better insights in the process.

"Summing up," LeBoeuf says, "the key to understanding the creative cycle is to realise that there are five distinct phases. There is the initial desire to create, followed by a lengthy period of investigating and information gathering. Then there is a period of incubation where the subconscious takes over. This gives rise to the moment of illumination when the results of the subconscious take place. And finally there is a period of refining and verifying the ideas created.

Certain conditions and attitudes can result in understanding how your creative abilities work. Above all you must give yourself an incentive. What's in it for you? A new and better career? A promotion? Self-satisfaction? The best ideas come from those hungry for success. In addition to giving yourself an incentive, you must also create a sense of urgency. Create the necessary pressure by giving yourself reasonable but challenging deadlines for coming up with new ideas.

Then, be sure to stick to them. Creative people show a spirit of intellectual playfulness. All of us can enhance our own idea producing capabilities by adopting a similar attitude—relax, avoid being too careful, think of creativity as fun even though the results of the fun may be very serious. No one can tell you what will work for you. Perhaps it's pacing the floor, or drinking coffee, or listening to music. The point is to use those things that work for you.

Creative thinkers have come up with some practical devices for stimulating and capturing new ideas.

Checklists

Make a list of verbs, such as magnify, minify, substitute, rearrange, reverse, and combine. Try to apply each of these verbs to the problem at hand. Attribute listing is another check-list technique. For example consider the screwdriver. It has the following attributes: it is round; steal shafted; wooden handled; with a wedge shaped-tip; and it is manually operated, by twisting. To design a better screwdriver, you then focus on each attribute separately and ask: could the round shape be made hexagonal so that the wrench could be used for turning with greater torque? What if we remove the wooden handle and design the shaft to fit an electric drill? What if we make several interchangeable shafts for different sized screws? The basic premise of attribute-listing is to look at each component and ask, "Why does this have to be this way?" This breaks down conceptual assumptions.

Recording Devices

Unless you make the effort to document your ideas you'll lose many of them, in the shuffle of the day to day activity. Since there's absolutely no way to predict when a great idea is likely to pop into your mind, be prepared at all times with a note pad, and pen or pencil, or better a micro cassette recorder. When that new idea comes get it on paper or tape.

Idea banks

Have a central place to store ideas related to a particular subject. The idea bank can be a file folder, shoe box, or a desk drawer. Whenever you have a good idea, write it down and bank it. Then, when you get ready to start some serious imagining, you'll have a number of previous ideas to get you started.

Make time work for you
Illumination can speak up in the middle of the night. If you're working on a problem, write down what is blocking your progress, forget it, go to sleep, and let your subconscious work on it. Frequently, you will be awaken with new ideas and solutions. Insomnia can also be put to creative uses. Instead of worrying why you can't sleep, pick an idea in which you can generate new ideas to help you achieve your goals. Who knows? You may come up with a very profitable idea. And thinking them up will often bring good sleep. Much of our daily living consists of routine that requires little or no mental effort. Why not put this time to creative use? Wasted moments can be turned into productive ones.

Most important, withhold judgement when you come up with new ideas, else you may be doing the equivalent of stepping hard on the accelerator at the same time you apply the brakes. Apply critical judgement only after you have come up with as many new ideas as you can.

On the job creativity
"The principal arena of creativity is the work day world of people who are confronted with getting a job done," says William Ellis. "On the job creativity is often merely a matter of imaginative combinations. It is *everybody's* property, and hundreds of people have discovered that it can make almost any line of work into an adventure, a career.

"Where do creative ideas come from?" asks Ellis. "For an answer, observe yourself. Do you do your best thinking at your desk or when you are away from the job? Do your hunches come in a flurry for several days, then dry up for several months or so? You can study and take advantage of these patterns. Do your ideas jump out at you when you are driving? Pull out of the traffic and write them down while the bloom is on them. Ask other people for their creativity tricks and adopt any that suit you.

"Many people abandon a good idea when they get stuck on a "missing link" that they can't resolve," says Ellis. "Professionals in creative jobs encounter the same gaps, but they leave them blank while they work out rest of the idea. Whatever the problem a good idea should keep burning a hole in the pockets of mind. Keep the idea simmering. Your subconscious mind will work on it while you're eating, sleeping, doing chores. Don't give up. Your hunches may be your future… Possibly the most important single element in bringing an idea into being is simply believing in it and hanging on to that belief."

"Accept your ideas are worthwhile until they have been proved otherwise," advises Le Boeuf. "Remember, almost every innovation came about because a determined person stubbornly believed in the product of his or her imagination. Trust yourself." Allow your imagination to fly, think creatively.

"Be brave enough to live creatively," tells Allan Alda. "The creative is a place where no one else has ever been. You have to leave the city of your comfort and go into the wilderness of intuition. You can't get there by bus, only by hard work and risk and by not quite knowing what you're doing. What you will discover will be wonderful. What you will discover will be yourself."

Chapter 10

Delightful Gift of Communication Skills

> *Self expression must pass into communication for its fulfillment.*
> **Pearl S Buck** (1892 – 1973)
> American missionary, author, Nobel Prize for literature 1938
>
> *There is a grace of kind listening as well as a grace of kind speaking.*
> **Frederick William Faber** (1814 – 1863)
> British oratorian, devotional writer

Language is one of the greatest gifts of human beings. It is a tool of thought, but we usually think it is a tool of communication. The two words 'communication' and 'information' are often used interchangeably, but they signify quite different things. Information is *giving out,* communication is *getting through*. Language is said to communicate others to understand meaning of our sentences and we in turn, understand theirs. Communication, of course, is not limited to language. We convey much information to others non-verbally, through gestures and other means.

When we speak one of the several languages of the world we draw on our underlying knowledge of the rules governing the use of language. This knowledge about language or linguistic competence, as it is called, is used automatically and almost effortlessly to generate and comprehend meaningful speech. Linguistic competence seems to be universal human species-typical ability.

The art of pleasing conversation

"Conversational give-and-take is among the most enjoyable and rewarding of mental activities," says James Nathan Miller. "Like study, it informs. Like travel, it broadens. Like friendship, it nourishes the soul. It calls, however, for a willingness to alternate the role of a speaker with that of the listener, and it calls for occasional ""digestive pauses" by both.

"There is a fundamental principle underlying good talk," says Gelett Burgess. "The principle—the basis of all good manners—is the avoidance of friction in social contacts, emotional friction caused by irritation, boredom, envy, egotism, or ridicule." Here are some of the rules to guide your conversation and make it a delightful game.

Avoid all purely subjective talk

Don't dwell on your health, troubles, domestic matters. Never discuss your wife or husband. Streams of personal gossip and egotism destroy all objective discussion of science, history, the day's news, sport or whatever. Such chatter bores the listener; and the talker, repeating what he already knows, learns nothing from others.

Don't monopolise conversation

People yearn for more quiet, comfortable talk with plenty of give and take. You couldn't help remembering what Sydney Smith wrote of Macaulay: "He has occasional flashes of silence, that make his conversation perfectly delightful."

Don't contradict

You may say, "I don't agree with that," but flat contradiction is a conversation stopper. One should seek to find points of agreement. In that way the subject develops interest with each person's contribution. "That is the happiest conversation," said Samuel Johnson, "where there is no competition, but a calm, quiet interchange of sentiments."

Don't abruptly change the subject

Some people, after patiently—and painfully—waiting for a talker to pause for a moment, jump into conversation with a totally new subject. It would be a good practice to have a rule that after a person stopped talking there should be a brief silence in which to reflect, digest, appreciate what had been said. It is a proper tribute for any one who has offered an idea for consideration.

Show an active interest in what is said
This brings out the best in a speaker. Prolong his subject, ask more about it, and he expands like a flower in the sun.

After a diversion bring back the subject
Often while a subject has not yet been fully considered it is lost in some conversational detour. There is no surer test of being able to converse well than to reintroduce this forgotten topic. Not only this is polite and gracious, but it is the best evidence of real interest.

Don't make dogmatic statements of opinion
The Japanese tea ceremony is perhaps the most refined social form ever practised. It is a cult of self-effacement. One may speak of anything, but never with an expression of finality. The remark is left in the air for the next to enlarge upon, so that no one is guilty of forcing any personal opinion upon others.

It is a good game, try it sometime with your friends. You may state facts as facts; but your application of them should be with such qualification as "Isn't it possible that—." Those who really know things speak thus, "meekness of wisdom," as St James says, while the ignoramus tends to make cut-dried pronouncements.

Avoid destructive talk
We are all likely to make unnecessary derogatory remarks. Evil, of course, must be condemned. But try to avoid the unnecessary criticism, the desire to raise a laugh through a ridicule, the tendency to look on the unpleasant side of life. Cynical comments may sound clever, but they make others feel uncomfortable.

So much for the negative side of conversational rules. How can you create an agreeable conversation? The secret is simple. To talk well one must think well. You must think underneath the subject, above it and all round it.

This kind of thinking is well-illustrated by the conversation of sport enthusiasts. Are they content with talking about the score of the game? Not at all. They discuss the teams potentialities, the characteristics of different players, the technique of the game. The same principle applies to all conversation. *"Any one who finds it hard to talk should learn to think about what he sees, hears and reads,"* says Burgess. "As you ponder, associate the subject with your own experience and observation. If you enrich your thinking in these ways you need not worry about your conversation. Every new experience will make your talk more valuable."

Listen to the speaker with interest
James Nathan Miller says, "Actually, a worthwhile exchange requires no more than thoughtful listening, and a thoughtful listener need be no brighter than the rest of us. He simply knows that a true conversation is an opportunity to learn something about one another, and from one another."

There is no such thing as worthless conversation, provided you know what to listen for. The attentive listener doesn't always tune his ear to what people think they're saying. Sometimes he listens for what people unconsciously reveal about themselves while they are talking. Thus he can derive meaning from a conversation even though the other person is talking nonsense. Sometimes, too, the listener can spot unconscious thoughts in an otherwise dull conversation that open up wide vistas of interest.

The question mark is mightier than exclamation mark. The good listener is not afraid to admit ignorance by asking questions. And questions are breath of life for conversation. The single most powerful tool for making a conversation worthwhile is the simple two-word question, "For instance?" It lets the speaker know that you're interested in what he's saying and simultaneously challenges him to move from the surface generality to the illustrative particular. Pressed for specifics, he often blossoms out with a wealth of first hand anecdotes—which can illuminate the most obscure subject.

The listener, in other words, leads the conversation. This is because most of us do not think very well while we are talking. Without help from those around us, we sometimes get lost in our own words. A good listener can help us to overcome this hurdle.

"The basic fact about conversation is this," says James Nathan Miller "it is a partnership, not a rivalry. Pit the most articulate best informed conversationalist against a non-listener, and the result is as if you tried to bounce a ball against a feather pillow. Conversely, subject an ordinary, run-of-the-mill 'dull talker' to the gentle, exploratory probing of a good listener, he often turns out to have wells of interest and information that nobody bothered to tap. The good listener, the person who does not regard lively talk as merely an exercise in self-assertion, adds immeasurably to the art of true conversation—and to the enjoyment of those around him."

The knack of asking questions in a conversation

"How wonderful when a conversational stone we throw out starts an avalanche of response; when our interest and concern open a wide path to another's personality!" says Nardi Reeder Campion. "So often we feel shut out, unable to establish real contact. Yet, by learning the magic power of asking the right question at the right time, we unlock the floodgates of communication." She says that our questions should not be conversation stoppers; instead they should call for thought provoking answers that can set the conversational stone rolling and start others. Consider the following points:

- Seize every possible chance to ask a searching question, *then keep quiet*.
  (When you're talking, you're not learning anything)
- One thoughtful question is worth a dozen inquisitive ones. The prod-and-pry approach makes people to close up.
- Questions that come close to the other person's true interest get the best answers—provided you are interested too.
- Be prepared to wait. Sometimes a long silence can be more rewarding than another question.
- *In every case*, the quality of an answer depends on the quality of attention given by the questioner.
- Questions must spring from honest enquiry, not from attempts at flattery or efforts to manipulate the other person's thinking.

- Questions that deal with a person's *feelings* are more provocative than those that deal with *facts*.
- "Really caring the other person" is the essence of communication.

Only a listening, with loving heart has power to penetrate the coat of armour that encases us all.

Listening

The most basic and powerful way to connect to another person is to listen. Just listen. Perhaps the most important thing we ever give each other is attention. A loving silence often has far more power to heal and connect than most well-intentioned words.

Perhaps, there is more grace in listening than in speaking.

The problem of spare time

Paul Cameron of Wayne State University in Detroit once made an interesting experiment in listening in a nine week course in introductory psychology for 85 college sophomores. A gun was fired 21 times at random, usually when Cameron was in the middle of a sentence. Students were asked to encode their thoughts and moods at that moment.

The results confirmed the worst fears of the professor.

- About 20 per cent of the students, men and women, are pursuing erotic thoughts.
- About 20 per cent are reminiscing about something.
- Only 20 per cent are actually paying attention to the lecture; 12 per cent are actively listening.
- The others are worrying, daydreaming, thinking about lunch or—religion(8 per cent)

We all like to think that we are good listeners. But the fact is, we all have a common problem. Most of us speak about 120 to 180 words per minute and think at four or five times that rate. Because of this disparity, we have a lot of spare time. So, our attention wanders, and we often pick up only about half of the other person's message.

Delightful Gift of Communication Skills   109

How can we improve our ability to listen

Yet, the ability to listen and respond can make all the difference in any relationship—on the job, in the home, with friends. How can we improve our ability to listen? To find out Margaret Lane talked with many professional listeners—psychiatrists, family counselors, social workers. Here is what they recommend:

Listen with your whole self

Tapping with your fingers or jiggling your foot is fine if you are listening to music—but not people. Nothing is more damaging to another person's ego. And if that person is your mate, employer or customer, nothing is more damaging to *you*. So try to block out all distractions. Show you are actively listening through eye contact, encouraging nod of head, a hand gesture that urges the speaker to go on. Even the way you sit, if it's relaxed and attentive, indicates interest as clearly as any words.

When the conversational ball bounces into your court, don't feel you've got to bang on it. Bounce it back.

Speaking and listening are complementary. If everybody talks while nobody listens, it would be like a chatter of monkeys in a zoo. That's what happens in parties. Basic truth is every talker needs a listener. A good listener is as welcome at a party—and as rare—as spring water in the midst of Sahara.

In order to be a good listener you don't have to be beautiful nor witty. When you are listening to a person, your attention should be complete. You should make the other person feel that he is the most interesting person on earth. A good listener has a powerful appeal, the ability, the magic, to make other person feel important.

Help draw the other person out by posing brief comments or questions that show you're listening—even if you are reduced to "Really?" or "Tell me more."

Talking to someone who does not respond is like shouting over a dead telephone: you will soon feel foolish and give up. When some one tells personal problems, we usually try to avoid the topic as we are afraid of prying into his private affairs. But what if we responded positively? "I don't wonder you can't sleep," you could say, "you must have gone through a lot of agony over this." Given a chance to release those pent-up feelings your friend will feel much better. Few of us are so self-sufficient that we don't sometimes need to tell our troubles to a friend who knows how to listen.

Develop sensitivity to what is left unsaid in most messages: the inner thoughts that words often hide.

Even with the people we love most, it's easy to hear the words and miss the real message. An angry attack – "What do you *mean* you are out of money? All this family does is spend, spend, spend!"— may have nothing to do with a family's extravagance. The real message? "I have had a terrible day at work. I'm ready to explode."

If you know how to listen, you'll recognize the hidden hurt and frustration behind the criticism. In a calmer moment, a few words that show you care ("You look tired, rough day?") can help the one who is hurting to vent his feelings in a more constructive way. What might have been a bitter quarrel becomes, instead, the quiet sharing that strengthens any marriage.

Listen without being judgmental
We are always eager to set standards of right and wrong, and hand down judgments. But by judging instead of listening we cut all lines of communication. Psychiatrist Dr Barbara Shipley of University of California says, that it is essential to show people you care about that, while you may not approve of their behaviour, you still approve of *them.*

When a teenager walks in at 3 a.m., it's not easy for concerned parents to keep in mind the importance of listening. The impulse is to shout, "I don't want to hear what happened." This reaction not only destroys communication but far more seriously—it weakens the teenager's regard for himself. By all means let him know how his behaviour has made you feel: "We've been terribly worried and upset." But permit him to tell his side of the story. Psychiatrists caution that it often takes years of therapy to rebuild the self-esteem of those who've grown up in a home where parents never listened.

"All of us hunger to be heard," says Lane. "Psychiatrists' offices are filled with people in need of a listener. "In most instances, communication gets blocked because there are no listeners—only talkers. Listening is an act of caring, a selfless act that permits us to escape the isolation of our separate selves and enter into the warm circle of human kinship –and friendship."

Active listening

Active listening is distinctively different from defensive listening. Active listening enhances our understanding whereas defensive, listening distorts what is being said. At the highest level, listening means, all concentration right *now* to understand what the other person says. That means expression of respect for the speaker and his words.

Active listening is practised by psychiatrists, psychotherapists, social workers and counselors. They pay more attention to the *feelings* and they give feed back to the other person. They help people to help themselves with their emotional problems. There are several reasons why active listening works so well. First, it takes the burden off you as a friend. Simply by being there to understand what is on a person's mind, it often makes it possible for the speaker to clarify his own thoughts. This means you don't have to know all the answers to help. Helping by active listening means, you don't need to guess at reasons or solutions that might not be correct. Thus, you and your friend are saved from wild guessing all possible and impossible solutions.

Second advantage of active listening is that it's a great way to get through hidden layers of meaning. Often people express their ideas, problems or feelings in strangely coded ways. Active listening can sometimes cut through to the real meaning.

Third advantage is that it's usually the best way to encourage someone to share more of himself with you. Knowing that you are interested in him will encourage less feelings of threat, and he will be willing to let down some of his defenses (the walls he had built around himself). In this sense, active listening is simply a good way to learn more about someone and a good foundation upon which to build a relationship.

When to use

Active listening is not appropriate in all situations when some one wants help. Sometimes people are looking for information and not trying to work out their feelings. Active listening is out of place at times like this.

People often hide an important feeling behind an innocent sounding statement or question, and in such cases active listening can bring their real concern into the open. Don't apply the technique unless you are convinced. Usually, if there is a feeling behind a question, you will recognise some accompanying cue—a change in your friend's facial expression, tone of voice, posture and so on. But, it takes attention, concentration and "caring" on your part.

"You should realise that your success in using skill will depend on the attitude you bring to the situation" say Ron Adler and Neil Towne. "Too often people think that active listening is a kind of gimmick they can use when some unpleasant situation arises. If you think about this technique this way, it is almost sure to fail. In fact, unless you truly mean what you say, you'll come across as being manipulative, phony and uncaring." So as you practice your listening skill, try to keep the following points in mind:

First, don't actively listen unless you want to help the other person. You will be doing both yourself and the other person a disservice if you pretend to care when you really don't.

Second, don't actively listen if you're not willing to take the necessary time. Listening with feedback takes time. If you are willing to make the effort, you will be rewarded, but you will only lose speaker's trust if you commit yourself and don't follow through.

Third, don't try to impose your ideas on the other person. Active listening means accepting the speaker's feelings and trusting he can find his own solutions. If you try to moralize, suggest, or otherwise change the speaker, you won't be really be actively listening, and it is less likely that you'll be of much help.

Fourth, keep your attention focused on the sender. Sometimes as you listen to another person share his feelings it is easy to become defensive, to relate his thoughts to your own life, or busy your self thinking of an answer. Remember active listening is a form of helping someone else. Try to keep your energy focused on this goal.

Public speaking

John Wolfe wrote an interesting article, "You Can Speak in Public." He says anyone can improve speaking skills. There are two steps involved in making a speech:

Preparation: Here are four rules for planning your talk.

- *Pick the right subject*: It should be a topic about which you have strong feelings. The only way to be comfortable in front of an audience is to know what you are talking about—and to believe in what you are trying to get across. Choose a topic of direct interest to your listeners and slant your message to them. Assume that you have come up with an idea to improve office efficiency. If you are called upon to sell your idea proposal to the board of directors, emphasise the profits it will bring; when presenting the plan to the people who will implement it, stress how it can make their jobs easier. Every one wants to know what's in it for me?

- *Organise your points logically:* You need a *beginning*—usually a brief description of the problem you intend to attack; a *middle* that enumerates the main points; and an *end* that summarises your entire presentation. An old rule for speakers is put in this way: "Tell them what you are going to tell them (introduction); Then tell them (the main points); and finally tell them what you told them (summary)."

- *Rehearse in private* : After you have planned your presentation, you need to practise delivering it. It's best to do in private not in front of a friend or spouse. You are rehearsing a speech to a group not a one to one discussion. Try to visualise the audience "see" and "hear" the positive responses you will be receiving. Whenever possible do a final review in the room where you will be speaking. This way you will feel at home during your actual performance.

- *Keep notes to a minimum* : The worst thing to do is to read your speech. It's virtually impossible to make reading sound spontaneous. If necessary, list your major headings on index cards—with only a few words on each card. A quick glance will trigger your thoughts. The less you refer your notes, the better you will communicate with your audience. Public speaking is essentially a matter of communication between you and your audience. For most speakers, copious notes is more of a hindrance than help.

Delivery : But no matter how you prepare, you also have to deliver the speech. Here are three rules:

- *Make friends with the audience.* There is no need for "oratory" in the old fashioned sense. Be yourself, you will seldom go wrong. Simple words and short sentences are the best. Examples and anecdotes also help to "build the bridge" to your listeners. Also be sure to look at the audience and maintain eye contact. Seek out friendly faces.

  For the platform professional "humour" is a requirement, but for the average person it is not necessary. Don't begin a speech by saying "Before I get into my talk, let me tell you a joke." That sort of thing adds nothing to your message and, in fact, can destroy your effectiveness.

- *Never apologise* : If you feel any shortcomings, ignore them. If you have a cold, don't mention it. To be confident, *act* confident. If you happen to forget what you are going to say next, keep to yourself (your listeners don't know unless you tell them). Instead repeat your last point, to give yourself a breather or go on to some thing else. Your audience wants you to do well, why disappoint it?

- *Build to a climax* : There should be a compelling purpose to your talk. Aim towards it throughout your speech. Close with a call to action. Don't wait too long to finish. Be sure you stop to speak before the audience stops listening. American entertainer George Cohan had the right idea: "always leave them wanting more."

The old saying "practice makes perfect" applies in public speaking too. So speak at every opportunity; the rewards can be enormous. Indeed with practice, you can use speaking as a spring board for success and a fuller, more satisfying life.

Presentations

The same principles can be used in presentations, using visual aids. Slide projectors, overhead projectors and transparencies, computer aided power point presentations, and video rehearsals are the order of the day. Live demonstrations of products and services are much more effective than explanations and appeals with pictures and photographs.

Persuasion

Plutarch tells us, "When Domesthenes was asked what were the three most important aspects of oratory, he answered "action, action, action." He emphasised the need for appropriate action to win people.

Until recently even the best of the speakers couldn't tell us what makes them persuasive. Now, after hundreds of studies, the researchers have concluded that persuasiveness is greatly enhanced by identifiable techniques that we can all borrow—keeping in mind persuasion is not a manipulation; it is a matter of creating right environment for your ideas and then communicating them effectively.

You can *"get your own way—the easy way"* with "subtle communication skills," says Morton Hunt. The ability to win people to one's point of view is invaluable. We would be far more successful in everyday situations—asking for a raise, ironing out a difference with a neighbour, helping children making their choices—if we used communication techniques of the great persuaders. Here are six ways to be more persuasive in everyday situations:

Use the home-ground advantage

Many people can be more persuasive in their own surroundings than in someone else's. That's why a canny negotiator strives to hold important meetings in his or her office rather than in that of the other side. Research shows that this technique does, indeed, work.

Look your best

We like to think we are more influenced by what someone says than by his or her appearance. But experiments show otherwise.

Psychologist Shelly Chaiken of Massachusetts University selected volunteers on the basis of physical appearance, speech fluency, persuasiveness, and intelligence. She found that the attractive volunteers were much more successful in influencing people than were their less attractive counterparts. Good grooming and appearance should be more appealing besides the persuasive words.

Identify with your listener

When you speak to people with a purpose in mind be friendly and sincere. The more you identify with the listener, the more persuasive the listener will find you. In part, that is due to a human tendency to believe what someone who is one of us tell us. Impress that you are one of them; never show you are different from them. People need that – and it works.

Psychologist Donald Moine discovered that top sales people "match the tone of voice, volume, rhythm, and speech of the customer and mirror body language, posture and mood. Unconsciously, they may even breathe in and out with him. In essence, the best sales people act as sophisticated bio-feedback mechanism, sending back the same signals the customer is sending them."

Reflect the listener's experiences

Good persuaders first create trust and empathy; they never jump right into their argument. The skilled persuader tends to reflect, not rebut, the other person's objections to his argument. He restates the objection, allows that it has merit and only then goes on to show that his views are more cogent. Several studies have found that when a presentation looks at both sides before coming to its conclusion, it seems more persuasive, than one that offers views of only one side.

Make a strong case

You will increase your persuasiveness by giving your listener a solid information instead of opinion. But in doing so, keep in mind that people who are uncommitted can be as much influenced by the *source* of the facts as by the facts themselves. When people hear strong, highly credible authorities cited, they're far less likely to defend their preconceptions against new ideas. But don't overdo citing experts; too much information may make the listener rebel.

Employ stories and examples

Great persuaders have always known that we are more easily influenced by individualized examples and experiences than we are by summarised evidence and general principles. Stories from persuader's personal experience are quite effective in influencing people. Successful people use realistic examples to show the listener that another individual has made the choice he is being urged to make.

In the past, persuasiveness seemed to be a mysterious and personal gift. Today we know that it is largely the result of certain communication skills and techniques that can be learnt. To convince yourself of this, just try it.

Chapter 11

Emotions and Feelings: Exclusive Gift to Humans

Let us not forget that the little emotions are the greatest captains of our lives and we obey them without realising it.

Vincent Van Gogh (1853 – 1890)
Dutch painter

Tune into your emotions, it will allow you to find your natural expression and grow toward a new life of accomplishment and emotional freedom.

Dr David Viscott (1938 –1996)
Pulitzer Prize winning psychiatrist

Human beings are richly endowed with the gifts of emotions and feelings. The ability to feel and be aware of other's emotions and feelings is a special quality of human beings. They are completely human; no other living beings have this faculty. Feelings are a 'living language' that keep us in touch with each other, not as spectators but as participants in a never ending drama of life.

"The mind leads, emotions follow," reminds Ayn Rand. Psychologists recognise that emotion is a subjective feeling which can influence our perception, thinking and behaviour; and that the brain is involved in the perception and evaluation of emotion. Just what is emotion? Surprisingly, this is not an easy question to answer. It almost seems as if there are as many definitions of emotion as there are writers on the subject. In one review 92 definitions were listed. Clifford T

Morgan et al say, "The reason for so many definitions is that emotions have numerous aspects to them; an emotion is many things at once."

Several psychologists tried to explain emotion with their own pet theories. Working definitions of emotions vary, but consensus is emerging that "emotions are multi-component response tendencies that unfold over relatively short time spans." Typically, an emotional process begins with an individual's assessment of personal meaning of an antecedent event, what R S Lazarus calls the "person-environment relationship" or "adaptational encounter". This appraisal process triggers a cascade of response tendencies which may manifest across loosely coupled component systems, such as subjective experience, facial expression.

Emotions differ from moods in that they are about some personally meaningful circumstance (i.e., they have an object); where as moods are free-floating or objectless. Emotions also differ from objective traits such as hostility, neuroticism or optimism. Enduring affective traits predispose individuals toward experiencing certain emotions, and so effective traits and emotional states represent different levels of analysis. So, much for the scientific explanation of emotions.

But we all understand what emotions and feeling are just as we understand electricity without ever bothering about the scientific explanations. Basically, we are not only rational beings but also emotional beings—more emotional than we often realise. Indeed, most of the affairs of everyday life are tinged with emotions and feelings. Joy and sorrow, excitement and disappointment, love and fear, attraction and repulsion, jealousy and envy, anger and frustration, hatred and contempt, disgust and despair, hope or dismay—all these and many more we experience in the course of our lives.

Role of emotions and beliefs

Emotions are our reactions to stimuli from the environment. Information conveyed by the senses is automatically categorised and placed in the context: a person's beliefs about the world and his/her function in it. Beliefs are accumulated memories acquired by the person during the process of socialisation, academic learning, personal experience; they give meaning to a stimulus that comes from outside.

This gives rise to automatic arousal of associated emotions, which are psychosomatic phenomena involving whole nervous system. When aroused a person literally 'becomes' the emotions. If memories and beliefs are bricks, emotions are the cement that binds them together. These emotions focus energy on limited learned processes. Then the strategy to respond is formed. Consciousness finally enters the process. It helps to determine appropriate tactics of carrying out the learned responses. Finally we respond to the stimulus, by appropriate behaviour and actions.

Emotions do rule our health

Psychiatrist Dr Don Dudley, a specialist in the field of behavioural medicine, says that there is a "link between a person's emotional state and disease." Dr Caroline Bedell says that anybody who does not believe this, is "ill-informed." Emotional strain and mental distress affect our health and bring in disabling bodily diseases. Investigators found that lung cancer patients tend to be individuals who bottle up their emotions. Researchers at John Hopkins University School of medicine discovered that physicians with established tendencies towards depression, anxiety or anger tended to fall ill at a younger age than those of calmer temperament.

"Medical experts have demonstrated that emotional upset triggers a chain of events involving the brain and the endocrine system," says Peter Michelmore. "This neuro endocrine response, which affects all vital bodily processes, is natural and necessary. Severe over stimulation, however, may have physical effects leading to disease."

According to one theory, says Dr James Henry, professor of physiology at the University of Southern California in Los Angeles, two patterns are beginning to emerge, depending on the type of emotion.

Such passive emotions as grief and despair, with feelings of loss or failure, register in the hippocampus, the part of the brain that activates the body's pituitary-adrenal- cortical network. Hormones like cortisol, needed for the regulation of metabolism, are secreted in excess quantities from the outer portion (cortex) of the adrenal glands. If this occurs too often or for too long, the immune mechanism is thrown out of order. Defences against infections and tumours diminish. And such auto-immune diseases as rheumatoid arthritis, myasthenia gravis, a progressive muscle weakening disease, may be more likely to develop.

More intense emotions like anger and impatience or a sense of threat to one's family, income or position, affect a different section of the brain—amygdala, which sets the adrenal-medullary system. The inner portion (medulla) of the adrenal glands releases chemicals known as catecholamines (adrenaline is one). These increase the heart rate, elevate blood-pressure and raise the level of free fatty acids in the blood. Faced with challenge our survival instincts prompt this response. But prolonged and repeated stimulation may lead to migraines, hypertension even coronary heart disease and stroke.

Everybody has setbacks in life; everyone experiences occasional losses or threats. Why do some people sail through such events, while others fall apart? "Effective coping involves a capacity to maintain psychological equilibrium without experiencing undue or prolonged neuro-endocrine arousal" says Dr Henry. "And this is enormously dependent on a person's self-esteem and social assets, the ties that bind him to others."

"But learning how to live with one's emotions is important. Denying that they exist causes problems," says Peter Michelmore. "A sense of mastery over one's destiny is an essential asset for good physical and emotional health. When feelings of helplessness or insignificance set in, the neuro-endocrine system shifts into overdrive and the disease may become far more likely."

What can you do to prevent your emotions from making you ill? "Learn to take care of your mind as well as your body," says Dr Dudley. "Recognising that emotions trigger physiological reactions—and vice versa—is half the battle," says Michelmore. "The other half, is knowing that the foundations of good health lie in love, laughter, and faith in oneself."

Don't be afraid to let your feelings show
Expression of feelings is a sign of health; while their suppression leads to serious illness. "Feelings can never be categorised as 'good' or 'bad',"

says Psychologist Beatrice Harris. "Feelings are symptoms of complex reactions." In an article *"Don't Be Afraid to Let Your Feelings Show,"* John Kord Lagemann says, "The secret of getting along with people is to recognise how they feel, and let them know you know."

"When some one is rude or quarrelsome, it is often a way of saying, "Pay attention to my feelings." When we say of someone "He understands me," we're really saying "He knows how I feel." Awareness of feelings in others comes naturally if only you let it. In difficult situations, "the right thing to do" is not hard to find if you let other people's feelings come through to you and acknowledge your own.

Share your feelings

Happiness, too, is greater for being shared. "I felt like it"—that is the best reason in the world to laugh, or to be generous, or to applaud something. And that is what moods are—"feeling like it." Why fight them? Like shifting of lights in the theatre, moods, enable you to see life in all its aspects. In melancholy mood you observe details that escape you in a mood of jubilation. Pensive, you filter out distracters and concentrate on deeper thoughts. Nostalgic, you capture the flavour of past events and see the meaning that escaped before.

We mistrust moods because they change. Yet changing moods are perhaps the surest indication of a healthy personality. It's when the mood *doesn't* change we should be worried. "Happiness is just a mood, there is little logic to it. Wonderful moments of joy or sheer well-being come over us now and then without warning; elation appears out of nowhere," says Lagemann. "Such moments of spontaneously shared feelings are unpredictable and fleeting. But they linger on in the atmosphere of the place."

Feelings provide reliable self-guiding system

"My feelings got the better of me," we sometimes say when we are moved to act kindly or courageously. It's almost an apology. Yet feelings welling up from depths of our personality, shaped by lifetime of experience, provide a reliable and almost automatic self-guiding system. But as Sigmund Freud once observed, in all the really fundamental issues of life, the final decision is best left to feelings. Lagemann says, "How else is one to decide whom to marry, whom to trust as a friend or colleague, what to do when faced with a sudden life or death emergency? Through feelings we gain self-insight, tap our creative powers, deepen and enrich our relationship with others."

But unfortunately we often deny our feelings, because we are afraid of facing consequences. Feelings commit us to one another, and this involves the risk of disappointment. They make us take sides, blurt out awkward truths, from personal preferences. "Playing it cool" on the other hand, means being "with it" until the going gets rough, then turning without regret to something else—another mate, another job, and an other cause. It may spare us a lot of heartache, self searching and struggle.

Relationship without feelings is empty
"But when you subtract feelings from marriage, friendship or work," asks Lagemann, "what is left? You can share money, food or sex with another and still remain complete strangers. In the end the only way you can mean anything to another human being is to share his feelings."

Be in touch with your feelings
"The first step in increasing your self-understanding is to look at how closely you're in touch with your emotions," say Ron Adler and Neil Towne in *Looking out/Looking in*. Before communicating your feelings to others you have to be aware of them yourself. This seems obvious, but many times we are not certain *how* we feel. People have trouble recognising their feelings. If you have spent some time with babies or young children you know that for them there is no gap between feeling and acting. When a one-year-old is happy she laughs not just with her face but with her whole body. When she feels pain she cries, and when she is angry you know it right away.. Children at this age do not know feel-think-act pattern, that is common with grownups; instead it seems that they are just angry.

Learn to decondition your conditioned reflexes
What happens in the way of this easy expression of feelings? Kids don't stop getting angry, having sexual thoughts or intense feelings; emotions can't be turned off or on as it will be like water from a faucet. But because we are taught that certain feelings are not ok, we

do learn to push them out of our consciousness so that pretty soon they become hard to recognise. In the process of growing up we learn to link-up our feelings with feel-think-act pattern.

Ivan Pavlov, a Russian physiologist and Nobel laureate, discovered what are called "conditioned reflexes" in human beings. In the process of growing up, our emotions and feelings get conditioned to respond to various external stimuli. Our behaviour is conditioned by rewards and punishments. Success is rewarded and failure is punished. So, we all learn to feel happy when we succeed and unhappy when we fail. As we grow into adulthood, our feelings of happiness and unhappiness become conditioned reflexes. Thus, free expression of emotions and feelings becomes very difficult if you impose a condition to be happy. Emotions and feelings are conditioned responses to social stimuli. If you want you can unlearn them. Once you master the new learning, you will be free to feel whatever you want, even happiness!

Chapter 12
Only One Life to Live Joyfully

Man can will nothing unless he has first understood that he must count on no one but himself; that he is alone, abandoned on earth in the midst of his infinite responsibilities, without help, with no other aim than the one he sets himself, with no other destiny than the one he forges for himself on this earth.

Jean-Paul Sartre (1905-80)
French philosopher, novelist Nobel Prize for literature 1964

We are not permitted to choose the frame of our destiny.
But what we put into it is ours.

Dag Hammarskjold (1905-61)
Swedish diplomat, Former Secretary General UN Nobel Prize for peace 1961

Story of man is writ large on our civilisation. But what historians have recorded is entirely different from what it actually is. Will and Ariel Durant tell us the other side of the story. "Civilisation is a stream with banks. The stream is sometimes filled with blood from people killing, stealing, shouting, and doing things historians usually record, while on banks, unnoticed, people build homes, make love, raise children, sing songs write poetry and even whittle statues. The story of civilisation is the story of what happened on the banks. Historians are pessimists because they ignore the banks for the river."

Let us consider what is happening on the banks here and now on the earth. You will notice that even today, as ever, "people build homes, make love, raise children, sing songs, write poetry and even whittle statues." That's life, bustling all around you and me. As we observe, people are busy with many activities to satisfy basic needs, achieve personal goals, make money, enjoy life and make themselves happy. In the process they encounter success and failure and experience all the associated feelings. Sometimes they feel happy and sometimes unhappy. When personal demands are not met and expectations unanswered they enrage themselves with helpless anger. And when the ordeal becomes tough and the situation difficult, they get frustrated; and when the problems frighten them, they suffer the trauma of stress and strain; and even experience psychosomatic health problems. Yet, people keep on working strenuously towards achievement of their goals, whatever be the outcome. With ceaseless efforts, they pursue happiness which seems to elude them. Before they end the relay race they hand over children the baton of family values, traditions and mores of the society.

Dr Lewis Thomas of Cornell University Medical College, New York, says,

> "One way of looking at Nature is to put together all the scientific facts learnt so far and conclude that we are here through the blind accident of an infinite series of random events, that we are trapped like insects in a pointless, centreless universe and have no responsibilities except our individual selves. We have the responsibilities, even though we are not sure just what they are, but we do not run this place. It runs itself, and we are part of this running."

Jaen-Paul Sartre also expresses similar views

> "Man can will nothing unless he has first understood that he must count on no one but himself; that he is alone, abandoned on earth in the midst of infinite responsibilities, without help, with no other aim than the one he sets himself, with no other destiny than the one he forges for himself on this earth."

Yes, man is all alone here. When you come to know that there is no other life form like man in the entire universe except the earth, the immediate feeling is frightening.

Yes, it looks as if you are abandoned here, like Daniel Defoe's character Robinson Crusoe, in a remote planet surrounded by endless universe. Since there is none to come to your rescue you have to count on yourself for everything. In other words, "you have to run your own race". Again, you are overwhelmed by endless responsibilities. You have the responsibility to look after your self, spouse, children and parents. Help your siblings in their struggle for existence.

Man is self-centered, but he cannot live all by himself. Family, spouse, work, and friends are the four pillars that support his life. He needs external support to sustain himself and his family members. Fortunately he has a lot of people around. As he learnt the necessity of interdependence, dealings with fellow beings assumes importance. As Henry Van Dyke says, "In the progress of personality first comes a declaration of independence, then the recognition of interdependence." We live in a society that thrives on interdependence, and we live on hopes of help and cooperation. This necessity of interdependence created groups, organisatons, and the society at the apex level. Robert Wright tells us, in *Non-zero*, that living organizations—both organisms and the groups they form—have been getting increasingly complex and well-integrated since life began, so it is a good bet that this trend will continue in the future.

A philosopher George Santayana says, "Life is not a spectacle or a feast; it is a predicament." There is some truth in the statement because life on earth is indeed a bitter-sweet predicament. And then there are pessimists like Thomas Fuller who says, "We are born crying, live complaining and die disappointed." On the other hand there are plenty of optimists like George Bernard Shah, who says, "Life is no brief candle. It's a splendid torch." Actually there are more optimists on earth who expect to live a joyful life.

"Let us live. Let us have the true joy of life," says Rabindranath Tagore, "which is the joy of the poet in pouring himself out in his poem. Let us express our infinity in everything around us, in works we do, in things we use, in men with whom we deal, in the enjoyment of the world with which we are surrounded. Let our soul permeate our surroundings and create itself in all things, and show its fullness, by fulfilling the needs of all times. This life of ours has been filled with gifts of the divine giver. The stars have sung to it, it has been blessed with the daily blessing of the morning light, the fruits have been sweet to it, and the earth has spread its carpet of grass so that it may have its rest. And let it like an instrument fully break out in the music of its soul in response to the touch of the infinite soul."

But then, he points out the necessity of moral standards in our lives. While speaking of man, he says that there is "dualism in his consciousness of what *is* and what *ought* to be. In the animal this is lacking, its conflict is between what *is* and what is desired.; whereas in man, the conflict is between what *is* desired and what *should* be desired. What is desired dwells in the heart of natural life, which we share with animals; but what should be desired belongs to a life beyond which is far beyond.

"So, in man, a second birth has taken place. He still retains a good many habits and animal instincts of his animal life; yet his true life is in the region of what *ought* to be. In this, there is continuation, yet there is conflict. This necessity of fight with himself introduced an element into his personality which is character. From the life of desire it guides man to the life of purpose. This life is the life of moral world. In this moral world we come from the world of nature into the world of humanity. We live and move and have our being in the universal man." Immanuel Kant says, "Morality is not properly the doctrine of how we may make ourselves happy, but how we may make ourselves worthy of happiness."

Human nature is so complex that there is a great diversity in human experience—in success and failure, joy and pleasure and pain and suffering. Every man's life is precious, in as much as it offers valuable lessons of life. There is a lot to learn from the personal experiences of people who have gone through the different trials of life. Let us consider what people say about their experiences in life and what they offer to other fellow beings.

Family life: the main source of our happiness

"Call it a clan, call it a network, call it a tribe, call it a family, whatever you call it, whoever you are, you need one," says Jane Howard. Family is the basic unit that makes communities and societies thrive. Charles Colson says, "The family is the most basic unit of government. As the first community to which a person is attached and first authority under which a person learns to live, the family establishes the society's most basic values." Yes, the traditions, customs and values of the society originate from our families. "A family is a place where principles are hammered and honed on the anvil of everyday living," says Charles Swindoll. "A family is the school of duties founded on love," says Felix Adler. Family is the place where man learns his sense of responsibility for self and the family members.

"Home is where the heart is," said Pliny the elder, a Roman historian, long ago. Family, indeed, is the first and the last solace for love and affection for every human being. When Admiral Byrd believed himself to be dying in the ice of Ross Barrierhe wrote some thoughts on happiness. "I realised I failed to see that the simple, homely, unpretentious things of life are the most important. When a man achieves fair measure of harmony within himself and his family circle, he achieves peace. At the end only two things really matters to a man, regardless of who he is : the affection and understanding of his family." John Bowring says, "A happy family is an earlier heaven."

Poet John Howard Payne wrote:

Mid pleasures and places though

We may roam,

Be it ever so humble

There is no place like home.

Parents: the source of our life

"Honour thy father and mother, that you may live long in the land," says one of the ten commandments which Moses is said to have received from God. Most of us were taught, in the early days of our schooling, a small prayer *"Pitru devo bhava, Matru devo bhava, Guru devo bhava."* It means: 'My father, my god, I bow to you (with reverence); my mother, my goddess, I bow to you (with love), my teacher, my god, I bow to you (with respect).'

In the Eastern world children stay with parents even after their marriage; they usually have joint families. Recent phenomenon of urbanisation is breaking this tradition; forcing people to live in nuclear families. Whereas in the Western world, children leave their parents when they grow up to establish their own families. Ted Cook says woefully, "Parents: Persons who spend half their time worrying how a child will turn out, and rest of the time wondering when a child will turn in." Parental feelings of attachment are for ever; distance cannot diminish their love and affection.

Father: source of support and learning
No one would have come into being without a father. He is the one who gave you identity and his family name. Every father has the responsibility to bring up children, and support them through their education, career, and settlement in life. George Herbert says, "One father is more than a hundred school teachers." Yes, he is the first teacher and mentor.

He shares his experiences with children and teaches them the intricacies of life. Arthur Gordon says that sharing a wonderful experience with loved ones establishes unforgettable bond. "Years have passed since then; most of the minor trials and triumphs of childhood have faded from my mind. But I remember that moment on the roof with my father as if it had happened yesterday. A magical day when—just for a moment, perhaps simply by accident—a chord was struck, a spark jumped the gap between generations, and a relationship was suddenly achieved so warm, so intense, that it was caught and held in the meshes of the mind, impervious to time." That is the kind of joy we all derive when a father shares joy with his children.

Mother: source of love and affection
A story is told how Solon, the Athenian showed his wisdom when he came in his travels to the court of Croesus, the king of ancient Lydia. The king having shown his riches asked him who he thought was the happiest of the men, counting that he would answer, "Croesus the king". But Solon said "Tillus the Athenian", for he lived honorably and begot noble sons and fair daughters, having given victory to his country." Then Croesus asking, "And the next?", Solon made answer, "Cleobis and Biton," whose mother prayed the gods to grant the best of all gifts to her sons for *the utter love and tenderness they had shown to her*(the italics are mine), and on the morrow the twain were found dead. For he is happiest who dies happily and no man may be counted until he is dead."

Yes, every living human being would be too glad to show love and tenderness to one's mother. Abraham Lincoln echoes, as if he is saying for everybody: "All that I am, or can be, I owe to my angel mother." Again, read a delightful narrative of William A Greenbaum II who admires his loving mother: "If there is anything one cannot do without, it is mother. Father loves her daughters imitate her, son ignores her, salesmen thrive on her, motorists hurry around her, teacher phones her, the woman next door confides in her.

She can be sweeter than sugar, more sour than lemon, all smiles, and crying her heart out within any given 2-minute period.

She likes detective stories, having her birthday remembered, church, a new dress, the cleaning woman, father's praise, a little lipstick, flowers and plants, canasta, dinner out on sunday, policeman, one whole day in bed, crossword puzzle, sunny days, tea, and the newspaper boy.

She dislikes doing dishes, father's boss, having her birthday forgotten, the motorist behind her, spring cleaning, junior's report card, rainy days, the neighbour's dog, stairs, and the man who was supposed to cut the grass.

She can be found standing by, bending over, reaching for, kneeling under, and stretching around, but rarely sitting on.

She has the beauty of a spring day, the patience of a saint, the appetite of a small bird, and the memory of a large elephant.

She knows the lowest prices, everybody's birthday, what you should be doing, and all your secret thoughts.

She is always straightening up after, reminding you to, taking care of, but never asking for.

Yes, a mother is one thing that nobody can do without. And when you have harassed her, buffed her about, tried her patience, and worn her out, it seems that the end of the world is about to descend upon you, then you can win her back with your little words, "Mom, I love you."

Sandra Day O'Connor grew up in a ranch but rose to become the first woman justice on the US Supreme court. What motivates a woman like her? Alan Loy McGinnis says, "Intelligence, of course, and inner drive. But the credit goes to a determined ranch mother sitting in her abode house, reading to her children by hour, and pushing them to do their best." But people take their mothers for granted till they grow up. W D Howells says, "A man never sees all that a mother has been to him until it is too late."

On married life

"Weddings have less to do with being married than with the fact that it is best to begin the most arduous journey surrounded by friends and wearing nice cloths," says Tony Early. Wedding is an event and marriage is an achievement.

"Love and marriage are like a garden that needs to be tended every day," says Bruce Willis. "A marriage must be created—it is not something that happens," says Wilfred Peterson the author of *The New Book of the Art of Living*. "And in the art of marriage little things are big things." Here are simple rules for successful marriage:

- It is never being too old to hold hands.
- It is remembering to say, "I love you," at least once each day.
- It is never going to sleep angrily.
- It is forming a circle of love that gathers in the whole family.
- It is at no time taking the other for granted, but making the courtship continue through all the years.
- It is doing things for each other, not out of duty or sacrifice, but in the spirit of joy.
- It is demonstrating gratitude in thoughtful ways.
- It is not looking for perfection, but cultivating flexibility, patience, understanding, and a sense of humour.
- It is having the capacity to forgive and forget.
- It is giving each other an atmosphere in which each can grow.
- It is finding room for the things of the spirit. It is a common search for the good and the beautiful.
- It is not only marrying the right partner, it is *being* the right partner.

Advice to young men

One of the oldest advices comes from Solomon, king of ancient Israel: "Enjoy life with a woman you love all the days of your allotted span here under the sun, empty as they are; for that is your lot while you live and labour here under the sun."

> "Drink water from your own cistern
> and running water from your own spring
> do not let your well overflow into road
> your runnels of water pour into the street;
> Let them be yours alone,
> not shared with strangers.
> Let your fountain, the wife of your youth,
> be blessed, rejoice in her,
> a lovely doe, a graceful hind, let her be your companion.
> You will at all times be bathed in her love,
> and her love continually wrap you around,
> where ever you turn, she will guide you,
> when you lie in bed, she will watch over you,
> when you wake she will talk to you."

Advice to a young wife

"Thirty-six years of being a wife have utterly convinced me that no job, no hobby, no activity on earth can compare with the drama and exhilaration of living with a man, loving him, doing your best to understand his infinitely complex mechanism and helping to make it hum and sing and soar the way it was designed to do," says Ruth Stafford Peale. "Is this easy? Of course not. It takes skill and selflessness. You have to use your heart and your head. But it can be done, and when it is—well, what *is* adventure? It's the discovery of new powers and new dimensions, the opportunity for self testing, the happiness that comes from high achievement. These are the promises hidden in every marriage—if only a woman will reach out and claim them." She offers some suggestions as to how to make and keep one's marriage exciting:

Study your man

Recognise that your man is a rare and fascinating animal—which indeed he is. ! Study him ceaselessly because he will be constantly changing. Take pride in his strengths and achievements, but analyse his areas of weakness, too. You are dazzled by his brilliance, his confidence, his charm. You have yet to encounter his uncertainties, and inadequacies. But this is where you can *really* love him, *really* help him, *really* be his wife.

Respect his work
When you marry a man, you also marry his job. At times you may even feel that the job comes before you. It doesn't really, but doing his work well means as much to a man as motherhood does to a woman—and for much the same reasons.

Learn the tricky and challenging art of absorption
Certainly a wife is entitled to love and loyalty. But she also has to be ready to absorb irritability on the part of her husband at times, flashes of displaced anger, discontent with his own performance. These things have to find an outlet somewhere. If a wife can think of herself as a kind of lightning rod that conducts fear and frustration harmlessly in to the ground, not only will she be of inestimable value to her husband but she will grow tremendously as a person herself.

Even when a man becomes successful, and know it, some hidden, sensitive, unsure part of him continues to need the unquestioning support and loyalty of a loving woman. Most men desperately need a sounding board against which to test ideas, hopes, dreams, ambitions, problems, inner conflicts that they can't resolve alone. They need a woman to whom they can confide their innermost thoughts and feelings without fear of ridicule and rejection.

Listen creatively
Listening involves response, communication, and exchange of ideas. Sometimes a wife has to be silent, has to bite her tongue, hold back the sharp words that will turn an argument in to a fight, or a bad situation into a worse one. No doubt her husband has equal responsibility. But think that a man's job is basically to tame the world; a wife's job is to control herself—and indirectly her husband.

Let him know you need him
If you think he is neglecting you, don't be angry. Go to your husband. Ask him to put his hands around you. When he does, say to him,

'Darling, I'm hurt. I'm unhappy, and I think you know why. I am your wife. Please hold me. Please help me.' The admission of your need of his love will work miracles that no amount of anger can.

Use your talents
Marriage need not limit your horizons. If you have a gift for design, or photography, or decorating, or writing poetry—any talent at all—don't let it gather dust; use it to expand your marriage. Use them to understand your husband, to run his home efficiently and keep yourself aware of what's going on in the world.

Commonsense do's and don'ts
Don't make an issue over small things. Overlook them and you will find your opinion carries a lot more weight in big things.

Don't be afraid to compromise. Compromise does not mean giving in. It's simply an adult way of acknowledging that there are points of view other than your own in this complex world, and realising that some of them may occasionally be right.

Don't be alarmed if you and your husband differ about some things. Marriage is a partnership not a merger of identities. Don't keep fretting over irretrievable mistakes. Everybody makes them. The best thing to do is to learn from them and then forget them.

Expand, develop the art of sharing—not just the big, serious things, but the little, delightful things: the book you are reading, the joke that you hear and hoard for him, the sunset you call him out to watch, the entrancing, the unbelievable thing your three-year-old said.

Try to please your husband
This is perhaps the simplest and most inclusive of all rules for successful wives. Does he like neatness? You can be neat. Does he like friends around him? Learn to entertain. Is his job an exacting one? Make his home an oasis of quietness in a noisy world. Does he want you near? Thank heaven—be available.

"To love and cherish, till death do us part," this is the great, soul-satisfying role of a wife" says Ardis Whitman. "And never make the mistake of thinking it a secondary role. Where the ship of matrimony is concerned your husband may be the engine, but you are the rudder—and it's rudder that determines where the ship will go!"

Death, grief and solitude

Death of loved ones is equally emotional but it invokes feelings of deep sorrow. Memories of loved ones linger on for a long time. The loss of a spouse is one of the most tragic events in anybody's life. The living life partner sometimes would like to do something in memory of the departed soul. When King Mausolus of ancient Caria died, his widow Artemisia decided that she would erect in his memory a most magnificent tomb – the Mausoleum, that the world had never seen or should ever see. It was completed after her death. Shah Jahan, a Mogul emperor had built Taj Mahal, a beautiful piece of architecture in memory of his beloved wife, Mumtaj Mahal. Both these monuments were regarded as the great wonders of the world. Though not on such a grand scale, many people continue to do similar things to keep the memories of their loved ones who left this world. As their memories linger on, living a lonely life becomes an ordeal for many.

As the dear ones leave this world, we are often left with grief and solitude. When American writer Max Wylie lost his wife and two daughters, he was left alone. He narrated how he dealt with such a deep sorrow in an article, "When Faced With Grief."

He says, "Immediately after a loss, when the shock is most acute there isn't much one can do. No one, when stranded by sudden loss, will believe that time will heal. All you can do is stand still and hurt, insensitive to pain but your own. But if you want to get your nerve back after any disabling catastrophe—whether it is job loss, crippling illness, death in the family, an agonising divorce, betrayal, rejection or sudden loss of normal powers—there are certain affirmatives to remember. However formidable your situation, you are not alone in it. You are not the first to go through it. Many others are there in it with you right this minute. Misfortune is the only true international currency the world has ever had."

"Now in retrospect, I know that I learned something of value. Some of your own grief departs when you take on that of another. It becomes a bit more bearable. Your own pain will never go away, but a true sharing of the perplexities of someone else will do much to push aside the monopolising and suffocating fog of great personal loss. In the course of months, I found that the more you can be concerned with the hard condition of another, the less you will be concerned about your own." Psychiatrist Eric Fromm says,

"To spare oneself from grief at all cost can be achieved at the price of detachment, which excludes the ability to experience happiness."

Solitude does not always lead to loneliness; but it remains a great emotional concern for every human being. "Like most important learning experiences, solitude is full of pain. No state of life can sour easily. We must use both craft and courage to prevent it from doing so," says Ardis Whitman:

Don't feel sorry for yourself
Self-pity separates us from people. Don't brood resentfully; instead learn to respond to people. You must contrive in solitude to love life and people dearly.

Search out the joys of solitude
Read your daily journal. List out the special joys: "Today a friend called me and brought me an unexpected gift.; I took a long walk and came back rejuvenated." Looking back in the pages you can watch yourself growing and discover how unpredictable and wonderful life can be.

Accept your solitude as a time to grow
Solitude is related to our lives as link to a chain. It is—if we let it be—a time to grow; a time to see both past and future directions of our lives.

Accept your solitude
Perhaps you will be alone at least for a part of your life. You have to learn to deal with it. But if there is something you want –remarriage, a new kind of work, new friends, transmute the longing into being worthy of these things when and if they come.

Deepen your life
Turn everything to account, to understanding. This is the special virtue of solitude. The power of life comes from within; go there.

Pray, meditate. Reach for those luminous places in yourself where, for most of your life, you have been a stranger.

Love, respect and enjoy your life

Do not castigate yourself for guilts that may have contributed to your loneliness. Rest. eat well, sleep. And give yourself rewards, surprises, joys. Say to yourself, "I have been hurt. I will allow myself a break, a comfort." Given a choice, few people would choose solitude as a permanent state. But one can choose to have it as a portion of life sometime, for without it we cannot be whole.

Whitman says, "Remember all of us are solitaries even when we are living in a house full of people. Everyone is born alone; find the meaning of this life alone; goes to death alone. The most important thing we can do is to learn to live with ourselves with courage, humility and beauty."

"Even in the ordinary rhythm of life, people are required to balance society and solitude," says Joan Mills. Solitude is "like a return to having a private place in which to know oneself, and grow." The setting must be just right for the ruleless, easeful time to spend. Serene hours, all for yourself. She says, "Alone, but not lonely, I postulate philosophies, explore my soul, and, in the modesty of solitude, expose my loves and angers, wishes and disappointments. I examine each and put it in its place. Alone, I redefine my appreciation of the people with whom I live."

Arthur Schopenhaur says, "He who does not enjoy solitude will not have freedom." June Callwood says happiness "is also part of an unembarrassed appreciation of leisure and solitude." According to Henrick Ibsen, "The strongest man is he who stands alone."

Birth, children and grand children

"So goes the world around. Time in its season, grace in moments of knowing. The children become mothers and fathers; and love begins again—at the beginning," says Joan Mills. "And there is something else: having a baby is one of those rare times in life when things you haven't even thought of come into focus and good happens in mysterious ways." And, "Grand children are the crown of old age and sons are proud of their fathers," says an ancient proverb.

"Our children are our greatest joy and treasure," says Pearl Buck. "In this most challenging age of human history, we need them all. Who knows what brilliant scientist, what talented artist, is lost in a slum? Our investment of love – wise, understanding, guiding love – is the best investment we can make. For our children are what we make them. They come to us helpless, malleable, dependent upon what we provide. They leave us as men and women, the next generation, the blessed or the doomed. Brought up in the security of love, our children are our strength, our future and our pride."

Upbringing and helping to grow

Remember that we are all formed by other people's expectations of us. Children are self-fulfilling prophecies. The development of a child's personality depends on the kind of treatment he receives from his parents. Our children are what we make them. Dorothy Law Nolte explains this in a beautiful poem:

> If a child lives with criticism
> he learns to condemn.
> If a child lives with hostility
> he learns to fight.
> If a child lives with ridicule
> he learns to be shy.
> If a child lives with shame
> he learns to feel guilty.
> If a child lives with tolerance
> he learns to be patient.
> If a child lives with encouragement
> he learns confidence.
> If a child lives with praise
> he learns to appreciate
> If a child lives with fairness
> he learns justice.
> If a child lives with security
> he learns to have faith.

> If a child lives with approval
> > he learns to like himself.
> If a child lives with acceptance and friendship
> > he learns to find love in the world.

But then there is no single theory that tells a parent how to do it. Lord Rochester once said, "Before I got married I had six theories about bringing up children. Now I have six children and no theories." Isadora Duncan says, "The finest inheritance you can give to a child is to allow it to make its own way completely on its own feet." Harry Truman said, "I found that the best way to give advice to your children is to find out what they want and then advise them to do it." A pat on the back develops character, if administered young enough, often enough, low enough.

Discipline

We are familiar with the proverb, "He who spares his rod hates his son. But he who loves him, disciplines him promptly." Alfie Kohn points out that, "nearly 40 years of research shows that the "rod" tends to produce children who are more aggressive than their peers. While physical punishment may suppress misbehaviour in the short run, it ultimately promotes nothing more than a determination to avoid getting caught."

"I know of no joy in life is greater than the joy of seeing a child grow in mind and spirit and body, the small self-absorbed creature changing into a responsible, eager, active human being. This is the happy child, feeling himself free and yet under firm discipline, one which teaches discipline," says Pearl S Buck

We all know the importance of discipline; yet we pamper children so much that we hesitate to be strict with them. We don't realise that discipline is the key to successful parenthood. "Say No to Your Children" says Ann Landers. She explains: "In my opinion, the theory of permissive upbringing is the most damaging concept ever thought up by a generation of mixed-up parents. What vast majority of children need is an end of being pampered, indulged, catered for, and made to feel that the world belongs to them. The key word in child rearing is discipline—and discipline should begin when the child is in the cradle. An infant knows whether or not he can manipulate his parents, if he can, he will. So don't be afraid to be boss. Children need to know there is someone stronger and wiser in the family.

When the situation demands it, stand up and say "No, you cannot go"; "No, you cannot have it." Your child may protest bitterly, and accuse you of humiliating him, of making him look like a baby in the eyes of his friends. But deep down he will be pleased that you love him enough to risk his anger and that you have the good judgement to protect his own lack of experience. Children are continually testing, to see how much they can get away with, how far you will let them go. Yet they scarcely hope you will not let them go too far. Beware of this testing mechanism the next time you are locked in bitter debate with your teenage son or daughter. The parent who tries to curry the favour of his child by giving him every thing he asks for and let him do as he pleases loses out on all fronts. He does not gain children's goodwill or affection.

To create fear in the mind of a child is a good thing. "Fear under certain circumstances is healthy' says Landers. "I am not recommending that children be terrified of their parents. There must be free and open expression on both sides. But the manner of expression should bear the hall mark of respect."

A child should be taught to vent his anger in ways that will not injure others, damage the property or hurt his own self esteem. Set limits for every thing: get mad as you like—but there must be no hitting, no yelling swear words so loud that the neighbours will hear, and breaking any thing you are not prepared to pay for. A child who knows how far he can go is relieved of a heavy burden. If there is a question as to whether you should give the edge to your child or yourself, take it yourself. And don't feel guilty. Rank has its privileges. Children need to practice the art of giving—and who is more deserving of consideration than one's own parents?

"Parents who genuinely love their children will teach and direct them, not just satisfy their every whim" says Landers. "For, in the final analysis, it is not what you do for your children but what you have taught them to do for themselves that will make them successful human beings." "The word *no* carries a lot more meaning when spoken by a parent who also knows how to say yes," says Joyce Maynard.

Give your child enduring values

"We are deluged by distorted value system," says, Max Lucado. "We see the most valuable things in our lives peddled for pennies and we see the cheapest smut go for millions."

"Why do we do what we do? Why are priceless mores trashed while senseless standards are obeyed? What causes us to elevate the body and degrade the soul?. What causes us to pamper the skin while we pollute the heart?

"Our values are messed up. Thrills are going for top dollar and the value of human beings is at an all time low… It all began when someone convinced us that human race is headed no where. That man has no destiny. That we are in a cycle.

"If a man has no destiny, then he has no *duty*. No obligation, no responsibility. If a man has no destiny he has no guidelines or goals. If a man has no destiny who is to say what is right and wrong? Who is to say a husband can't leave his wife and family? Who is to say you can't abort a fetus? What is wrong with shaking up? Who says that I can't step on someone's neck to get to the top? Its your value system against mine? No absolutes. No principles. No standards. Life is reduced to weekend pay checks, and quick thrills. The bottom line is disaster. …If a man has no duty or destiny, the next logical step is he has no value."

Again look at the skewed priorities in life. What has now become important for some students is a powerful motor bike, branded luxury clothing, shoes that cost a fortune, and latest model of mobile phone –studies take least priority. Girls are not far behind. Some of them value fashion designs, designer wear, herbal beauty care, and make up tips from top models—modesty and family values come last. Brainwashing is being legitimised for material gains by business houses. They are trying to build customer preferences using brain washing techniques through advertisements. Propaganda is assuming special importance in political and religious campaigns. Marketing departments are trying to build brand loyalties. Watching satellite TV and drinking soft drinks are much easier these days than procuring drinking water for the villagers. Even poor people are being convinced that a colour TV is far more important than basic needs –food, clothing or children's education. Governments are eager to spend billions on nuclear weapons and space programmes, while they pay lip service to the basic minimum facilities like roads, electricity, drinking water, nutrition, healthcare, and housing. Millions of innocent animals are being killed in the name of experiments, to glorify achievements in science. Wars are being fought in the name of peace, no matter if millions lose their sons.

This state of affairs has its roots in our upbringing, in our learning, and the values practised by our parents, peers, friends, and all the people who influence us. Values should be nurtured in our families; children should be taught right values so they can appreciate when they grow up. Ardis Whitman, has written *Five Enduring Values for Your Child*. Children these days are saying, "So what? Everything's different now. We don't go by your values." But she reminds, "Times change. So do customs—and even moral codes. But certain qualities abide. No matter how times change we will always have the same need our ancestors did to live out our lives in joy and courage; to get along with our fellowmen; and to hold to those values which show us how to grow, to learn and to become better people."

Joy

"First, teach a child to be happy. Happiness by no means life's greatest goal, and it is not necessary to be happy all the time. But the *habit of being pleased* has sustained many a broken heart, just as fretful inability to enjoy has dissolved many lives in bitterness. Happy experiences help to make generous and outgoing personalities. They give us lovely memories to warm the history of our lives."

"We need to teach them how to hold on to this quality into adult life. And you can do that best by making your own grown-up years a good and rewarding time. Enjoy your self; enjoy your world; and your child will catch joy from you."

Love

Second, I would teach a child how to sustain love. A child needs a kind of love that is trustworthy as the rising of the sun. If a child is to grow up to truly join the human race, he needs to know how to keep love alive.

A child should learn not merely to love but to be a loving person, to make love his stance in the world. "Love" may come and go but a loving person, like the sun itself, never loses his shining warmth. How does one channel these seedling signs of love in to the permanent and mature expressions of a loving person? By making sure that your child is in daily contact with a loving adult—yourself.

Honesty

Third, I would teach a child that integrity matters. Nothing will ever change the need for that—it is impossible to imagine any livable society without it. Integrity is *the quality of being able to be trusted*. It means that we don't lie to each other; that what we say we'll do, we'll do; that the affection we profess is genuine and the praise we give is honest.

We teach integrity, by the way we live ourselves. Perhaps a child learns trustworthiness best of all when he has tasks to do. Children never learn responsibility without help. Parents in the process of teaching have to hold a child to a task until it is finished; it means trusting him to do things on his own which he may spoil in the process.

Integrity means also that a child is taught to accept blame when that is what he ought to do. Integrity doesn't come without a price, and this is best taught when the child is small.

Courage

Fourth, I would teach a child to be brave. He needs this if he is going to live with integrity. He also needs it to sustain life's griefs and failures without being thrown by them. How to tell a child to be brave? Should you tell a happy child that pain is coming? I think you should. Even a little child finds out that grandma dies; a puppy is hurt; childhood friends leave and betray. The best thing to tell a small child too young for philosophy is simply that this is the way things are.

Comfort the child when he is in tears. Let him know you understand. But do not stanch the flow of tears. Accept a grieving child's feelings and permit him to express them. When the tempest of grief has quieted say "Let's see what you can learn from this; let's see how you can begin to get better." Life is for growing, we should tell him; and all experience, good and bad, can be useful in that growth. Finally, you can prepare the child for pain by teaching him to feel a bond with others who suffer. Many a person has put heartache behind him by finding someone who needs him.

Faith
Fifth, I would give a child something to believe in. Things to care deeply about come in many kinds and sizes, from a small boy's dream of being a pilot to a Martin Luther King's vision of freeing his people. But how can parents "give" a child a good dream? In the strict sense, we can't. But we can listen lovingly and respectfully to a child's plans and hopes, however naive they may seem, and when ever possible help to make them come true.

We can also open to our children the world of books, music, art, because these are the lodging places of many a dream. And finally we can offer them a religious faith, the most spacious of all things to believe in. It's like finding a path through a dark wood.

What if we have no belief ourselves? Tell a life-time is not too long to try to find out whether God is, and what he is like. Meanwhile, teach your child to transfer belief into action. We learn to believe by acting out our faith, and so do our children. Ardis Whitman considers these values are the most important things a child can learn.

Give your child the greatest gift : self-esteem
"The child is an individual in his own right and from birth should be so treated," says Pearl Buck. "With self-respect comes certain virtues, including pride in one's own behaviour. Some thing is expected, and pride in one's self, which is totally different from conceit, responds to expectation. At the same time satisfaction with one's self removes inhibitions. Self-confidence, once gained, provides a kind of security which helps make a person dare to live and with joy."

Many of our children become victims of flawed standards society uses to assess the worth of our children. Not everyone is seen as worthy or is accepted. Instead we reserve the praise and admiration for the few who have been blessed from birth with characteristics we, wrongly, value most highly—beauty, brains or riches. It is a vicious system and, we must counter-balance its impact by helping young people develop self-esteem.

All children are created worthy and are due the right to personal respect and dignity but how can we, as parents, build strong egos and indomitable spirits, despite the strong forces that prevail? Psychologist James Dobson suggests strategies by which we can instill confidence and self-worth in our children:

Examine your own values

A sizeable portion of a child's self-concept emerges from the way he thinks you see him, even reading your spoken attitudes. When a child is convinced that he is loved and respected by his parents, he is inclined to accept his own worth as a person. Many children know that you would give your life for him, yet still detect your doubts about his acceptability. You are nervous when he speaks to guests. You butt in to explain what he was trying to say, or laugh when his remarks sound foolish.

Parents need to guard what they say in the presence of their children. Parents must also take time to introduce children to good books, to fly kites and play ball with them. Listen to the skinned-knee episode and talk about the bird with broken wing. These are the building blocks of self-esteem.

Teach a "no knock" policy

One characteristic of a person who feels inferior is that he talks about his deficiencies to anyone who will listen. While you are blabbing about your inadequacies the listener is formulating an impression of you. He will later treat you according to the evidence you've provided. If you put your feelings into words, they become solidified as facts in your mind. Therefore, we should teach a no-knock policy to our children. Constant self-criticism can become a self defeating habit.

Help your child compensate

Our task as parents is to serve as a confident ally, encouraging when children are distressed, intervening when threats are overwhelming, and giving them the tools to overcome the obstacles. One of those tools is *compensation*. An individual counter-balances his weaknesses by capitalising on his strengths.

Perhaps a child can establish his niche in music. May be he can build model aeroplanes, or raise rabbits or play basket ball. Nothing is more risky than sending a child into adolescence with no skills, no unique knowledge, no means of compensating. He must be able to say, "I may not be the most popular student in the school, but I am the best trumpet player in the band."

Dobson recommends that, "the parents assess a child's strengths, then select a skill with the best chance for success. See that he gets through the first stage. Reward, push, bribe if necessary, but make him learn. If you find you have made a mistake, start over on something else. But don't let inertia keep you from teaching a skill to your offspring!"

Help your child compete

A parent who opposes the stress placed on beauty, brawn, and brains knows his child is forced to compete in a world that worships those attributes. Should he help his younger become as attractive as possible? Should he encourage his "average" child to excel in school?

Dobson gives his opinion: "I am obligated to help my child to compete in this world as best as he can. If his teeth are crooked, I will see that they are straightened. If he flounders academically, I will seek tutorial assistance. We are allies in his fight for survival. But while helping my child to compete, I also instruct him on the true values of life: love for mankind, integrity, truthfulness, and devotion to God."

Discipline with respect

Does punishment, and particularly spanking break the spirit of the child? The answer depends on the manner and intent of the parents. A spanking, in response to willful defiance, is a worthwhile tool, but belief in corporal punishment is no excuse for taking out your frustrations on little Johnny; it offers no license to punish him in front of others or treat him with disrespect.

It is important to recognise, however, that one way to damage self-esteem is to avoid discipline altogether. Parents are symbols of justice and order and a child wonders why they would let him get away with doing harmful things if they really love him.

Keep an eye on the class room
Make certain a child has learnt to read by the end of his second year in school. Self-esteem has been assassinated more frequently over reading problems than any other aspect of school life. Tutorial help can pull a child through a rough spot academically. Sometime change of schools—or change of teachers in school—can be in the child's best interest.

The slow learner is even more likely to have self-esteem problems. What can parents do? De-emphasize school achievement. Anything your child *cannot* accomplish, despite his efforts,

Avoid over protection
Preparation for responsible adulthood is derived from training during adulthood. A child should be encouraged to progress on an orderly time table, at the level of responsibility appropriate for his age. Each year a child should make more of his own decisions. A seven-year-old, for example, is usually capable of selecting his own cloths for the day. He should be keeping his room tidy and making his bed.

An overly protective parent allows the child to fall behind his normal time table. As a ten year old, he finds it hard to make decisions or exercise self-discipline. A few years later, he will steamroll into adolescence unprepared for the freedom and responsibility he will find there.

The importance of parental concern in a child's development of self-esteem has been confirmed by numerous studies. One found three important characteristics that distinguish those with high self-esteem: (1) The children were more loved and appreciated at home. (2) They had parents who set firm guidelines. (3) Their homes were characterised by democracy and openness.

There are ways to teach a child to appreciate his genuine significance, regardless of the shape of his nose or the size of his ears or the efficiency of his mind. *Every* child is entitled to hold up his head in confidence and security. It can be done. James Dobson says, "Self-esteem—that precious sense of personal worth—can provide our child with the inner strength to survive the hazards of growing up."

Allow children to play and appreciate beauty

"If I were asked what element is most important in a child's life, I would say the element of beauty," says Pearl Buck. "Children crave it, they accept with ecstasy, but they can not always create it or even find its whereabouts. They must be taught to discover beauty in nature, in art, music and books, in noble human beings, living or dead, in the loyalties of friendship and family, in the love of country and God. Without the perception of beauty the wings never spread, the mind lives in shadow, and the heart fails.

Shown what beauty is, however, the child pursues it and in the pursuit he discovers his own talents and so himself. He tries many pathways of experience. At school, beyond his books, he tries music drama and sports. In church he learns the beauty of worship and of the soul inspired. In museums he sees the work of other dedicated men and women, those who devoted their lives to creating beauty through art. In the presence of the great dead, he finds the dedication to the great demands of the country and mankind. The flag becomes a symbol and he knows himself one of the great company called nation.

When a child learns to read, it comes to know a greater host of men, women, and children and to be identified with them. Above all a child learns the joy of learning. His world is infinitely enlarged, and ahead of him he sees the illuminated path of more and more to know, as long as he lives.

There must also be time and space for play: solitary play, when the mind can create fruitful loneliness, play, too, in which the whole family shares. Outdoor play is essential. Blessed are the children who live in peaceful places, in space and beauty. But anywhere children are, they play, imitating the life they see about them. In play the child finds satisfaction for his entire being, his body is strengthened, his mind refreshed, his imagination inspired.

For adults the most satisfying hours of life are those spent in interesting and absorbing, exciting work. What such work provides for adults is provided for children in play, stretching their capacity to enjoy, to perform, to achieve. The child discovers in play the lasting values of life.

Friends : the secret to a longer life

"Friendship is one of the sweetest joys of life; many might have failed beneath the bitterness of their trial had they not found a friend," says Charles Haddon Spurgeon. According to Robert Louis Stevenson, "A friend is a gift you give yourself." That is the reason why everyone needs a friend. "We cannot tell the precise moment when friendship is formed," said Samuel Johnson. "As in filling a vessel drop by drop, there is at last a drop which makes it run over, so in a series of kindnesses there is at least one that makes the heart run over." Liking a person takes a long time; love can happen at first sight. According to Thomas Moore, "A friendship like love is warm. A love like friendship is steady." Friendship is a heart to heart relationship that sustains our life. Sharing joyful experiences with friends enhances our happiness; sharing the sorrowful moments gives relief and comfort. "It brings comfort to have companions in whatever happens," said Saint John Crysostom.

"I can not imagine where I would be today were it not for that handful of friends who have given me a heart full of joy," says Charles Swindol. "Let's face it, friends make life a lot more fun." Amanda Bradley says, "Celebrate the happiness that friends are always giving. Make everyday a holiday and celebrate just living."

There is solid scientific evidence that friendship can extend life. "Friendships play far more important role in maintaining good health and having a long life than most people realise," says Shelly Taylor, a research psychologist at the university of California, Los Angeles. More than a hundred studies attest to the health benefits of friendship. People with strong social networks are shown to:

- Boost their chances of surviving life-threatening illness.
- Have stronger, more resilient immune systems.
- Improve their mental health.
- Live longer than people with social support.

Just as the body cannot survive without life, a friendship between individuals or nations cannot thrive without genuine trust and mutual respect. There is a lot of truth in the statement that 'trust begets trust'. But if you trust those who are not trustworthy you are likely to be cheated. Be discerning in choosing your friends. The Thalmud says, "Thy friend has a friend. Thy friend's friend has a friend; be discrete." "Associate with men of good quality if you esteem your own reputation; for it is better to be alone than in bad company," said George Washington. Our friends influence our character just as we influence them. People can know you from the kind of friends you have.

In our eagerness to make friends we make a lot of mistakes; and most of the time they are unintended. This happens because of differences in upbringing, family values, traditions, perceptions, and attitudes. Because of misunderstanding sometimes friends appear to be doing the wrong things to us. We must learn to forgive the mistakes of our friends. "A friend should bear a friend's infirmities," wrote Shakespeare in *Julius Caesar*.

"It takes a great soul to be a true friend," said Anna Robertson Brown. "One must forgive much, forget much, and forbear much." Henry Ward Beacher says, "Keep a fair-sized a backyard to bury the faults of your friends."

How to win friends

People have been using, Dale Carnegie 's book *How to Win Friends and Influence People,* for the last six decades, to improve their ability to get along with people. The approach he suggested is still relevant today. Let us consider what he says briefly:

Be genuinely interested in people

To learn how to win friends, Carnegie suggested that we better study the technique adopted by man's best friend. When you get within three meters of him, he will begin to wag his tail. If you stop and pat him, he will almost jump out of his skin to show you how much he likes you. A dog makes friends by getting genuinely interested in people and not vice versa. Yet people blunder through life trying to bulldoze others into becoming interested in them. It doesn't work, because people are not interested in you. They are interested in themselves.

Make them feel important and appreciated
You want approval, recognition of your true worth. You want to feel that you are important. You crave sincere appreciation, not cheap, insincere flattery. So treat others as you would want them treat you. Where should you begin the magic touchstone of appreciation? It is needed more at home than anywhere else. Show appreciation and nourish the self-esteem of your children. Your spouse has good points, too, but how long has it been since you expressed your admiration? *Do it* ! And bring a smile in addition, and some warm words of affection. All of us can use the philosophy of appreciation of the other fellow. You can work magic almost everyday with little phrases: "I am sorry to trouble you," "Would you be so kind as to…" when you appreciate people, they love to make friends.

Listen intently with genuine interest
Once Carnegie happened to meet a botanist in a party. He listened to his fascinating talk about the humble potato. After the party, he heard the botanist complementing him as the "most interesting conversationalist." He said hardly anything. What all he did was, he listened intently because he was genuinely interested, and he felt it. David Ausburger says, "The golden rule of friendship is to listen to others as you would have them listen to."

Get the other person's point of view
Another bit of advice about the fine art of human relations came from Henry Ford: "If there is any one secret of success," he said, "it lies in the ability to get the other person's point of view and see things from his angle as well as your own." That is so obvious that anyone ought to see the truth of it at a glance; yet 90 per cent of the people ignore it 90 per cent of the time.

Talk about what the other person wants
We know fish prefer worms; so when you go fishing think about what the fish wants. It is childish to talk about what *we* want. The only way to influence the other fellow is to talk about what he wants and show him how to get it.

Let the other person discover it himself
But when you have a good idea, instead of making the other person think it is yours, why not let him cook and stir the idea himself? Don't you have more faith in ideas that *you* discover than those that are handed to you on a silver platter.

Some years ago, Carnegie planned to go fishing in Canada. And wrote to a tourist bureau for information. He was bewildered by scores of letters and booklets from camps and guides. Then one camp owner sent him names of several New Yorkers he had served and invited to call them to discover himself what he had to offer. He happened to know one of the men on the list. He telephoned him and found out what his experiences had been and then wired the camp the date of his arrival. He says, "The others had been trying to sell me on their service, but one chap let me sell himself."

Avoid arguments
"Arguments, particularly unnecessary arguments, are a sure way to dissipate goodwill," says Carnegie. He says he learned this lesson one night at a banquet. The man next to him told a humorous story that hinged on a quotation. He mentioned that the quotation was from the Bible. Carnegie knew it was from Shakespeare and he appointed a committee of one to correct him. But the other gentleman stuck to his guns. An old friend of Carnegie, who devoted years to the study of Shakespeare, was also at the table. The story teller and he agreed to submit the question to this friend, who listened, kicked him under the table and said, "Dale you are wrong. It *is* from the Bible." Later he told his friend he was certain that the quotation was from Shakespeare. "Yes, of course," he replied. "But we were guests at a festive occasion. Why prove to a man he is wrong? Is that going to make him like you?" We don't win friends by arguments, we lose them.

Since then, having watched the effects of thousands of arguments, he concluded that there is only one way to get the best of an argument, avoid it. He says, "even if you win it, you lose it. Why? You feel fine, but you have made the other person feel inferior, and he will resent you."

Emphasise on things you both agree
Socrates was one of the wisest persuaders who ever influenced this wrangling world. His technique was based upon getting "yes" response. He asked questions with which his opponent would have to agree. He kept on winning one admission after another until he had armful of yeses. Finally almost without realising it, his opponent found himself embracing a conclusion that he would have denied bitterly a few minutes ago. The next time you are smarting to tell a man he is wrong, remember Socrates and ask a gentle question—one that will get the yes response.

Kindliness, friendly approach and appreciation can win people
This lesson comes from Aesop's fable about the sun and the wind quarrelling over which one was stronger. The wind said, "I'll prove I am. See that old man wearing a coat? I bet I can make him take his coat off quicker than you can." So the wind blew until it was almost a tornado, but the harder it blew, the tighter the old man wrapped his coat about him. Finally, the wind gave up, and the sun came from behind a cloud and smiled kindly on the old man. Presently, he mopped his brow and pulled of his coat. The sun then told the wind that gentleness and friendliness are stronger than fury and force.

And so it is today. The sun can make you take off your coat more quickly than the wind; and kindliness, the friendly approach and appreciation can make people change their minds more readily than all the bluster and storming on earth.

How to nurture old friendships
Just as scientists are discovering more ways that friendships enhance our lives, over-stuffed schedules make it hard to keep up with our pals. But many friendships need just a little nurturing to help them flourish. Here are some tips from sociologist Jan Yager, author of *Friendshifts* and *When Friendship Hurts*:

- Stop feeling guilty that you can't spend lots of time with old friends, like you did long time ago. Acknowledge that your lives have changed, and do whatever you can now to maintain the relationship. Use e-mail, instant messaging and other electronic devices to stay in touch when you have small bits of time.

Only One Life to Live Joyfully   155

- Meet for coffee or early morning walk before you start your working day.
- Schedule a regular "friends time out," in which you set aside one-week night a month, for example, to catch up with your buddies.
- Invite your friend to share everyday activities you normally do alone, like exercising, doing errands, or going to your kids soccer game.
- Try to be there for the key events in your friend's life—weddings, graduations, funerals. Your presence will make a difference.

Interacting with people

Before you approach the package called 'people' read the warning in small print:. "Caution: Human beings, handle with care." Since human beings are very sensitive, if we don't handle them with sensitivity, human relations can become fragile. It is imperative that we have to be careful in dealing with people. William Blake warns, "You throw the sand against the wind. And the wind will blow it back again." Be careful.

Our dealings with people and their reactions to us will have tremendous impact on our lives. "It was my first brush with the profound and painful knowledge that people heal and people destroy" says Ardis Whitman. "When I am with you, I grow or diminish according to how you make me feel. And, in my turn, I invite you to live or to die, by walking with you or retreating, by holding out my hand with you or not holding out, by opening my heart to you or keeping it closed."

Loneliness is one of the desperate problems of our age. "People are lonely because they build walls instead of bridges," says Joseph Fort Newton. If you want to understand people you have to build special bridges to reach them. Don't miss the fun of talking to strangers. The world is full of people waiting for you to speak first. "I know now that the world is not filled with strangers. It is full of other people—waiting only to be spoken to," says Beth Day. "Approaching a stranger is not really difficult. Don't bother with generalities. Try to pick up a clue about his interests. Every one is an authority on something. The trick is to find what that subject is." That will be the 'open sesame' kind of a door that opens for you. "It takes as much energy to be rotten as to be nice," says George Burns. "I would rather put my energy into being nice. I'll tell you something else—when you give energy into being nice, you usually get more back than you give out."

Dr Albert Schweitzer pleads that we must give to every will to live the same reverence for life that we give to our own. If we would invite a person to live we must accept the "otherness" of that person. We must see what is best in him and allow it to be and grow. For growth is the very insignia of every living creature, the heart of life process—life is a growing tree, not a statue.

Make distinctions

"Never judge people, don't type them too quickly; but in a pinch always assume that a man is good and at worst he is in the gray area between good and bad," said Gordon Dean former chairman of US Atomic Energy Commission. "The greatest tragedies in the world and personal events stem from misunderstanding."

"It is a complex world," said Alan Alda. "I hope you will make distinctions. A peach is not its fuzz, a toad is not its warts, a person is not his or her crankiness. If we can make distinctions we can be tolerant, and we can get to the heart of our problems instead of wrestling endlessly with their gross exteriors.

Once you make a habit of making distinctions, you'll begin challenging your own assumptions. Your assumptions are your windows on the world. Scrub them off every once in a while, or the light won't come in. If you challenge your own, you won't be so quick to accept the unchallenged assumptions of others. You'll be a lot less likely to be caught up in bias or prejudice, or be influenced by people who ask you to hand over your brains, your soul or money because they have everything all planned for you".

Ten commandments of Human Relations

Sometimes we feel like reading a crisp presentation of all the rules at one place that tell us how to establish rapport with people. Here are Robert G. Lee's Ten Commandments of Human Relations:

1. Speak to people. There is nothing as nice as a cheerful word of greeting.
2. Smile at people. It takes seventy-two muscles to frown, and only fourteen to smile.
3. Call people by name. The sweetest music to anyone's ears is the sound of his own name.
4. Be friendly and helpful. If you would have friends, be friendly.
5. Be cordial, speak and act as if everything you do is genuine pleasure.
6. Be genuinely interested in people. You can like almost any body if you try.
7. Be generous with praise – cautious with criticism.
8. Be considerate with feeling of others. There are usually three sides to a controversy; yours, the other fellow's and the right one.
9. Be alert to give service; what counts in life is what we do for others.
10. Add to this a good sense of humour, a big dose of patience and a dash of humility and you will be rewarded many fold.

Adjust with changes in life

World is ever changing as observed by Heraclitus, a Greek philosopher. We live in the kind of world in which the only constant factor is change and some of the changes are unhappy ones. But change is as inevitable as the turning of seasons and the tides. To try to keep it from our door is to try to shut out life itself. For everything that is alive is in constant change. As our cells die and new cells replace them, as our very personality change, so do we live. How much regret we could spare ourselves if we would regard change for what it is—a chance to grow.

"The most common of all human dreams, is to stop life in its tracks, to hold on to what we cherish, to keep change away from us and all we love," says Ardis Whitman. Perhaps it would work if we *could* make our lives stand still. But we can't. The biggest reason we don't adopt ourselves to change is what Gilbert Murray calls "failure of nerve". When we suffer such a failure of nerve, staying put is defence against disappointment. It is when we fail to change that we fall behind living, and our spirits age. Perhaps you can remember in your own experience – how, despite the wrench it gave you, discarding of an old way of life made you feel young again. Some rare people know instinctively that change is life asserting itself, and they renew themselves by keeping pace with it.

People who accept change anticipate progress. They accept new things and innovations. They raise new hopes and look forward to opportunities for growth. "While some people can move agilely to absorb new information and points of view, for others advancement is frightening," says June Callwood. "It may lie not so much in the glittering heroic act as in stubborn persistence or acceptance of change." She says that it requires courage to accept change.

Our only choice is how well we will face the inevitable changes which come to us. "The best way to face changes is to welcome them. Above all, learn to extricate yourself from the bondage of the past," says Ardis Whitman. Keep the past as a treasure in your heart, but don't waste time longing for its happiness. Changes are sure to come, and it is possible to prepare oneself to meet them. Perhaps we can not alter the course of our lives so radically' but we can, day by day, make small adaptations to keep ourselves flexible and venturesome. Practise flexibility you will be surprised to discover how eventually your days will become. You will always feel young, for you will be keeping up with life rather than passing it by.

Human qualities

Let us consider some qualities that represent sublime values of human beings. Just as the serene blue waters of the deep sea reflects the beauty of the blue sky, these qualities reflect the nobility of human character. We all recognise them, though we are not in a position to define them. Just as we understand love without ever defining it, we can understand and deal with them. The best way to understand them is to read what great people have actually said about them, in their own words (i.e. quotes).

Love, hatred and indifference

The ancient Greeks, poets, authors and philosophers all puzzled, over the question but nobody really knows what love is. Apostle Paul describes love in a letter written to Corinthians: "Put love first. Love is patient; love is kind and envies no one. Love is never boastful nor conceited, nor rude; never selfish, not quick to take offence. Love keeps no score of wrongs; does not gloat over other men's sins, but delights in the truth. There is nothing love cannot face; there is no limit to its faith, its hope, and its endurance. Love will never come to an end." And he says, "In a word, there are three things that last for ever: faith, hope, and love; but the greatest of them all is love."

Life in general

A naturalist, Henry David Thoreau advocates simple way of living:

> "I am convinced both by faith and experience, that to maintain one's life on this earth is not a hardship but a past time, if we live simply and wisely. I would say to my fellows, once for all: as long as possible live free and uncommitted. It makes but little difference whether you are committed to a farm or jail."

There are people who advocate exemplary life, besides simplicity and refreshing attitude toward life. Thomas Hesburg says "It is easier to exemplify values than teach them." Thomas Morrel says "The first great gift we can bestow on others is a good example."

Many people believe that man finds meaning in living. "A person lives," says psychotherapist Sidney Jourard, "as long as he experiences his life having meaning and value, and as long as he has something to live for. As soon as meaning, value and hope vanish from a person's life, he begins to stop living; he begins to die." Alan Alda says, "Life is absurd and meaningless—unless *you* bring meaning to it, unless *you* make something of it. It is up to us to create our own existence."

There are people who look for a purpose in living. Thomas Carlyle says, "A man without a purpose is a ship without a rudder, a waif, a nothing, a no man. Have a purpose in life and having it throw such strength of mind and muscle in to your work as God has given you."

On the other hand there are people who look for luck and destiny in life. Richard Wiseman, a psychologist at the of the University of Hertfordshire, recently published the results of a 10-year long study *The Luck Factor.* Having studied the luckiest and the unluckiest people, he came to the conclusion that people are not born lucky but create and enhance their own good fortune as they go through life. He found that those with charmed lives are, without realising it, using four basic principles to create good fortune for themselves.

The first principle of the lucky is that they maximise their opportunities. They are skilled at creating, noticing and acting upon chances through networking, adopting a relaxed attitude to life and by being open to new experiences. Second, Wiseman discovered that people who appear to have good fortune tend to make effective decisions by acting on their intuition and feelings. Third, lucky people go through life expecting good fortune and in the certainty that the future will be positive. These expectations become self fulfilling prophecies, by helping lucky people persist in the face of failure and shape their interactions with others in a positive way. The fourth principle, Wiseman found is that the lucky people have the ability to turn bad fortune into good luck. They usually employ various psychological techniques to cope with and often even thrive upon any ill fortune that comes their way. For example, they spontaneously imagine how things could have been worse, do not dwell on any ill fortune and take control of the situation.

We come across considerable amount of literature on "destiny" in human life. But many people believe that waiting for fate or looking for destiny is not a wise thing to do." Dag Hammarskjold said, "We are not permitted to choose the frame of our destiny. But what we put into it is ours." William Jennings Bryan says, "Destiny is not a matter of chance, it is matter of choice; It is not a thing to be waited for; it is a thing to be achieved."

"Attachment is the source of all pleasures now," says Swami Vivekananda. "All misery and pain comes from attachment. That man alone will be able to get the best of nature, who, having the power of attaching himself to a thing with all his energy, has also the power to detach himself when he should do so. We have to detach ourselves to enjoy. If only we had power to detach ourselves at will, there would not be any misery." Therefore The Gita says, "work constantly: work, be not attached, be not caught."

God-fearing life

"The greatest question of our times is not communism versus individualism, not Europe versus America, not even the East versus the West, it is whether men can bear to live without God. Can civilisation hold together if man abandons his faith in God?" asks historian Will Durant.

Solomon, son of David, and the wise king of Israel said 'all is empty' in human life. "What does man gain from all his labour and his toil here under the sun?" "So I commend enjoyment, since there is nothing good for a man to do here under the sun but to eat and drink and enjoy himself; this is all that remain with him to reward his toil throughout the span of life which God grants him here under the sun." "Fear God and obey his commands; there is no more to man than this. For God brings every thing we do to judgement, and every secret, whether good or bad."

"At the day of Doom men shall be judged according to their Fruits. It will not be said then, 'Did you believe?' But, were you Doers or Talkers only," said John Bunyan. But Albert Camus, a Nobel-laureate, warns, "I shall tell you a great secret, my friend. Do not wait for the last judgement, it takes place everyday."

On the other hand there are people who mock at the way people talk about God. "Man is certainly stark mad, he cannot make a worm and yet will be making gods by dozens," said a French writer Michel Eyquem de Montaigne. Both the statements, 'God created man,' and 'Man created god' are essentially beliefs. Let us consider the logical possibilities. If Mr X believes that there is God, he will follow ethical standards in his life. If God exists, he will have no problem facing the final judgement of God. If God does not really exist, he will at least have the satisfaction that he lived a morally satisfying life. On the other hand consider Mr. Y who does not believe in God. This belief will lead him to live a carefree life with or without morals. If God really does not exist, he will be happy because his belief has come true. On the other hand, if God exists, proving his belief wrong, then he will have a big problem facing the final judgement of God. So, decide yourself which belief you would like to hold.

What is really worthwhile?

"Only one life to live!" points out Anna Robertson Brown, in her book *What is Worthwhile*. "We all want to make the most of it. How can we accomplish the most with the energies and powers at our command? What is worthwhile?" "To find ourselves what makes life worth living is a risky business, for it means that once we know it, we must seek it. It also means that without it life will be valueless," says Marsha Sineter in *Ordinary People as Monks and Mystics*. Philosopher Joseph Campbell warned consequences of not searching for meaning: "If a person insists on a certain program, does not listen to the demands of his own heart, he is going to risk a schizophrenic crack," he wrote in *Myth and Quest for Meaning*. "When you are in touch with your inner wisdom, you have a way to choose what is right for you(and what is not)."

Finally, we all go to the same place: all come from dust, and to dust we all return. Yet, we human beings are really greedy; we expect great things in our lives. Indeed, it is too much to expect in so short a life! Abraham Lincoln said, "And in the end it's not the years in your life that count. It's the life in your years." Barbara De Angelis says, "At the end of our time on earth, if we have lived fully, we will not be able to say "I was always happy." Hopefully, we will be able to say, "I have experienced a life-time of real moments, and many of them were happy moments."

Chapter 13

Sanity in Accepting Reality

> *Happiness is a function of accepting what is.*
> **Werner Erhard** (John Rosenberg 1935—)
> American philosophical thinker
>
> *Let us face our lives bravely as we are. For only a philosophy that recognizes reality can lead us into true happiness, only that kind of philosophy is sound and healthy.*
> **Lin Yutang** (1895 –1976)
> Chinese American writer

We, human beings, are predisposed and programmed to construct *reality* of the world with the help of our brain and senses. We see the world with human eyes. The world we live in – all that we see, hear, touch, smell, taste, and feel – is a thing created by our mind. In other words, the world we know is essentially a mental construct. But many people do not appreciate the 'constructive nature' of our reality. You must open your eyes to this fact, so that you may create more than what is, and instil the world with new and greater meaning. At the same time, you must not be blind to the realities of this world. Walking on the tight rope of reality is indeed an admirable balancing feat that ensures joyful living.

Errors of reality

Human beings, however, are likely to commit two types of errors while constructing reality. The first error is *failing to accept or disrespect reality*. Facing reality means, accepting as facts those aspects of your life you believe cannot be changed. It also means accepting those things and relationships you could change, but in which you are not willing to invest time and energy necessary to do so. People who refuse to accept reality often suffer from superiority complex. People who refuse to face reality, will have to face its wrath; and account for their follies. They will be frustrated and their energies will be wasted; their actions will become unproductive.

This kind of error can be overcome by respecting reality. You must realise that you are one of the 6 billion people living on the earth. The world is not created to serve you personally. Remember reality has no respect for your wishes. It is the same for everyone. Courageous people start with what *is*, rather than what they think *it should be*. You must learn to eliminate *shoulds*, *oughts* and *musts* in your life. Reality is not fair; so don't demand and expect it to be so. Have a good perspective. Don't dodge reality.

Second error of reality is *disrespecting self*. People fail to realise all the possible alternatives when that reality is faced. Unaware of the possibilities, the frustrated people feel hopeless and helpless. They believe they are the passive victims of powerful forces of life and other people. They do not realise that they have full control of their personal interpretations of this world that ultimately affects them.

The first step in overcoming this error, begins with your belief in yourself. Learn to face any situation realistically. Develop most productive ways of viewing the situation. Generate more perceptual alternatives. Choose the more effective realistic alternative. Take personal responsibility for making changes in life. This will lead to long-range goal attainment. Neither your heredity nor the environment is the determining factor. Remember, you alone are responsible for your life. Your success and failure are invariably linked with your perception of reality. Once you realise this, you will feel a sense of power over yourself.

Resistance to reality

"There is something in us which has a liking for myths, for notions about ourselves that have little to do with reality," says Father Eugene Kennedy. We all have some beliefs about this world. Many times our beliefs do not match with the reality out there.

Christiaan Barnard, the famous cardiac surgeon, says that when people resist reality, they entertain false beliefs : "I will be healthy for ever. I will stay young forever. I will live forever. This immortality wish is common to all mankind." He says, "It comes out as a strange reluctance on the part of the patient to face facts—a kind of resistance to reality based on the "what you don't know won't hurt you" philosophy. Note his words: *resistance to reality.* He says "nothing is more important than personal health… We don't often get a second chance." He tells us to respect reality if we want a trouble free and peaceful life.

Unrealistic expectations cause failures

We have every right to believe what we wish to believe. But very often the reality out there differs with what we believe it to be. "Every time I close the door on reality, it comes in through the window," says Ashleigh Brilliant. Yes, that is true, we all have the similar experience; yet we foolishly ignore the presence of reality. When the gap between *reality* and our *beliefs* widens we tend to have *unrealistic expectations* from everything we do. Most often, the reason we fail is because we are unable to handle the difficulties in life in realistic ways. This leads to unrealistic expectations in life. They in turn lead to inappropriate actions and negative consequences. This is often the main source of our unhappiness.

Your success depends on your ability to sight *realistic* opportunities. But a lot of it hinges on your expectations, which are products of your experience. Perception of *real* opportunities and formulating *realistic* expectations will lead to achievable goals. Clear objectives and well-planned strategies will prompt result oriented actions; appropriate and timely actions will result in success. Therefore *realistic* expectations from life is the first requirement for success.

Dangers of flights of reality

There is a twilight zone that divides reality and imagination. Once this thin border line is transgressed people encounter delusions that have disastrous consequences. People who choose to ignore the limits of reality will suffer. Those who stray in to the unrealistic world may not be aware of this lurking danger. They "short circuit the most fanciful imaginations that step beyond the realm of reality and enter absurdity", says Max Lucado. This is confirmed by many psychiatrists.

Such people get lost into their absurd imaginations; and lose touch with reality They confuse the real with the unreal. Indulging in elaborate fantasy may make it difficult to arrive at practical judgements in any situation. Unless one switches back to the present and lives in reality, he continues to suffer. Some of them become schizophrenics. Most of them end up in mental asylum where insane people take refuge. Have you ever seen psychotics? These are the people who lost touch with reality. They have no realistic perception of the world. They develop disorganised thinking, confused views and eccentric behaviour. Because of their flights of reality they often talk irrelevant nonsense. One distinguishing feature is that they have no conscious awareness of persons, places and time.

It is difficult for such people to revert back to normal life, but it is not impossible. Dr John Forbes Nash Jr, a mathematical genius, suffered a devastating breakdown and was diagnosed as a schizophrenic. After leading a ghostlike existence for a decade he has re-emerged to normal life and won the Nobel Prize in 1994. In *A Beautiful Mind,* Sylvia Nasar narrates the story of his mysterious mind, the genius, madness, and the awakening. It is, indeed, one of those rare events of a 'second chance' in life.

"All our negative thoughts tend to distort reality", says Dr Aron Beck of University of Pennsylvania. "By correcting erroneous beliefs we can clamp down or alter excessive, in appropriate emotional reactions". If you don't follow the path of reality you may have to face its wrath. For peace of mind resign as general manager of the universe. Otherwise, you will pay the price in terms of poor mental health.

Need for reality check

Meaning for any organism lies outside itself. This is where the sense of reality ultimately comes from. The world is real just to the degree that determines experience. "We have seen that forms of things and their changes have no absolute reality at all. Their truth dwells in our personality, only there it is real and not abstract," says Rabindranath Tagore.

But then we must learn to live in the reality of this world. If you stray into imaginary world and act on the basis of unrealistic dreams, consequences could be disastrous. Mismatch between subjective reality and external reality is the main reason. A reality check could avert that danger. "Balance" is the single word which describes two things: 1. Your emotional and psychological need based strivings, and 2. Your intellectual abilities that appraise positive risk /reward and accept reality.

Realistic approach is essentially a proactive approach. It considers possibilities and probabilities rather than enthusiasm or expectations. It relies more on what is within you and within your reach rather than what is outside you. It relies more on your personal strengths rather than depending on others. It takes into account all the realities and requirements of a given situation, such as skills, means, resources time, and effort etc. You must therefore think what is possible and feasible, before you attempt anything. If you try anything within your reach you have greater chances of reaching it. Be realistic in setting your goals. Make realistic expectations and appropriate actions. Realistic perception can lead you to profitable opportunities. Have a realistic perspective of your problems, and then plan to solve with practical approach. Anticipate realistic risks and be prepared to take necessary precautions. Remember, realistic approach is the first requirement for the success of any endeavour.

Seek blessings of reality before you venture anything in life, you will never be disappointed. Reality is an impartial guide. Sane people who cherish the limits of reality will flourish; and those who ignore will perish. If you want to be successful in life you have to learn to accept reality. All you have to do is to walk on its safe path. Your experience is an excellent guide and the reality a great teacher. Imagine what cannot be achieved if these two giants are on your side!

Remember, happiness is a function of accepting what is!

Chapter 14

Happiness in Satisfying Needs

What we call happiness in the strictest sense comes from the (preferably sudden) satisfaction of needs which have been damned up to a high degree.

Sigmund Freud (1856 –1939)
Austrian psychiatrist

There are two ways of being happy. We must either diminish our wants or augment our means — either may do —the result is same; and it is for each man to decide for himself and to do that which happens to be easier.

Benjamin Franklin (1706-1790)
American statesman, diplomat, inventor

All human behaviour is purposive. It is mainly concerned with satisfaction of basic needs and achievement of personal goals. Human 'needs' give rise to 'wants'; if we are hungry we want food, if we are thirsty we want water. If these needs are not satisfied in time they cause tensions; and we are prompted to do anything to get food or water. Thus unsatisfied needs cause 'tensions' that propel us to take some 'action.' And when we get what we want, we are satisfied; otherwise we become unhappy. We learn early in life that our happiness is invariably linked with satisfaction of our needs.

Human wants are unlimited but the resources that can satisfy man's needs are limited in the world. Entire field of economics is based on this fact. As Vivekananda rightly said, human "desire is infinite, its fulfillment limited. Our desires are constantly changing, what we would prize today we would reject tomorrow. The satisfaction of desire only increases it, as oil poured on fire but makes it burn more fiercely. There is no limit to man's desire, he goes on desiring and when he comes to a point where desire cannot be fulfilled, the result is pain." As Rabindranath Tagore said, "his needs are not only great in number and therefore requiring larger field for search, but also are more complex, requiring deeper knowledge of things. This gives him greater consciousness of himself."

We can get what we want, if it is within our reach "He who hunts for flowers, will find flowers. He who loves weeds, will find weeds," says Henry Ward Beacher. When we crave for things that are not within our reach, we are destined to be disappointed. That is the reason why most philosophers find the root cause of our unhappiness in our desires. Swami Vivekananda says "Desire, want, is the father of all misery." John Stuart Mill said, "I have learned to seek happiness by limiting my desires, rather than attempting to satisfy them."

Hierarchy of human needs

Abraham Maslow identified a hierarchy of human needs. Firstly, we have physical needs: Food and Thirst, Sleep, Health, Body needs, Exercise and Rest and Sex. Next in importance are the Safety Needs: Security and Safety, Protection, Comfort and Peace, No Threats or Danger, Orderly and neat surroundings. Since man is a social being he has Love Needs that are often called as Social Needs: Acceptance, Feeling of belonging, Membership in a Group, Love and Affection, and Group Participation. Higher needs include Self Esteem Needs: Recognition and Prestige, Confidence and Leadership, Achievement and Ability, Competence and Success, Strength and Intelligence. Highest in the hierarchy are the Self-actualisation Needs: Self-fulfillment of potential, Doing Things purely for the challenge of Accomplishment, Intellectual Curiosity and Fulfillment, Creativity and Aesthetic Appreciation, and Acceptance of Reality and Transcendence – the need to help others in their self-fulfillment and realise their potential. During his last days Maslow also recognised the need for happiness and peace.

Psychologists have found other human needs. The need for achievement is a need to succeed and strive against standards of excellence; it serves to motivate an individual to do well. The need for power is the need to influence the behaviour of others. The need for affiliation is the need to associate with other people.

All human beings generally satisfy their physical needs, safety needs, and social needs. Whereas the self-esteem needs require some striving for their fulfillment. Self-actualisation needs often get neglected for some reason or the other. The need for achievement, need for power and the need for affiliation generally get the opportunities to satisfy at the place of work. Of all the needs, sex is being given undue importance because of the pleasure it offers.

Sex is our strongest need, after hunger

Sex, after hunger, is our strongest instinct and greatest problem. Primary purpose of sex is procreation and the perpetuity of human race; the joy associated with sex is the incentive for this purpose. Since happiness is the ultimate goal in life, pleasure giving sex activities occupy great importance in everybody's life. Most often people look for the joy in sex, even avoiding to fulfil its basic purpose. Sex has the power to bind people for a life-time; and it has the built-in advantage of making a family which is the basic unit of our society.

Since sexual behaviour depends, in part, on physiological conditions, it may be considered as a biological motive. According to socio-biologist Edward O Wilson the purpose of an individual's life is to pass along genetic material to the next generation of the species; evolutionary forces are at work to make individuals, alone and in groups, better adapted to their environments so that they will survive to pass on the genes. Bonding of man and woman is nature's need to perpetuate the race.

Sex is more than a biological motive. It is a social motive too. Sexual motivation is social because it involves other people and provides the basis for social groupings in higher animals—behaviour of baboon troops and human family, and sexual behaviour is powerfully regulated by social pressures and religious beliefs.

In *symposium, Greek* philosopher Plato says, "Love's function is giving birth in beauty both in body and in mind." He goes on to say that "sexual intercourse between men and women is a kind of birth.

There is something divine in the process. This is how mortal creatures achieve immortality." But the act of intercourse has been considered primarily an issue of lust, even when it is physical manifestation of a higher form of love for another person.

Sexual love remains to be the most compelling need that keeps people together. Sex in this sense is psychological; it is an important part of our emotional lives. And the intense pleasure associated with sex activity—those moments of infinite joy, ecstasy, and bliss, both real and vicarious—takes supreme importance in everybody's life. "When you are in love it's the most glorious two-and-half minutes of your life," says Richard Lewis. "When people learn to enjoy the experience of sexuality rather than focussing on how often, how long and how much; then sex will always be something to look forward to," says Richard Carroll, director of the Sex and Marital Therapy Program.

Sexual attraction between couples reinforces a bond of love and lifelong friendship. But "It's absurd to put love and friendship in the same category," says French essayist Michel de Montaigne. "Sexual love is impetuous and fickle, a feverish flame subject to sharp swellings and flickerings, fits, lulls, spurts, and interruptions. Friendship on the other hand, is a constant warmth, moderate and even, smooth and gentle, with no pain or bitterness. Moreover, love is a frantic chase for whatever eludes us; once desire is satisfied, it is extinguished, enjoyment kills it. Friendship, on the other hand, is constantly nourished and never dwindles; enjoyment only increases it." But when the blessings of love between a couple manifests in lifelong bond of love and companionship their relationship is doubly reinforced.

On the other hand, the flip side of sex is not so desirable. The attraction of sexual pleasures may induce habituation; this in turn may force the individuals into lustful activities, sometimes bordering on crime. No society is immune from this menacing disease. Every government is compelled to tackle this problem, though not successfully. This ends up in a world of misery rooted in indiscriminate sex.

Sex preoccupies the minds of young people; they innocently or ignorantly carry on the delightful sex activities unaware of the dangers involved. Their world is flooded with all sorts of things associated with sex—blue films, vulgar songs of sex, pornographic materials, strip tease shows, nude displays, maddening sexual orgies. It also has its flip side that causes agony—rapes, sexual violence, unwanted pregnancies, abortions, venereal diseases, AIDS, and tragic deaths. By the time people realise the danger lurking behind indiscriminate sex, it is often too late.

As the age progresses interest in sex takes secondary importance, in view of other needs yet to be satisfied. The general opinion in many societies has long been that older people have little or no capacity for sex. Now the findings of new survey of 4,246 American men and women aged 50 to 93—the largest study ever made—explodes this myth. The Consumer's Union survey revealed that age does not whither the sexual attraction between the opposite sexes. It shows that most people will, or could, remain sexually active into their 70s and beyond, and the warmth, excitement and comfort of sexual love will still be important in these years. Older people may find that sex is not only a way of being close and expressing love but a source of good feeling about one's self. It gives many of them a sense of vitality, of aliveness.

Morton Hunt warns that "this report ought not be taken as a blueprint of what they *should* do but only as a picture of what they *could* do if they wish, assuming they have the capacity. Some people in the survey seem relieved to be done with sex; others, who still want sex but whose spouses can't or won't have it, are happily married and reasonably satisfied. But to most older people today, sex is nature's great gift that keeps on living.

Allen Frank and Carol Anderson studied 100 happily married couples to find out how important is sex to a happy marriage. They say, "Indeed the prime conclusion we drew from this study is that sexual difficulties are normal—and sex, per se, isn't crucial for a happy marriage... Apparently the crucial issue for marital satisfaction is the ability to work out a pattern acceptable to both partners."

But sex *isn't* everything

"Our ancestors played this sex impulse down, knowing that it was strong enough without encouragement; we have blown it up with a thousand forms of incitation, advertisement, emphasis and display, and have armed it with the doctrine that inhibition is dangerous", says Will Durant, an eminent American historian. "Whereas inhibition—control of impulse—is the first principle of civilization."

But today there seems to be a kind of sexual permissiveness in the Western world. "One of the most pervasive current myths is that sex is the driving force of all human behaviour; in short, sex is everything," says Father Eugene Kennedy, professor of psychology at Loyola University, Chicago. "The myth would have us believe that no action is undertaken, no glance exchanged, no creative message set sparkling, that is not motivated by sexual impulse of one kind or the other. And the person who is not sensuous is somehow badly disconnected from the current impulses of his culture. To be mature, we are told, means to be sexually responsive in all moods and seasons."

This idea is so far at variance with what most human beings are really like that it is ludicrous. More important, it destroys the meaning of romance. It is sexual tyranny, because it imposes a uniform response to everyone irrespective of difference in age, personality, and situation. The myth of sex-is-everything has another effect: it has promoted sexual intercourse as a means of dealing with non-sexual problems.

When everything is linked to sex, it becomes difficult to determine and appreciate what is truly sexual. True sexuality is a function of the total personality, and is experienced and expressed only in the lives of truly mature people. The distorted view of sex we find around us confuses rather than enlightens. The myth urges us, often prematurely, into sexual intimacy we can neither understand nor appreciate. This makes it difficult to integrate fully our sexual impulses into our own personal identity. When we fail to meet these challenges in adolescence, we enter adulthood unprepared emotionally. It is no accident that many of us seem adolescent in terms of sexual maturity.

"The myth of sex-is-everything can be dispelled only through a deepening of our entire culture's appreciation of real values and meaning of life itself," says Father Kennedy. "For, despite all the myths, sexuality fits best into the lives of people who love each other. To believe that sex takes on its real significance when it is expressive of a loving human relationship is about as old-fashioned an idea as one could espouse. It is also true. "People everywhere are speaking of the 'new morality,' the 'new freedom' or the 'sexual freedom.' They add up to the same thing—a contagious spirit of permissiveness, of anything goes, in all areas of social conduct, in manners, dress and sexual relationships. "What concerns many is that, if it proceeds too far and too fast, liberty will become license and libertinism, and society may die of moral decay, as earlier civilizations have done," says William Nichols. "There is reason for such concern when reports appear about sex clubs, wife-swapping, orgies, drug addiction, sexually deviant behaviour."

Psychoanalyst Eric Fromm pointed out that current sexual freedom in no way contributes to a true sense of "aliveness" or "richness of experience." There is a significant report from Sweden, which for so long prided itself on removing moral restraints and encouraging sexual freedom. Yet the human toll has been so great that there is now a movement to put an end to sexual laxity.

"The fact is that in every area of human existence *the wheel turns*. What's up today will be down tomorrow. What was "in" yesterday is "out" today. And this happens in morals too," says William Nichols. "Sooner than most cynics believe a new set of values will emerge. There are people who build, and people who break down. It's time a stand was taken on the side of the people who add spiritual health rather than subtract from it. Each day things happen which make the wheel turn. And it's up to today's adults which way it goes."

Strive for self actualisation

While the satisfaction of sexual desire is being overplayed, self-actualisation needs are underplayed. According to psychologist Maslow, there is a tendency in *everyone* of us towards self-actualisation. He referred to "capacities clamouring to be used", a restlessness for self-development, accomplishment and self-esteem. One's potential emerges not by adding skills but first unlocking the door to internal resources waiting to be tapped. He emphasises the need for bringing out the hidden potential in everyone of us. Self fulfillment of potential is the highest need in the hierarchy of needs. Most of us do not know what is our hidden potential. Unless we realise inner talents and abilities they remain unused for ever.

Many individuals do things for the sheer pleasure of accomplishment. You can learn more about this from the Guinne's Book of World Records. Look at the mind boggling variety of things people do to prove their unique talents and achievements. There are great things like climbing the highest peaks without oxygen masks, walking alone all the way to the North Pole, sailing alone on a home made raft around the world. There are also trivial things like growing the longest nails or longest moustaches, fastest peeling of a coconut by teeth, spitting cherry pits to the longest distance. It doesn't matter what you do. Achievement is doing things that others cannot do!

Another area is the intellectual curiosity and fulfillment. Sir Isaac Newton's curiosity led him to discover the principle of gravitation. Herschel's curiosity led him to discover the planet Uranus and its satellites. We have plenty of examples from the scientific research, where people devote their lives for the sake of fulfillment of their desire to find the truth about the curious things in this world. We also heard about Albert Einstein's Theory of Relativity, and the genius of Stephen Hawking's theories of the origin of the universe.

Creativity and aesthetic appreciation are perhaps most admired by one and all. Consider the example of Leonardo da Vinci and his creative genius. Many of our technological achievements like aeroplanes, rockets, parachutes, armoured cars, tanks, were conceived and designed by him long ago. You must have heard of Michelangelo, the master sculptor who devoted his life creating the world's most prized artistic works. Vincent van Gogh devoted his life for painting, though he could sell only one of his works in his entire life; surprisingly each piece today is being sought after for millions of dollars.

Accepting reality is also seen by many people as a need deserving utmost attention. While refusal to accept reality is wrought with disasters in life, accepting reality promises peace and harmony. Since reality is right all the time, what better way is there for happy living than following the royal road of reality.

"No matter what our age or condition, there are still untapped possibilities within us and new beauty waiting to be born," says Dr Dale Turner. Yes, we all have a lot of hidden potential. Who knows what potential you have? Discover your hidden capabilities, infinite possibilities, and exciting opportunities. Discover your talents that are clamouring to come out; give them a chance to grow and flourish. Thus far, you must have devoted a lot of time to satisfy many of your needs. But there are important things that deserve your attention, particularly your self-actualisation needs. Think about them and do what you can. Psychologist Martin E P Seligman strongly advocates: "Realize your potential abilities for lasting fulfillment. They are the source of enduring happiness."

Chapter 15

You Need Money: Not the Craze

It is a spiritual snobbery that makes people think they can be happy without money.

Albert Camus (1913 –1960)
French novelist, Nobel Prize for literature 1957

It is good to have money and the things money can buy; but it is good to check up once in a while to make sure you haven't lost the things that money can't buy.

George Claude Lorimer (1838- ?)
American clergyman

Money hits you directly, in every walk of life. "Money, which we see and hold, is diabolically hard to comprehend," says James Buchan. Yet it plays important role in our lives. "Money reveals where our interests lie; it can direct our attitudes; it can even expose us to the danger of worshipping it; it represents value. Money not only talks, it screams," says Leslie B Flynn.

Ever since the Phoenicians invented it in Lydia (Asia Minor, now part of Western Turkey, 620-600 BC), money has not lost its charm for the mankind. There is nothing like money today that attracts man. Its importance is inherent in its exchange value. Simply by exchanging money, people can get anything they want. Because of this function, money has become absolutely necessary for every human being in the world. While the nature has created man and woman, they in turn have created the worldly trinity of *man, woman* and *money*. What was once an inseparable dyad has now become an interlocked triad of mutual attraction. Men and women love each other; and they both love money. They chase money as passionately as they chase each other. Every man and woman loves money as it delights every heart.

The pursuit of money has now become the point of life for many people, because it can fulfil any mortal purpose. Money indeed plays important role in everybody's life. James Buchan says, "Money is a frozen desire." How right he is? Undoubtedly, money has become the supreme need of mankind. Since it rules the present world, we may call this era as *The age of money*.

Since money can buy many things in this world, the need for money occupies a special place in the minds of human beings. Every body is now talking about money, directly or indirectly, as if the need for money has superseded all other human needs. Financial interests no longer remain in hidden agendas, they are now being discussed openly, everywhere. All our attitudes lie where money is. 'How to make money' and 'how to spend money' are the topics of the day. The broad spectrum of human relations is now being built on the profound foundation of economic values and financial interests. Most of the money in the world continues to change hands and move in global markets. Financial negotiations are transcending national and international politics. Financial markets have become the epicenters of human activities.

There are so many avenues to save and preserve money. Cash is often stashed in bundles in lockers and safe boxes. Sometimes it becomes bulky in its original form; so people convert it into precious metals such as platinum, gold or jewellery. Diamonds of course, are preferred by the richie rich. Some prefer to invest in permanent assets like real estate that are supposed to appreciate in the long run. But unfortunately, such men forget the eternal truth. Nothing lasts long, even life.

Sometimes a comparison with rich neighbours generates unconscious feelings of inferiority. Remember, money does not make much difference in the personal worth of people. Your personal worth is independent of the money you possess. No matter how much money you make, your worth as a person does not change. You must realise that no purpose is served if you go on ego trips. It is always better to keep your heart far from your money.

It is important to recognise that everybody's view of money is affected by one's mindset. When you are playing with money stakes, it is dangerous to play games with your mind. If you are obsessed with money your mind can cause serious troubles. They generally surface when you are losing big or gaining big in such games as stock trading or commodity trading. When you are losing heavily you tend to question your trading decisions. You may even panic and develop unconscious tendency to fall short of your potential. Nameless unreasoning, unjustified terror may paralyse the needed efforts to convert failure into success. When you are gaining big, you are likely to inflate your ego thinking you are invincible, and whatever you do is profitable.

How one makes money is not important for many people. Ends justify means, they say. Can anybody justify making money of other's misery? US actor Vincent Price has made much money acting in horror films. "The end," he says justifies "the meanness." How can anybody approve making money from illicit arm dealers, terrorists, ransom money from kidnappers, stolen money of the criminals, black money from illegal businessmen, arm dealers. Do you approve the money made from drugs that cause misery, and guns that kill people? It is up to you to choose your means of making money. But remember, the old saying. "Ill-gotten wealth brings no profit; uprightness is a safeguard against death."

Recent concern for money the world over is perhaps unprecedented. Never before has the world witnessed such a phenomenon. It has now become a universal craze reaching epidemic proportions. It is causing untold misery to people hankering for money. Recently the advertising giant Lowe & Partners, conducted a research study of five Asian cities Hong Kong, Singapore, Shanghai, Bangkok, and Jakarta. It was reported that the people in Hong Kong are the most stressed because of the pressure to make money quickly." "You are out there on your own," was the cry of Hong Kong people. This is perhaps true of all the people who go after money.

Over a period of time, money making becomes what psychologists call "functional fixedness"; people continue to make money even after it has served their purpose. Craze for money justifies the undesirable means, induces dishonesty and deceit and encourages fraud and embezzlement. Meanness for money degrades man. When tons of money gets accumulated, people do not know what to do with it. If a man's fortune does not fit him it is like the shoes in the story: if it is too large it trips him up, if it is too small it pinches him.

Elbert Hubbard says, "I don't like money. I don't like asprin. But it seems I always need both, sometimes for the same reason." As G K Chesterton said, "To be clever enough to get a great deal of money, one must be stupid enough to want it." Do we really need megabucks, in excess of what we need? That is the question one should ask. Think about it!

Herbert Casson says, "If money is all that he makes, then he will be poor—poor in happiness, poor in all that makes life worth living." Many people who make money, gain all the outward signs of success. But they seem to feel emptiness in life. They lack the capacity for creative living. Life is boring to them. They travel here and there but nowhere can they escape their emptiness. Having acquired money, they equate it with success; but in their heart they feel its emptiness. The empty person feels that he is a criminal because he thinks he has stolen something which he does not deserve. Thus he feels guilty and turns his victories into failures.

Money is a material thing, but happiness is psychological. Money once lost may not return; if it does by any chance, it may take a long time. Happiness comes to you in seconds, because you are capable of feeling happy whenever you want. Remember that your happiness transcends money. At some point in life all of us would realise that there are things other than money that can give more happiness

People have different opinions regarding money and happiness. Leo Rosten says, "*Nothing* brings happiness to some people: *anything* brings happiness to others. By and large, money brings more happiness than the absence there of." Yes, money can buy many things that satisfy our needs; it enables us to enjoy some comforts. But it does not guarantee happiness. Sometimes, as Spike Milligan says,

"Money can't buy you happiness, but it does bring a pleasant form of misery." Therefore, "let us all be happy and live within our means, even if we have to borrow money to do it," says Charles Farrer Browne. Another best advice comes from Jim Rohn: "Learn how to be happy with what you have while you pursue all that you want."

Listen to the advice of Will Durant:

"Build an economic basis under your life, but don't get caught in the rat-trap of moneymaking as a profession. That, like sex, can be consuming fever which brings only fitful pleasures, no lasting happiness. If you become an employer, your relations with your employees are more important than adding a zero to your wealth. Give every employee the full equivalent of his share in the product. Don't live in a boastful luxury based on taking more from the world than you give."

Lastly, listen to the wise King Solomon:

If you love money you will never be satisfied;
If you long to be rich you will never get all you want.

Chapter 16

Joy of Realising Dreams and Achieving Goals

If you want to have a happy life, tie it to a goal, not to people or things.

Albert Einstein (1879 –1955)
Philosopher, physicist, Nobel Prize for physics 1921

Men must have goals, which in their eyes merit effort and commitment and they must believe that their efforts will win them self-respect and respect of others.

John Gardner (1912- 2002)
US Administrator, Professor, Stanford university

Life is short but there is always time for achievements. "It is one of the strange ironies of this strange life that those who work the hardest, who subject themselves to the strict discipline, who give up certain pleasurable things in order to achieve a goal are the happiest men," said Brutus Hamilton, Olympic decathelete. "When you see 20 or 30 men line up for a distance race in some meet, don't pity them, don't feel sorry for them. Better envy them."

According to Richard Bach, anyone can achieve anything in this world. "The trick is" one should stop seeing oneself "as trapped inside a limited body". We must try "to overcome our limitations". If we can see unlimited potential in us, we will be able to achieve our goals. Since you do not know what potential is hidden inside, it is not wise to underestimate yourself. You must look past your limitations and eliminate negative forces that sidetrack you from your goals. Remember, you can do many things in life, if you try sincerely.

Dare to live your dream

All people dream every night; but only a few are able to turn their dreams in to reality. One must learn to "turn possibilities into realities," says Colm McLoughlin. "What if you *could* realise your dream that you put away in a tissue paper, the talent you never developed—and give yourself a life you love, instead of one that's just okay?" asks Annie Gottlieb in an interesting article *"Dare to Live Your Dream."* She says any one can realise dreams, set personal goals, and achieve them. She describes a few principles developed by Barbara Sher, a New York city psychotherapist and career consultant. First choose a goal you love, work out a practical route to it, and draw untapped resources we all have—the ideas, skills, contacts, and support of friends and family. No miracles are necessary. All the resources are within you and around you. Here is how to get started:

Find out what you love

"There is at least nothing in this world (and probably more than one) that makes your heart beat faster," says Sher. Anything that makes you forget what time it is can become the key to your life make-over. They are the sources of energy and joy in your life, and they connect to something central in your life, the unique configuration of talents and drives hidden in you like a seed. In other words, you have to take your dream seriously.

Tell somebody

"Find a witness to your wish," says Sher. Pick a person who cares about you, someone you can trust to take you seriously—a good friend, your spouse—tell him or her. Another person's eyes make your wish real—and make you accountable to someone outside yourself. Since you have committed it to another trusted person, you will be propelled to act on it. You'll feel worse about letting down a friend or spouse than you would about disappointing yourself.

Brainstrom

If you tell your friend what you love to do, he might suggest how to go about. A freewheeling session can be done alone, writing down every idea that props in your head, however crazy. But it works out better if you and your friend or a group of friends, do it together. "We have more and better ideas for one another than we have for ourselves," says Sher.

Get your feet wet
Become involved in what you love right now, without any more skills, credentials or money than you already have. The mistake most of us make is to assume that the traditional way of doing something is the only way. You don't need degrees or experience to start any thing. There are inexpensive, basic ways to jump into almost any field you love. You can almost always barter skills, borrow equipment or buy it second hand, take a low-priced course. "Isolation is the great dream killer", says Sher. Aim for a situation that involves you with other people. When you find an idea you can actually do right now, *do* it. This is the threshold where panic strikes—fear of failure, fear of change. The only cure is action—immediate action.

Clarify your goals
The gap may seem awfully large between dabbling in something and doing it as a full time professional. But, in fact the beginning of your life make-over is the most important step—because once you get out where the action is, you will feel as thrilled as if you'd already arrived at the top. You will soon discover the *joy is in doing what you love*, not in the end result. Soon one thing will lead to another, and you'll meet people, learn things, and hear about opportunities that will draw you deeper into the field. A time may come when you want to make more formal commitment. Then the experience, contacts and know-how you have acquired will stand you in good stead. You will know the basic principle of wish-craft: talk to people. You will know how to tap the wealth of resources and the willingness of help that are right in front of you.

"Best of all," says Barbara Sher "you will have a sparkle in your eyes and a new spring in your stride. Your twenty-four-hour day will have shrunk, but you will love getting out of the bed in the morning." Yes, people need a goal, a direction, a passion in life—something that would make them happy to get out of bed in the morning. If you have the passion for achievement, you can realise your dream with perseverance in the face of obstacles. You never know to what lengths you would go to achieve your goals. Believe in yourself and your realistic goals, pursue with commitment; you will soon find achievement within your reach. Henry David Thoreau assures, "If one advances confidently in the direction of his dreams and endeavours to live the life which he has imagined he will meet with a success unexpected in common hours."

Set realistic goals

Most of us have some ideal and socially desirable goals. But we often get lost in the thoughts of ideal goals. We talk more instead of doing anything worthwhile. The purpose of such socially desirable talk is only to please others, but not to achieve anything. Some times the intention may be good, but we aim too high beyond our reach. Swami Vivekananda says, "Our greatest defect in life is that we are so much drawn to the ideal, the goal is much more enchanting, so much more alluring, so much bigger in our mental horizon, that we lose sight of the details altogether." Think what is possible and practical. Anna Robertson Brown says, "there is a great danger of substituting intellectual ambition for ordinary human affections. Let us keep in bounds; let us see to it that it holds a just proportion in our lives". In others words, keep your ambitions in check.

"Creative living today means steering your mind to productive goals," says Maxwell Maltz. Your personal goals are your first priority. It is certainly not a self-centered thinking; rather it is a highly responsible behaviour. You would like to enjoy life doing what you love to do. "Nothing great was ever achieved without enthusiasm" says, Ralph Waldo Emerson. Do whatever you do with zest for life.

"Principles without programmes are platitudes," said George Bernard Shaw. In the same way goals without actions are mere slogans. Unless you initiate result oriented actions nothing can be achieved. Doing a job successfully means doing whatever is needed to achieve goals. Successful people set realistic goals. You must set achievable goals that make sense to you.

"Choose your goals and make sure they're really your own, not something imposed on you by others," advises Dr Hans Selye. We often set exciting and challenging goals; some times they induce stress. The Yerkes-Dodson curve shows us that up to an optimal point stress can aid performance, so long as the goal is seen as challenging but within reach. But after a certain point a goal can turn into a threat, when we begin to feel the pressure in the case of reaching the set targets. At this point even a little stress becomes 'distress,' because we feel our targets are beyond our reach. At a time like this we usually scale down the targets, into a zone of 'achievable targets.' In other words, we venture into what we know best and set them at a level we hope to reach with confidence, and pursue until we achieve success.

Unprepared first attempts are usually discouraging. If at first you succeed, try to hide your astonishment! Analyse your desires and define your problems in not achieving your objectives. Focus on pivotal problems instead of running around in all directions. There is nothing wrong with aggressiveness, properly channeled. To reach your goals, sometimes you may have to be aggressive. But if frustration is the major cause of your aggressiveness it is likely to be misdirected. It blocks the goal oriented behaviour. It is usually linked up with unrealistic goals which cannot be achieved.

You must believe in your success, otherwise you can not achieve anything. Therefore it is necessary to convert achievable goals into actual beliefs. It involves a process of communicating with the subconscious, so that the latter automatically accepts your goal as being valid call on its energy.

Ensure the help of subconscious mind

In practice, defining achievable goals in a positive way transmits important information to the subconscious mind. There are two ways of doing it: *visualisation* of goals and *writing* them down. They can provide a clear picture of the goals to the subconscious. Both provide powerful reinforcements. In fact, only one experience is actually more powerful. That is, the final realisation of the goal itself. The process takes time and commitment. But those who persisted with it have confirmed its power.

Another important thing to do is the act of *focused attention* on the objective to be achieved. It transfers the details of that objective into the subconscious. It is in effect a way of convincing your subconscious that your goal deserves investment of potential energies yet to be utilised.

Goal setting strategy

The first task is to convert your achievable goals/objectives into actual beliefs about your future. While setting your goals, make a clear distinction between, what is *desired* in terms of results, gain, profit, or success, and what can actually be *expected* at the moment. Analyse your desires and define your problems in not achieving your objectives. Examine what is needed—resources, experience, plans, strategies, methods, time, effort, help etc. Specify in detail your resources that would be necessary to achieve the desired objective. Then equip yourself with all that is required for reaching your goals. State your objective in operational terms—for example, a target marks of 90 per cent and above or a minimum income or profit.

Remember, your goals are not targets. Goals belong to the future, where as achievements belong to the present. Achievements attract and manipulate emotional energy. Diversion of focused attention to strategy is critical. If you focus your attention to what can be achieved now huge resources can (and will) be released from unfulfilled desires and unpleasant emotions and can be used to deal with tasks at hand.

A good strategy is required for the immediate task on hand. The word 'strategy' is a military term, meaning the art of conducting a war campaign against the enemy. It involves meticulous planning and thorough preparation to meet all the foreseeable contingencies of war. It includes the provision of required resources, tools, and methods etc. Wise King Solomon once said, "Wisdom prevails over strength, knowledge over brute force. For wars are won by skillful strategy, victory is the fruit of long planning." Every task in hand requires a strategy for success.

We must give attention to means. Swami Vivekananda says, "I have been always learning great lessons from that one principle, and it appears to me that all the secrets of success is there : to pay as much attention to the means as to the end... When ever failure comes, if we analyse critically, in ninety nine per cent of the cases we shall find that it was because we did not pay attention to the means... If we take care of the cause, the effect will take care of itself. The realization of the ideal is the effect. The means are the cause: attention to means therefore is the secret of life."

"As a general rule, the most successful man in life is the man who has the best information," said Benjamin Disraeli. "The trick of successful problem solving is to assemble all relevant information—every fact and clue—and evaluate each possible combination," say Karen Billings and Alice Kaseberg Schwandt.

Another important thing is to remember the triad of success: goals—means—effort. In this combination the goals must be realistic and achievable. The means and strategies should be appropriate. And then when it comes to effort it should be sustained effort, that requires steady and persistent work. It also means commitment with indefatigable zeal in spite of setbacks or failures.

There are several advantages of realistic goal setting. It increases one's capabilities to a meaningful extent. You will become more confident and be able to put in sustained effort. You will be more patient in waiting for the outcome. It reduces the gap between expected outcome and actual outcome. Nothing is difficult to achieve. Think what is possible, and aim at what you can do. Define achievable limits. Set your sights on realistic goals. Isolate your realistic goals, then draw up a plan—for the next five years, year, month, and day—listing specific actions to achieve those goals.

Lastly, remember the words of John Condry: "Happiness, wealth and success are the by-products of goal-setting; they cannot be goals themselves."

Chapter 17

Fun in Capturing Opportunities

To find what one is fitted to do, and secure an opportunity to do is the key to happiness.

John Dewey (1859 – 1952)
American philosopher and educator

A pessimist sees the difficulty in every opportunity, an optimist sees the opportunity in every difficulty.

Sir Winston Churchill (1874-1965)
British soldier and statesman
Nobel Prize for literature 1953.

"Four things come not back: spoken word, the spent arrow, the past, the neglected opportunity," said Omar Ibn Al-Halifa, the second Calif. Then, what is an opportunity? "An opportunity is a course of action that is possible," says Professor Edward de Bono. Obviously it is worth pursuing. It can be seen everywhere, only when we look for it. "Therefore if a man looks sharply and attentively, he shall see fortune, for though she be blind, yet she is not invisible," said Francis Bacon. Once it is seen, it exists for you. Opportunities don't come knocking every time. You have to seize them when they do. Be prepared to capture them before they vanish. If you look for opportunities you will find them.

"Effective people are not problem minded; they are opportunity minded. They feed opportunities and starve problems", said Peter Drucker. Benjamin Franklin once said, "The opportunities that I did seize have invariably enriched my life and contributed to growth even though at times it seemed as if I'd made a mistake and seized the wrong opportunities."

Edward de Bono recognised the importance of looking for profitable opportunities. But he warns that you can reap the benefits only when your *perception* of an opportunity matches with the *reality* of its existence. Otherwise there are two possible dangers.

First, if you look with hind sight you might miss them as well as the potential benefits and profits. If you have illusions of opportunities you will see them everywhere, even in their absence. Eric Hoffer says "We usually see things we are looking for – so much so that we some times see them where they are not." That reminds a familiar story from Vajrakarur, a village in Anantapur District (A.P., India). Every rainy season, a sort of 'diamond rush' wakes up this sleepy village. Prospectors descend on the scene to try their luck. Soon after the rain showers they rush to the fields, with a lot of excitement looking for diamonds. Suddenly some thing dazzles at a distance. Something tells a prospector that he should not miss this rare chance. He is reminded of the familiar saying: ' opportunities are never lost, the other fellow takes those you miss.' His mind reminds him that he must seize it before others do. Immediately, he runs to grab what seemed to be a life-time opportunity. Heightened focus sometimes blurs vision, every minute thing catches attention. Even the shining pebbles appear as brilliant diamonds. He forgets two things here. Diamonds are rare in nature, and as such cannot be found everywhere. The brilliance of a cut diamond is extremely rare in raw diamonds. Yet, some believe what they found are real diamonds until some expert tells them the truth. That is true, excited people tend to see opportunities in everything they see.

Second, apart from such illusions of opportunities, there are delusions that are very dangerous. It is quite baffling to know even highly intelligent people fall into a hypnotic trance dreaming opportunities. Their greed mesmerises them to believe and see the ghosts of opportunities as the real ones. Believing in their existence people make all sorts of preparations to capture them. They spend substantial amounts of money, with the fond hope of profiting from such opportunities. They actually encounter disaster when they act on their delusions. Obsessed people, tend to see opportunities in every thing they believe. Their beliefs do not have any realistic basis. When they walk on the tight rope of reality, they sometimes fall into the oblivion. Unless the wisdom dawns on them there is no hope for their survival. In his book *Opportunities,* Edward de Bono gives many examples of business ventures that were virtual disasters, for the single reason that they were based on unrealistic obsessions of opportunities.

"Fortune favours the prepared mind", says Louis Pasteur. You may think that one should be lucky to find opportunities. Field marshal Viscount Slim says, "Luck means being in the right place at the right time to see an opportunity." Since opportunities do not show up frequently, what seems an opportunity could be a trap. Opportunity knocks only once in a while, but human temptation leans on every thing. You must guard against this possible danger. You know the proverb, ' look before you leap.' Before jumping into action, ensure what you see is a *real* opportunity. When you are convinced, make your efforts in its direction. At the same time, be alert to correct yourself, if it turns out to be a red herring. You must develop that uncanny knack of identifying the *real* opportunities. Only then you can make realistic expectations, formulate appropriate plans and execute them with confidence.

De Bono says that opportunity search involves both problem finding and solution finding. He advocates lateral perception—a creative approach to find opportunities. Possibility of finding them will increase with focused thinking. He says that ideas give direction; but direction is different from destination. Your destination is an opportunity. To convert an idea into an opportunity you need the means: thinking time, and thinking effort.

First thing is to look for perceptual alternatives. You need market pull information not technology push information. Look in all directions—different routes, obvious and not so obvious, less risky, better tried, cheaper, reliable, to be improved, to be simplified. Since information is generally inadequate, start with what you have. Don't use killer phrases such as, "The same as." You need special glasses to look at information: ideas as frames of reference. Stop looking at things in fixed ways, be flexible. Look sideways, look for new routes. Switch from one way to another. There is always another way! Look for it. Develop new ideas, new ways of thinking, new ways of putting things together, change your concepts. He advocates such techniques as Function extraction, Plus, Minus, Interesting provocation, Stepping stones, Tailoring an idea, DPA (Difference, Practical Advantage) rating, Spell it out, Information available, Required information, Satisfy and define.

Once a destination has been identified it becomes possible to examine the means of getting there. Then formulate your idea, get information, assess benefits, work out feasible action. He advocates such tools as "if-box maps," and such strategies as 'scan approach' and 'deliberate search.' De Bono says, "Man's progress depends on Opportunity Search. We cannot afford not to look for opportunities". He advocates establishment of Opportunity Search departments in every business organisation.

Steve Marshal Cohen gave a framework for evaluating a business opportunity. It involves examining important questions:

1. How much money it is going to take, to start the venture?
2. What is it for? Analyse sources and uses.
3. How the money is returned to the investor?
4. Does it pass the reality test? Is the product real? Is the market real?
5. Does it pass competitive test?
6. Does it pass value test? Is it worth it? Examine Risk, Profitability, Return on investment.
7. If it is technology based venture, is the perspective real?
8. Are there any hidden unknowns or overriding factors?

Take charge: Turn adversity into an opportunity
Would you want to go through that mill again? Think it over. Shouldn't be looking for greater challenges? At exploring new adventures? At pioneering something?

Who knows what is in store for you? Whatever it is, the first requirement is, you should stop the blame-game; and take the responsibility for your life. Recharge yourself with enough courage.

Remember, when you are in charge of yourself you will regain your power to make your own destiny.

After interviewing 632 people who were able to turn adversity to their advantage, Robert and Jeanette Lauer of US International University in San Diego, California, have discovered that most of them made the best use of a *watershed event*—a turning point in life—to their advantage. It can be any event, positive or negative, that significantly affects the course of a person's life. They have come up with four strategies for mastering life's most unpredictable moments and transforming them into opportunities for growth.

Assume responsibility for yourself

Everyone encounters disappointments in life; and many people do not fully recover from the crisis, despite the promised healing of time. "It is important, then, to deal actively with painful experiences such as illness, divorce, or the loss of a job," say Lauer and Lauer. "Some people cope by blaming God, fate or others. But the simple truth is: ultimately we have to assume responsibility for our lives." A person should go beyond the hurt and make something of his life. He should accept responsibility for his life and do the best he could.

Make tough choices

People who gained most from watershed experiences felt that it is not possible to grow by avoiding risk and hoping all will turn out well. They should not hesitate taking the risk of trying new and tough options in life. Risk frequently pays large dividends. Chrysler chairman, Lee Iococca writes that decisiveness—the ability to make a decision and act on it –is the mark of a good manager. It is also the mark of anyone else willing to risk—and grow and become his or her own person.

Seek relationships that enrich your life

Relationships are web of life; they influence how we think, feel and behave. At times they affect the course of our lives. Successful people frequently told that they had friends or mentors who guided them through the early years of their careers. Even a casual acquaintance or a stranger may have deep impact on our lives. They instil the inspiration and courage, at a time we require them most.

Affirm self-worth

Typically, a crisis undermines one's self-esteem, which in turn, makes it difficult to deal with the crisis. Lauer and Lauer say, "We found that those who were able to affirm a sense of self-worth were less likely to feel helpless and more likely to influence events—and explore options—when faced with adversity."

We don't automatically incorporate good ideas into our lives. We grow by choosing to grow, by responding positively to what happens to us. We must learn to use our watershed experiences as opportunities to grow. Lauer and Lauer say, "All it takes is recognising a watershed experience for the life-shaping value it has—and *acting* on it." Wayne Dyer, the author of *Manifest Your Own Destiny* says, "Decide you are going to be the one in control of your life." Surely, you will find your own destiny.

Besides you need to commit yourself. Your sense of self —call it self-respect, self-esteem, being your own best friend—is the back bone of the move towards taking charge of your self. "A sense of control," according to Craig Anderson, of Rice University in Houston, "is the litmus test of success. The optimist feels in control of his own life."

"Getting a second chance means believing that change is within your grasp—and that you can benefit from it," says Barbara Bartocci. Life is full of second chances for all of us to find fulfilment in what we do, to change failure to success through a new endeavour or a different attitude. We don't have to limit ourselves. All we need for a second chance is the ability to recognize it and the courage to act.

When written in Chinese the word 'crisis' is composed of two characters: one represents 'danger' and the other 'opportunity". Yes "In the middle of difficulty lies opportunity," says Albert Einstein. But "It is often hard to distinguish between hard knocks in life and those of opportunity," says Frederick Philips. We are often carried away by the problems we encounter in life; and they may induce us to give up. Joe Kogel says, "The worst thing in your life may contain seeds of the best. When you see a crisis as an opportunity, your life becomes not easier, but more satisfying." Yes, who knows what crisis may prove to be your watershed in life. Remember, procrastination is the natural assassin of opportunity; look at obstacles as opportunities and whisper for yourself, "What's in it for me?"! Finally what matters is the courage to take on the difficult challenges offered by, what the British Prime Minister Tony Blair calls, the "opportunity society". "It is a great challenge to be better than your opportunities," says Sarah Jessica Parker, a successful Hollywood actress.

"He that awaits fortune is never sure of dinner," says Benjamin Franklin. Yes, it may take a long time before you find any opportunity in life. Then, don't waste your time doing nothing, waiting for opportunities to come by. A Polish proverb says, "If there is no wind, row." In the same way, if you are not lucky enough to find opportunities never stop working. Do anything that interests you, that is where opportunity of happiness may be waiting for you!

Chapter 18
Cheerful Actions Lead to Accomplishments

Happiness lies in the joy of achievement and the thrill of creative effort.
Franklin D.Roosevelt (1882 –1945)
Former US President

The persons born with a talent they are meant to use will find their greatest happiness in using it. What you can do or dream you can, begin it; boldness has genius, power and magic in it.
Johann Wolfgang Von Goethe (1749 – 1832)
German Poet, novelist, and scientist, natural philosopher.

All human behaviour is purposive and goal directed. Psychologists E G Boring, Langfeld and Weld explained that the human behaviour follows a sequence:

Stimulus—Organism—Behaviour —Accomplishments

The stimulus situation includes the people around, the environment, job routines, light, sound, and objects etc. The individual is the organism. Many of his personal factors contribute to his behaviour—heredity, intelligence, motivation, needs, knowledge, learning, attitudes, values, and beliefs. Behaviour includes all his actions, doing, talking, facial expressions, emotional responses, thinking, feelings etc. Accomplishments include, survival, escape, change in stimulation, and achievements.

Life is about choices; and our actions are the choices we make. Every human action is purposive, goal-directed and motivated. It is integrated with our needs and wants, cognitions and emotions. It is linked to our goals in life. It involves instrumental acts. It has some reference to other actions. It is the result of or cause of other actions.

Our actions speak louder than words. They speak about us— our needs, our intentions, our character. Our actions are central to our personality. Our actions result in accomplishments; and we are rewarded for our actions. And that is why people can judge us by our actions.

Do what you will

Do what you want to do. Don't bother about critics. "A critic is a man who knows the way but can't drive the car," says Kenneth Tynan. "Do what you can, with what you have, where you are," said Theodore Roosvelt. Forget what should be done. "Don't follow any advice, no matter how good, until you feel as deeply in your spirit as you think in your mind that the counsel is wise," says David Seabury. Just do what you will, and the best you can. Eric Raymond says, "People do their work when they are passionately engaged in what they are doing." Lee Iococca says, "Right upfront, tell people what you're trying to accomplish and what you are willing to sacrifice." When you publicise your intentions, you force your ideas set into motion, your mind moves from a state of inertia to a state of action.

Human behaviour is pulled towards goals – Goal seeking behaviour tends to persist. This driving and pulling of forces is called by psychologists as motivation, which results in persistent behaviour directed toward particular goals. David McClelland says that achievement motivation is responsible for rise and fall of nations with particular reference to economic activity. As Jean de la Bruyere said, "It's motive alone that gives character to the actions of men." Motivate yourself to achieve and accomplish the best you can.

Besides you need other ingredients for the success of your actions. Be enthusiastic about what you are doing. "Nothing great was ever achieved without enthusiasm," said Ralph Waldo Emerson "Loss of enthusiasm is a form of premature death. It is like accepting defeat without having been defeated," said Roberto Sapriza.

"No one can possibly be satisfied and no one can be happy who feels that in some permanent affairs he failed to take up challenges of life," says Enoch Arnold Bennet. Therefore, be courageous in whatever you do. As Sir Winston Churchill said "Courage is the first of human qualities because it is the quality which guarantees all others."

Another important input is your persistence. "Nothing in the world can take the place of persistence," says Calvin Coolidge. "Talent will not, nothing is more common than unsuccessful men with talent. Genius will not, unrewarded genius is almost a proverb. Education will not, the world is full of educated failures. Persistence and determination alone are omnipotent." Remember, no hurdle can stand before the might of your persistence; and no realistic goal is beyond your reach!

Concentrate on action

Thomas J Peters and Robert H Waterman Jr have reported in *In Search of Excellence*, eight attributes that characterise innovative excellent companies. Among them, "A bias for action" stands out as the most important requirement for excellent performance. All other seven attributes are secondary in importance—close to the customer; autonomy and entrepreneurship; productivity through people; hands on, value driven; stick to the knitting; simple form, lean staff; simultaneous lose tight properties.

Even when we consider individual achievement, this attribute stands out. Ludwig Van Beethoven exemplified a bias for action. He arose at daybreak and immediately began composing until 2.p.m. when he would have his dinner. He worked long stretches of unbroken time to allow his thoughts to unfold and flow uninterrupted. You must learn to have a bias for action. Remember what Benjamin Disraeli said, "Action may not bring happiness, but there is no happiness without action".

A secret formula for peak performance

Timothy Gallwey discovered a profound formula for achieving peak performance while playing tennis: it is sheer *concentration* on action. Seeking to improve his game, he gradually became aware of a constant commentary going on inside his head as he played—*Come on, get your racket back earlier.. Here comes another high backhand like the one you missed last time. Damn it, you missed it again...* "I was surprised to discover that there are two identities within me," he said. "One was playing tennis; the other was telling me how to play."

Gallwey called these identities Self 1 and Self 2. He made the following distinction:

Self 1.	Self 2.
It is verbal and conceptual, capable of understanding the rules for task.	It is the complex combination of mind, senses, nerves, and muscles that makes possible the accomplishment of any activity.
It decides whether or not we play tennis or type or sell a computer.	It will do the learning and, ultimately, the performance.

Gallwey observed that when he was playing his best, there was no noise in his mind; Self 2 seemed to respond automatically to the challenge of hitting the ball. We have all known such moments of "peak performance" when we "forget ourselves."

After experimenting with himself on the tennis court, Gallwey concluded that the key to peak performance is in *silencing* Self 1. All its instructions, and its doubts, fears and criticisms, only confuse Self 2. Of course turning off Self 1 is not that easy; for most of us, that barking voice in the head *is* what we think of as ourselves. But if Self 1 can be *turned off* at the right time, Self 2 can get on with the job. And near miracles will result.

How can we go about this Inner Game? Based on Gallwey's ideas, Samuel Schreiner Jr, has formulated five rules for achieving peak performance:

Keep your eye on the ball

Applied literally in sports like tennis, this phrase is also a metaphor for concentrating on the most important matter in any activity. How do we do this? Gallwey believes that *concentration* is not a matter of the will but a "fascination of the mind." In tennis, for example, he advises that you "learn to 'love' the ball," that you stop *ordering* yourself to watch it and simply let your eyes see it—its texture, its seems, its shape, its trajectory. "When I managed to do this myself," says Schreiner Jr, "I discovered that a kind of magic took over. Soon I was getting shots I didn't believe possible."

"Actually," Gallwey contends, "in a game where there is no ball, the first problem is deciding what "the ball" should be. In selling, the ball is the buyer. Watch the buyer as you would a tennis ball—the 'seems' are things like a yawn, a shift of the eyes, a change in the voice. Even if you don't make the sale, you'll learn from the buyer's signs of resistance where your sales talk went wrong."

Trust yourself
Self 1 inside us, is highly *critical*. Often it gives up on Self 2, the doer, saying, "You can't do *anything* right." This is *wrong*. Far from criticising Self 2, Self 1 should stand back in awe of human capacity. We all trust Self 2 to perform without conscious thoughts of such daily feats of coordination as tying shoe laces, threading a needle or driving a car. Mistakes set in, however, when we take on tasks of measurable achievement. That also involves the ego. With our self-image at stake, we become afraid to leave it all up to an "unconscious" Self 2.

How do we learn to trust Self 2 ? By practice! "Let go and let it happen," says Gallwey. Suspend Self 1's judgment as to whether the particular challenge—the ski turn, the golf putt, the difficult passage in a Beethoven sonata—is being done right or wrong.

Focus on here and now
Self 1 won't be at peace unless it does *something* useful—and that can be observing and monitoring the performance of Self 2. Concentrate on what *is* happening rather than what you fear or hope *will* happen. "Anxiety is fear about what may happen," Gallwey writes. "But when your attention is on the here and now, the actions that need doing have the best chance of accomplishing."

Don't worry about winning
Gallwey is convinced that worrying is the most insidious trick Self 1 plays on Self 2. It tightens muscles and tense nerves—the most

common causes of error. Self 2, Gallwey claims, will do its best only when Self 1 stops giving impossible commands.

If you stop consciously trying, you can perform with what Gallwey calls "effortless effort." Self 2 will live up to its potential, which is the total of its natural equipment plus what it has learnt in practice. Gallwey discovered that the less we worry about end results the better they are likely to be. "'Abandon' is a good word to describe what happens to a tennis player—or to any other player, for that matter—who feels he has nothing to lose," Gallwey says. "He stops worrying about the outcome and simply plays without regard for consequences". Ironically, when that state is achieved, the results are always the best possible.

Don't question your potential

Self-doubt is almost invariably fulfilling. The golfer who always thinks as he steps on to the green, *I always miss one-metre putts,* will always do so. Self-doubt can be banished only if you silence Self 1 and concentrate on the present. One woman in a Gallwey class claimed she was "frightened to death" to face an audience. How did she know she was frightened? asked Gallwey. Because, she said, her knees shook. Gallwey asked her to measure shaking of her knees on a scale of zero to ten. "About nine" she said, and her voice was already calmer. Then Gallwey got her to face the class. The woman's fascination with feeling her own fear made her lose it.

When the shaking dropped to nearly zero, she was able to talk to the group about her experience—to make the first speech of her life—and has since become a television and radio commentator.

Gallwey thinks that a wider understanding of the Inner Game and its ramifications could help our whole society. Whether that is true or not, the evidence *is* strong that playing a good Inner Game can at least improve the performance of any individual involved in a specific task. If, that is, we don't *try* too hard.

Time your actions

King Solomon said, "One more thing I have observed here under the sun : speed does not win the race nor strength the battle. Bread does not belong to the wise, nor wealth to the intelligent, nor success to the skillful; time and chance govern all." "Every activity and every purpose has its proper time." "A wise man knows in his heart the right time and method for action. There is a time and method for every enterprise, although man is greatly troubled by ignorance of future, who can tell him what it will bring." "Life is about timing," says Carl Lewis.

Avoid procrastination

"Procrastination is the fear of success," said Ella Wheeler Wilcox. "People procrastinate because they are afraid of the success that they know will result if they move ahead now." The key, differentiating factor is that the lucky people had a do-it-now philosophy that the comparatively unlucky seemed to lack.

George Clason writes in *The Richest Man in Babylon* :

> "In my younger days, I thought it was my poor judgement that caused me to lose many profitable deals. Later I thought my losses were caused by my stubborn disposition. At last I recognized it for what it was a habit of delaying where prompt and decisive action was required."

Dr Norman Vincent Peales wrote *You can Do It Now,* Stephan Bechtel wrote *How to Do Today What You Could Put Off Until Tomorrow.* Both on how to deal with procrastination. Let us summarise what they said :

Stop regarding procrastination as a harmless subject
Businessmen fail because they put off making key decisions. People die because they put off going to a doctor. Procrastination is not an inconsequential habit: it can thwart your ambitions, destroy your happiness, even kill you.

Pick one specific area where procrastination plagues you
Identify those aspects of your life that are being put off; take one specific area at a time try to conquer it. If you can break the hold procrastination has on this area, the sense of relief and triumph will help you eliminate it from others.

Try "Swiss cheese" approach
Instead of taking on an entire project at once, "poke holes" in the work by taking whatever time you have—five minutes, half an hour—to do

one small part of the overall work. That way it is easier to get started, you learn to consider each half-hour's work an accomplishment in itself, and you may eventually even complete the job.

Don't dodge the most difficult ones
It is a human tendency to do easier thing first. But putting off difficult things leads to greater difficulties later. Tackle them head on. The lift you get will carry your light through the reminder of the task.

Learn to set priorities
Decide to take up important tasks first, and set priorities. Then take up one at a time. Once you complete one task, a part of the project, the other uncompleted tasks will pull your attention to complete them. You will also feel a sense of achievement.

Give deadlines
If you set deadlines of your own you will probably ignore them later. But if you set deadlines in the presence of someone close to you, your friend or spouse, you will have to save your face if you don't meet your commitment. Your pride will make you finish the job on time. It 's much harder to be a public procrastinator than a private one.

Recognise that the finished project does not have to be perfect
If you aim perfection, the fear of failure may haunt you. Instead, aim to complete the task. That itself is an accomplishment, because what was put off for a long time is now got done.

Learn to transfer the energy to other projects
Once you have your work momentum in doing any project of your choice, you can transfer some of the energy generated to other things you have been putting off. That way, you can avoid the problem of initial inertia for doing those unpleasant tasks. You will probably find it easier than starting later from zero.

Reward yourself
Reward yourself by scheduling a pleasant task after you've completed a boring or unpleasant one. If your personal war is against putting things off, don't expect instant results. But remember: each small gain

brings you closer to the long-term goal of ridding yourself of the procrastination habit. "Look around and you'll agree that the really happy people are those who have broken the chains of procrastination, those who find satisfaction in doing the job at hand" says Peale. "They are full of eagerness, zest, productivity. You can be too."

Manage your time

Napoleon Bonaparte once said, "I may lose a battle but I shall never lose a minute." He knew the value of every minute, because it is one thing that can never be recovered once it is lost. All sensible people know that time is the essence of life. The secret of getting the maximum out of life is in intelligent use of available time. Have you ever marvelled at how some people, working with same number of hours we all have, seem to get so much more done? How do they do it?

"For one thing, they don't squander the bits and pieces of time that punctuate our days," says Dale Turner. "Rather than wasting energy getting irritated waiting for a phone call or a repairman, they capture those moments creatively. They keep tools handy—a pen, a book, a pair of scissors, a needle, whatever."

"Remember most time is wasted in minutes, not hours. The average person wastes enough minutes in ten years to have earned a college degree." Yet some people make constructive use of small bits of time available to them.

Successful people develop techniques for getting the maximum benefit from minimum investment of time. Edwin Bliss gives ten tips to help you manage your time:

Plan

You need to plan your day. Otherwise, you will allocate your time according to whatever happens to land on your desk. And you will find yourself making the fatal mistake of dealing primarily with problems rather than opportunities. Studies proved that "the more time we spend in planning a project, the less total time is required for it."

Concentrate

Concentration is more basic to time management. People who have serious time management problems invariably are trying to do too many things at once. The amount of time spent on a project is not what counts: it's the amount of *uninterrupted* time.

Take breaks

Working long periods has side effects: Energy decreases, boredom sets in and physical stress and tension accumulate. You should not think of a "rest" break as a poor use of time. Not only will being refreshed increase your efficiency, but relieving tension will benefit your health.

Avoid clutter

Clutter hinders concentration and can create tension—a feeling of being "buried under." Whenever you find your desk becoming chaotic, take time out to reorganise. Go through all papers and divide them into categories: 1) Immediate action. 2) Low priority. 3) Pending. 4) Reading material. Put the highest priority item from your first file in the centre of your desk, then put everything else out of sight. Remember, you can think of only one thing at a time, so focus all your attention on the most important one. Clearing the desk completely, or at least organising it, each evening should be standard practice. It gets the next day off to a good start.

Don't be a perfectionist

There is a difference between striving for excellence and striving for perfection. The first is attainable, gratifying and healthy. The second is often unattainable, frustrating and neurotic. It's also a terrible waste of time.

Don't be afraid to say no

Of all time-saving techniques ever developed, perhaps the most effective is frequent use of the word no. Learn to decline tactfully but firmly, every request that does not contribute to your goals. If you point out that your motivation is not to get out of work but to save your time to do a better job on the really important things, you'll have good chance of avoiding unproductive tasks. Remember, many people who worry about offending others wind up living according to other people's priorities.

Don't procrastinate
Procrastination, the habit of putting off things, is a deep rooted habit. Decide to start changing as soon as you read this. Don't try to do too much too quickly. Just force yourself right now to do one thing you have been putting off. Then, beginning tomorrow, start each day by doing the most unpleasant thing on your schedule: an overdue apology; a confrontation with a fellow worker; an annoying chore you know you should tackle. Whatever it is, do it before you begin your usual morning routine. This simple procedure can well set the tone for the day. You will get a feeling of exhilaration from knowing that although the day is only 15 minutes old you have already accomplished the most unpleasant thing you have to do all the day.

Do not permit exceptions. Be tough with yourself, for few minutes of each day, for the next two weeks; you will realise that you have acquired a new habit of priceless value.

Apply radical surgery
Time wasting activities are like cancers. They drain off vitality and have a tendency to grow. The only cure is radical surgery. If you are wasting your time in activities that bore you, divert you from your real goals and sap your energy, cut them out once and for all.

This principle applies to personal habits, routines and activities as much to ones associated with your work. Check your appointment calendar, your extracurricular activities, your reading list, your television viewing habits, and axe everything that does not give you a feeling of accomplishment or satisfaction.

Delegate
If you try to do everything yourself, when you have people around to do things, you are wasting your time. Giving subordinates jobs neither you nor anyone else wants to do isn't delegating, it is assigning. Learn to delegate challenging and rewarding tasks, along with sufficient authority to make decisions. It can help to free your time. You can concentrate on major decisions.

Don't be a workaholic

Most successful executives work long hours, but they don't let work interfere with really important things in life, such as friends and family. This differentiates them from the workaholic who becomes addicted to work just as people become addicted to alcohol. Symptoms of work addiction include refusal to take a holiday, inability to put the office out of your mind on weekends, a bulging briefcase, and a wife, son or daughter who is a stranger. It can affect your health. You may not be able to give enough to yourself or your children and spouse.

Above all else, good time management involves awareness that today is all we ever have to work with. The past is irretrievably gone, the future is only a concept. John Ruskin had the word "TO DAY" carved into a small block that he kept on his desk as a constant reminder to "Do it now." But bliss gives his favourite quotation by an anonymous philosopher:

> "Yesterday is a cancelled cheque
> Tomorrow is a promissory note
> Today is ready cash. Use it!"

He reminds us a verse of Julia Fletcher Carney:

> Little drops of water,
> Little grains of sand,
> Make the mighty ocean
> And the pleasant land.
> So the little minutes,
> Humble though they may be,
> Make the mighty ages,
> Of eternity.

Many people say that they are not able to find time. Oscar Schisgall says anyone can find time. "The trick is to create an hour and use it wisely. If you devote but one hour a day to an engrossing project, you will give it 365 hours a year, the equivalent of more than 45 full working days of eight hours each. This is like adding one and half months of productive living to every year of life!"

In *The Seven Habits of Effective People,* Stephen R Covey says, "the essence of best thinking in the area of time management may be captured in a single phrase: *Organise and execute around priorities.* Two factors that define an activity are *urgent* and *important. Urgent* means it requires immediate attention. It's "now!". Urgent things act on us. A ringing phone is urgent. Most people can't stand the thought of just allowing the phone to ring. *Importance* on the other hand, has to do with results. If something is important it contributes to your mission, your values, your high priority goals. Consider the matrix with two dimensions—urgent and not urgent on X axis and important and not important on Y axis. Let us examine all the four quadrants.

	Activities	Results
Quadrant I Urgent Important	Crises Pressing problems Deadline-driven projects.	Stress Burn out Crisis management Always putting out fires.
Quadrant II Not urgent Important	Prevention, Production Capability activities Relationship building Recognising new opportunities. Planning, recreation	Vision, perspective Balance Discipline Control Few crises.
QuadrantIII Urgent Not important	Interruptions, some calls Some mail, some reports Some meetings Proximate, pressing matters Popular activities.	Short-term focus Crisis management Reputation-chameleon character, See goals and plans as worthless. Feel victimised, out of control Shallow or broken relationships.

Quadrant IV	Trivia, busy work	Total responsibility
Not urgent	Some mail	Fired from job
Not important	Some phone calls	Dependent on others
	Time wasters	or institutions for
	Pleasant activities.	basics.

Quadrant I is both urgent and important. It deals with significant results. We usually call the activities in Quadrant I as "crises" or problems. We all have quadrant I activities in life. But Quadrant I consumes many people. They are crisis managers, problem minded people, deadline driven producers. As long as you focus on Quadrant I it keeps getting bigger and bigger until it dominates you. Some people are literally beaten up by problems all day everyday. The only relief they have is escaping to Quadrant IV.

There are other people who spend a great deal of time in "urgent but not important" Quadrant III, thinking they are in the Quadrant I. They spend most of the time reacting to things that are urgent, assuming they are also important. But the reality is that the urgency of these matters is often based on the priorities and expectations of others.

Effective people stay out of Quadrant III and Quadrant IV because, urgent or not, they aren't important. They also shrink quadrant I down to size by spending more time in quadrant II. It is the heart of effective personal management. It deals with things that are not urgent, but important.

The only place to get time for Quadrant II in the beginning is from Quadrants III and IV. You can't ignore urgent and important activities of Quadrant I, although it will shrink in size as you spend more time in Quadrant II. But the initial time for Quadrant II should come out of Quadrants III and IV. You have to be proactive to work on Quadrant II because Quadrants I and III work on you. To say "yes" to important Quadrant II priorities, you have to say "no" to other activities. Covey says that to be effective in life, one has to become Quadrant II self-manager.

"The question of life is not, How much time we have? The question is, What shall we do with it?" says Anna Robertson Brown.

"Dost thou love life? Then do not squander time, for that's the stuff life is made of," says Benjamin Franklin. "Time is the coin of your life," says Carl Sandburg. "It is the only coin you have and only you can determine how it will be spent. Be careful lest you let other people spend it for you." Learn to make the best use of every minute available to you. That is one of the secrets of great achievers. What matters is the enjoyment you derive from every minute of your life. If you take care of minutes, happy days, months and years will fill your life.

Take risk to achieve

A lot of people approach risk as if it's the enemy when it's really fortune's accomplice. Robert Kriegel with Louis Patler, has written *Do You Take Enough Risk to Succeed*. If you find yourself shying away from mistakes, here are five tips to help you tap into the adventurous spirit buried in us all.

Take your dream seriously

Take your dreams seriously. Don't bother about sceptics. None of us know what our limits are especially when we have passion, the dream, that make us persevere in the face of obstacles. Believe in your ability and make your dreams come true. Set your sights on some thing more realistic.

Take it in little steps

When starting something new, don't focus on the whole task in front of you. Figure out a first step and make it one you are reasonably sure of accomplishing. Having done the first step successfully, look at what you *could* do; then you can do rest of the things confidently. Lots of these little steps will eventually enable you to reach your goal.

Don't say don't

At times when facing a new situation, people rehearse their own defeat by spending too much time anticipating the worst. They don't want to fail; they don't want to face the embarrassment; they don't want to feel miserable. They become victims to their "don'ts," a form of negative goal setting. The don'ts can be self-fulfilling because your mind responds to pictures. Research shows that an image in the mind fires the nervous system the same way as actually doing something.

That means when a golfer tells himself *Don't hit the ball into the water,* his mind sees the image of ball-going-into-water. So guess where the ball is likely to go? Consequently, before going into any pressure packed situation, *focus only on what you want to have happen.* In all probability, you will see things happening the way you imagined.

Make your own rules
Most successful people are mavericks whose minds roam outside traditional way of thinking. Instead of trying to refine old formulas, they invent new ones. Creative people often share their secret of success: Innovations don't require genius, just a willingness to question the way things have always been done. They question the conventional wisdom, traditional methods, prescribed solutions. They make their rules that work for them; and make their own way to success.

Learn from your mistakes
No matter how much you prepare, one thing is certain: when you are doing something new, you *will* make mistakes. No one can escape failures if he continually challenges himself. In any walk of life disappointments will precede success. As Walter Wriston, former chairman of Citicorp, said "Failure is not a crime. Failure to learn from failure is." "If you are making mistakes, that means you are taking risks, and you won't grow unless you take risks," said Robert Wood Johnson the Chairman of Johnson & Johnson.

By embracing risk, you will accomplish more than you ever thought you could. In the process you will transform your life into an exciting adventure that will constantly challenge, reward and rejuvenate you.

"The most important thing when you are starting out is not to let the naysayers steal your dreams," says Barbara Grogan, president of a construction and consulting firm. "The world is full of negative people. They have thousand reasons why your dreams won't work, and they are ready to share them with you at the drop of a hat. You just have to believe in your ability and make your dreams come true."

All of us have our psychological strengths and weaknesses. They determine who we are. Our ability to feel happy or unhappy is the most important strength that separates us from all other living things.

Yet, paradoxically, sometimes it becomes our weakness. Emotional reactions to success and failure and profit and loss often cloud our judgments and influence our behaviour. When we succeed or make good money we feel highly elated and when we encounter failure or lose heavily we tend to become upset. If you are not careful these invisible forces can drive you mad.

Learn to enjoy your work

A science student from Delhi wrote a letter to Albert Einstein in 1953, telling him that he was 32, a bachelor, penniless and, although weak in science, wanted to spend rest of his life studying physics and mathematics. He disliked having to earn a living, because this was against his "inner nature."

"I was impressed, "replied Einstein, "by your ardent wish to continue to study physics. I must confess, however, that I can in no way agree with your attitude. We are all nourished and housed by the work of our fellow-men and we have to pay honestly for it not only by work chosen for the sake of our inner satisfaction but by work which, according to general opinion, serves them. Otherwise one becomes a parasite however modest our wants might be. This is more so in your country, where the work of educated persons is doubly needed in this time of struggle for economic improvement." All the comforts of life, which we enjoy, come from the work of other fellow beings. It is therefore our obligation to give our best to our fellow beings through our work.

We earn our livelihood by our actions and service. Since we devote half the time of our wakeful hours to work, it assumes great importance in our lives. King Solomon says, "so I saw that there is nothing better than that a man should enjoy his work, since that is his lot. For who can bring him through to see what will happen next?"

Anna Robertson Brown says that you must value your work, but not any kind of work. Ask yourself "Is the work vital, strengthening my own character, or inspiring others, or helping the world."

"Love your work," says Alan Alda. "If you always put your heart into everything you do, you really can't lose. Whether you wind up making a lot of money or not, you will have had a wonderful time, and no one will ever be able to take that away from you."

It is the sense of intense interest in what they are doing that propels people to success. One of the greatest sources of energy is pride in what you are doing. "If you can surrender yourself to the simple pleasure of a job well done, even if the work is not your choosing, you already have the basis for happiness and success," say Psycho analysts Mildred Newman and Bernard Berkowitz.

"For adults the most satisfying hours of life are those spent in interesting and absorbing, exciting work," says Pearl Buck. "What such work provides is provided to children in play, stretching their capacity to enjoy, perform to achieve." Sometimes we refer to it as a *calling*. Individuals with a calling see their work as contributing to the greater good, to something larger than they are. The work is fulfilling in its own right, without regard for money or advancement. When money stops, promotions end, the work goes on. Traditionally, callings were reserved to very prestigious and rarified work—priests, justices, physicians, and scientists. Professor Amy Wrzesniewski (pronounced rez-NES-kee) and her colleagues at the New York University discovered that any job can become a calling and any calling can become a job. "A physician who views the work as a job and simply interested in making a good income does not have a calling, while a garbage collector who sees the work as making the world cleaner, healthier place could have a calling."

Enjoy the fun in fun

Sometimes, "You know you have achieved success in your field when you don't know whether what you are doing is work or play," says Warren Beaty. We often forget that work can become play –a source of joy. Scott McNealy, CEO and Co-founder of Sun Microsystems says, "You spend more time working than any activity in your life, so it is absolutely ok to have fun."

"Whenever we are involved in activities that are rewarding in and of themselves, a joyful feeling—'flow'—emerges," says Psychologist Mihaly Csikszentmihalyi (here after "Dr C") at the University of Chicago, "it develops when we are completely immersed in what we are doing and lose a sense of self and time. In this state, a person gains a heightened awareness of his physical involvement with activity, and his enjoyment is enormously enhanced." Dr C believes, this feeling of flow is the "fun" in fun..

Dr C found that the extrinsic rewards are less stimulating to the spirit than the intrinsic pleasure of the "flow." He says that some people devote a great deal of energy to activities that do not return any extrinsic rewards; their real reward—was flow, an altered state of being that occurred when people were enjoying their activity most.

- People in flow undergo an intense centering of attention on the activity. Though they do not *try* to concentrate harder, concentration comes automatically.
- In flow, the individual experiences an altered sense of time. "Time passes a hundred times faster. In this sense it resembles the dream state," said one chess player.
- Sometimes the centering of attention produces a spatial alteration. In his prime, golfer Arnold Palmer could look at a putt and see a line on the green from ball to cup.
- There is no sense of self. A tennis player in flow is not bothered by such thoughts as "Am I doing well?" If the moment is split so that the player perceives his action from outside, then flow halts.
- Another factor is the clarity of response that the individual gets from the activity—the internal sense of rightness. But the person in flow does not stop to evaluate this sense.

  He is too involved with the experience to reflect upon it.
- Flow can make a person feel an almost godlike sense of control. All of life's conflicts seem resolved.

According to Dr C, to induce flow, an activity must allow an individual to meet a challenge at the outer limits of his capability, without testing him *beyond* those limits. If an activity is too simple, he is bored. But if the test is too severe, he begins worrying about its severity, and about himself. Anxiety stops flow. To facilitate a centering of attention, suggests Dr C, the activity should have a ritual preceding it.

A surprisingly diverse number of activities have the potential of producing flow. It can help improve our attitude towards work.

Putting more emphasis on the intrinsic quality of work itself could put flow back into work and thus enrich your life.

Mark of man

Jerome K Bruner, a Harvard psychologist explained in his book *On Knowing : Essays for the Left Hand,* the ideas of philosopher Papadopolous on what distinguishes a man from others. It is certainly not his riches; because personal worth based on wealth goes away when it is stolen. It is not his social position—it vanishes in the absence of people. It is not his beautiful body—it is likely to be crippled by accident or disease. What establishes the identity of a man on this earth is the products of his creative mind and his accomplishments—a piece of poem, a book, a work of art, a creative idea, a scientific theory etc.

Lastly, remember the profound words of Ben Stein, the speech writer to President Richard Nixon and Gerald Ford: "The human spirit needs to accomplish, to achieve, to triumph to be happy." There fore, as Paul Hawkins said, "Always leave enough time in your life to do something that makes you happy, satisfied and even joyous. That has more of an effect on economic well-being than any other single factor."

Chapter 19

Thrill of Success In Spite of Failures

"Within you, never forget this, are success instincts, and if you activate them you have within you a chain reaction of reaching- out- to- achieve- goals- mechanism."

Maxwell Maltz (1899-1975)
Plastic surgeon turned psycho-cybernetics guru

Believe that you succeed, you will succeed.

Dale Carnegie (1888-1955)
Pioneer of Personality Development

Human desires include all our needs to satisfy and the goals to achieve. As Vivekananda said, our "desires are bound by the laws of success and failure." All the human beings therefore have the natural urge to be successful in life. "One fundamental truth is that we all have within us instincts for successful survival in the world," says Maxwell Maltz the psycho-cybernetics guru. "Within you, never forget this, are success instincts, and if you can activate them you have within you a chain reaction of reaching-out-to- achieve-goals-mechanisms." According to him every human being has a predisposition toward successful achievement of personal goals. He calls these instincts as success mechanism, according to him every person has the natural tendency to achieve success. Professor Bernard Meltzer says, "Success is getting what you want. Happiness is wanting and being content with what you get."

Mortimer Adler says,

"Human beings, I believe, *must* try to succeed. This necessity is built into our biological background. Without trying to define success, it is enough to say that it is related to continuous peak performance, to doing tasks and solving problems as they come along. It is experiencing the exuberance, the joy, the 'flow' that goes with unimpeded exercise of one's human capabilities".

He says that life offers few pleasures more invigorating than the successful exercise of our faculties. It unleashes energies for additional work. Doing a job successfully means doing whatever is necessary with persistence. Success means never feeling tired to achieve whatever is important. And to accomplish success one should be prepared to work hard. There can be no improvement without effort, and effort means sustained work. This is what winners do and the losers don't.

Hope of success and fear of failure

Interplay of hope of success and fear of failure is common in every human endeavour. The behaviour of every successful man reflects his relative position between these opposing forces. Psychologists have confirmed in their studies that hope of success facilitates human achievement and fear of failure impedes progress. David C McClelland and D G Winter reported that, for people in whom the fear of failure is low relative to their need for achievement, achievement motivation expresses itself in many ways.

A failure is easy to recognise; it usually involves loss of money, self-esteem or status. It is simply not getting what you want. It can teach you how to become smart by learning from mistakes. Rabbi Harold Kushner says, a failure "teaches something about your strengths and acquaints you with your limitations. This is an important part of maturity". Many psychologists confirm that people who willingly risk failure and learn from their mistakes have the best chance of succeeding in whatever they try. They overcome failure by adequate preparation to succeed. On the other hand, unsuccessful people instinctively avoid risk due to fear of failure, even when a smart gamble might pay off. "Ninety nine per cent of failures come from people who have the habit of making excuses," says George Washington Carver.

Failure and losses are inevitable in human endeavours. Sometimes, even successful people encounter failures. "Everyone gets a chance. No one lives a fail proof life for ever" says, Amitai Etzioni, a professor of Social Economics in Washington. Failures are part of life of every human being. Failures are not permanent; and the same is true of successes. People who wish to achieve success should be willing to make honest mistakes and risk failure and try to learn from them. Vic Sussman says, "don't fear failure. It is the normal way to map the unknown—and can be your greatest tutor". You should therefore try to reduce your fear of failure and learn from your experience.

"It's easy to avoid failure," says Eugene Brice a priest from Kansas. "I have never lost a match in tennis tournament. Never been defeated in race for public office. Never choked up while singing solo. That's because I never tried those things. Only who try something run the risk of failure." Top performers in any field get to the top by confronting things they are afraid of. Cus D'Amato the legendary American boxing trainer, once said "Heroes and cowards feel exactly the same fear. Heroes just react to fear differently." "A man's life is interesting primarily when he has failed—for well I know. For it's a sign he has tried to surpass himself," says George Clemeceau. "Success is often the result of taking a miss-step in the right direction," says Al Bernstein.

"For every success, there are a hundred disappointments," said Saira Mohan an Indo-Canadian supermodel. "I have to deal with a lot of rejections." True, indeed, who ever seeks success must be prepared to deal with failures and disappointments. After all, you can not find a rose without thorns!

Belief in your ability to succeed is important
"They won because they think they can," said the Roman poet Virgil while speaking of a winning team of a boat race. In *War and Peace* Leo Tolstoy wrote "We lost because we told ourselves we lost." Yes, our beliefs predetermine success or failure. Once Norman Vincent Peale was invited to address a mass meeting of war veterans. A wave of panic swept over him. The thought of standing before 50,000 people and disappointing them terrified him. But Theodore Roosevelt Jr, son of the late President the guest of honour, encouraged him. He

said "Son, stop focusing on failure. You are a clergyman aren't you? Here you have a chance to comfort all the grieving mothers. You can tell them how much we love them for the sacrifice they've made. You can tell them how proud their country is of the sons and husbands they have lost. So get up there and talk, and I'm going to sit right behind you and visualise you loving these people and helping them and holding them spell bound for the next twenty minutes. I have a picture of this in my mind, and it's so strong that I know it's going to happen." The talk went pretty well. Afterwards, Roosevelt told him, "Now, you see, if you think you can, or somebody believes in you thinks you can, why, then you can". That's the power of positive-imaging. Peale says that your image of success should be stronger than the image of failure.

A golfer once said, "the essence of golf, especially at the pro-level, is visualizing success." "Think negative you might as well go home." All players believe they can win. This belief should stay during the course of action, no matter what. Holding on to this belief, one should be relentless during the course of action. This belief in personal success should continue till the end. "Your abilities count," explains psychologist Michael Sheier of Carnegie-Mellon University in Pittsburg, Pennsylvania, "but the belief that you succeed affects whether or not you will." "If my mind conceives it, my heart believes it, I know I can achieve it," says the reverend Jesse Jackson.

Focused determination to achieve

"I should have had an inkling of such focused determination would take that young man wherever he wanted to go," said Blanche Caffiere, a librarian at View Ridge School in Seattle, USA. "What I could not have guessed, however, that he would become a wizard of Information Age: Bill Gates, Tycoon of Microsoft and America's richest man." That's it. That is the power of focused determination to achieve. That's what brings out the courage to accept challenge, the hidden potential, the innate energies, perseverance and the sustained effort. That's what Caffiere says, "the billion dollar secret" of great achievers. Achievement requires serious preparation and continual application. It involves desire plus discipline plus determination.

Aim for success not perfection

David Burns, a psychiatrist, says that compulsive perfectionism actually lowers performance and gets in the way of success. As a part of a study of productivity and emotional health, he studied 150 salesmen with high income. Tests revealed 40 per cent of them were perfectionists. Predictably, this group felt under great stress than their non-perfectionist peers. Were they also successful? Surprisingly the answer was no. While the perfectionists clearly experienced much more anxiety and depression in their lives, there was not one shred of evidence that they were earning any more money. In fact, the discouragement and pressure that so often plagues perfectionists can lead to decrease in creativity and productivity. Burns says, "the perfectionists are so paralysed by their fear of failure that their productivity is far below that of many of their colleagues."

Ingredients of success

"In every human being there is a predisposition toward successful achievement of goals," says Maxwell Maltz. He describes the ingredients necessary for achieving success in life in the following acronym:

S : *Sense of direction.* You must set goals which make sense to *you.* You must know where you are going.

U : *Understanding.* Many of your goals center around other people. We must understand how they think and what they want; and how we interact with them. And to understand the communication they send to us.

C : *Charity.* Show compassion (or charity) to others. Compassionate attitudes toward other people and, most important, toward one self – are necessary because, in understanding people, one becomes conscious of many frailties which are basic to human nature. Compassion to yourself is necessary when you face failures.

C : *Courage.* — Setting goals purposefully, understanding and relating to people—you are on your way to success. But you must have the courage to *do,* the courage to take plunge off the diving board, or your success mechanism is incomplete. When you have the courage to take action, your goals will mean something to you in the world.

E : *Esteem.* — You must appreciate your own worth as a human being – and that of others. Unless you feel esteem for yourself, your goals are of little value; and even if you achieve them, the victory will be hollow. At the heart of your being, must be your feeling that there is a lot of good in you. If you don't feel this, your success may impress others, but you will know better.

S : *Self-confidence.* — Your self-confidence is the product of your successes; we have confidence in ourselves when we remember that we have succeeded in the past. We all have failures in life as well as successes, but we can develop the self-confidence that triggers our success mechanism if we concentrate our thinking on our successes, seeing ourselves at our best again. Not that we deny our failures; this would be unrealistic. We should use our blunders as guides to learning, then forget them. Then we should bring into our mind the images of our triumphs to cement our feelings of confidence in ourselves.

S : *Self-acceptance.* — You must accept the fact that everyone is imperfect. You are not an exception. You must not look to others for acceptance; this is something you must give yourself.

Remember, your surest guide to success is your acceptance of yourself, living the best you can.

"These are the basic ingredients of the success mechanism," says Maxwell Maltz. "Read them and reread them. They will help you toward the purposeful execution of your goals. They are success oriented; they point to goal attainment, to satisfaction in living."

Successful people see problems in new ways. They redefine, reconceptualise, reformulate in their own ways. Willing to cope with novel situations. Undertake sensible risks, and face challenges. Prepared to face failures, a prerequisite for growth. Willingness to grow is the key for going beyond the first success. They count on their self-confidence, to overcome the obstacles and to correct mistakes ultimately. They courageously uphold their convictions. As a consequence they get support from self and others. They employ intrinsic motivation. They love what they do. Their focus is on the task and the means but not so much on the goal. They seek supportive environment. It helps to spark and support new ideas. These ideas serve as basis for evaluating and correcting other ideas. The successful people are not the people who don't fail. They are the people who learn from their mistakes as well as those of others. They recognise their limitations and set realistic goals.

Profiles of high achievers

According to David C McClelland of Harvard University, the need for achievement is the need to succeed and strive against standards of excellence, it serves to motivate an individual to do well. He studied people with high need for achievement. They prefer to work on moderately challenging tasks that promise success. They prefer moderately difficult tasks and take calculated risk. They are likely to be realistic in the tasks, jobs and vocations they select. They tend to raise their levels of aspiration in realistic ways; so that they move on to slightly more challenging and difficult tasks. They tend to be persistent in working on tasks they perceive as reflecting their personal characteristics involved in "getting ahead". Another important point is that they like tasks in which their performance can be compared with that of others; they like feedback on "how they are doing". They "like to work in situations in which they have some control over the outcome; they are not gamblers".

At the Gallup Organisation, George Gallup, Alec Gallup and William Proctor have focused on the question, *What successful people have in common?* They conducted a survey probing the attitudes and traits of 1,500 prominent people selected at random from the American version of *Who's Who*. The main criterion for inclusion in *Who's Who* is not wealth or social position, but current achievement in a given field. Their research pinpoints a number of traits that recur regularly among top achievers. Here are five of the most important:

1. *Commonsense.* This is the most prevalent quality possessed by the respondents.

    Seventy-nine per cent awarded themselves a top score in this category. And 61 per cent said that commonsense was very important in contributing to their success.

    To most, commonsense means the ability to render sound, practical judgements on everyday affairs. To do this, one has to sweep aside extraneous ideas and get right to the core of what matters. Commonsense can be developed, through debates in school. Another way to increase your store of commonsense is to observe it in others, learning from their and your own mistakes.

2. *Knowing one's field.* Specialised knowledge in one's field is the second most common trait possessed by the respondents, with three-fourths giving themselves top rating in this category. "Nothing helps success more than knowing what you are doing. It reduces the risks and works like an insurance policy for your own ability."

    Once obtained, specialised knowledge is not something you should take for granted.

    The learning process continues even after the major peaks have been scaled.

3. *Self-reliance.* Top achievers rely primarily on their own resources and abilities.

Seventy per cent gave a top rating for this trait. Self-reliance is not how you feel or how good you are; rather, it's whether you have the gumption to take definitive action to get things moving in life. It includes plain old will power and the ability to set the goals. Two-thirds of respondents said they had clear goals for their lives and careers.

And half of those who were interviewed gave themselves a top rating in will power.

Among other capabilities, the will power encompasses the ability to be a self-starter and preserver after the project has begun.

4. *General intelligence.* This is essential for outstanding achievements because it involves your natural ability to comprehend difficult concepts quickly and analyse them clearly and incisively. At least that's the way the respondents saw it—43 per cent said it was very important ingredient of their success, and another 52 per cent said it was fairly important. It was confirmed in the study that the general intelligence of the respondents consisted of three elements besides IQ: an extensive vocabulary, good reading and writing skills. These top achievers aren't just talking about an innate capacity when they speak of intelligence. A finance executive summed it up: "An enquiring mind and broad ranging interests are fundamental to success."

5. *Ability to get things done.* Nearly three-fourths of the high achievers rank themselves "very efficient" in accomplishing their tasks. And they agree at least three important qualities have helped them to do so: organisational ability, good work habits and diligence.

The study concluded with the following remarks: "Besides the five listed here there are other factors that influence success: leadership, creativity, relationships with others and, of course, luck. But commonsense, knowing your field, self-reliance, intelligence and the ability to get things done stand out. If you cultivate these traits chances are you will succeed. And you might even find yourself listed in the *Who's Who* some day."

Charles Garfield of University of California studied 1,500 outstanding achievers in nearly all walks of life. He found that they all have certain traits in common—traits that are not innate but which *can be learnt by any one*. This does not mean everyone can become a company president or win a Olympic medal. It *does* mean that all of us can learn to make much more of the gifts we have. Based on Garfield's research, Morton Hunt tells us the seven secrets of peak performers:

1. *Lead a well-rounded life.* High performers are willing to work hard but within strict limits; for them work is not every thing. They know how to relax, could leave their work at office, have prized close friends and family life, and spend a healthy amount of time with their children and intimates.

2. *Select a career you care about.* High performers choose work they truly prefer. They want *internal* satisfaction, not the *external* rewards such as raises, promotions and power. In the end, of course, they often have both. Because they enjoy what they are doing, their work is better and their rewards higher.

3. *Rehearse each challenging task mentally.* Before any difficult or important situation—a board of directors meeting, a public appearance, a key tennis match—most peak performers run through their actions in their minds over and over. Jack Nicklaus, for example, never takes a golf shot without first mentally visualising the precise trajectory of his swing, the flight of the ball, the spot where it lands. Nearly all of us daydream about important coming events. But idle day dreaming isn't the same as a deliberate mental work out that hones the skills actually used in the activity.

4. *Seek results, not perfection.* Many ambitious and hard-working people are so obsessed with perfection that they turn out little work. High performers are almost always free of the compulsion to be perfect. "They don't think of their mistakes as failures," and "instead they learn from them so they can do better next time," says Garfield.

5. *Be willing to risk.* High performers are able to take risks because they carefully consider exactly how they would adjust—how

they would salvage the situation—if, in fact, they did fail. Constructing a "worst case scenario," as Garfield calls it, allows you to make rational choice. If you remain immobilised by fear you have no choice at all

6. *Don't underestimate your potential.* Most of us think we know our own limits. Much of what we "know" isn't knowledge at all but belief—erroneous, self limiting belief. "Self-limiting beliefs" says, Garfield, "are the biggest obstacle to high level performance." This is not to say there are *no* limits on how fast a human being can run—or on how much weight a person can lift or how well one can do any particular task. The point is: we rarely *really* know what these limits are. Thus too many of us too often set our individual limits far below what we could actually achieve. High performers, on the other hand, are better able to ignore artificial barriers. They concentrate instead on themselves on their feelings, on the momentum of their effort and are therefore free to achieve at peak levels.

7. *Compete with your self not with others.* "A certain amount of opposition is a great help to man. Kites rise against, not with the wind," says John Neal. High performers focus more intently on bettering their own previous efforts than on beating competitors. In fact, worrying about competitor's abilities—possible superiority—can often be self-defeating. "The trouble with being in the rat race is that even if you win, you are still a rat," says Lily Tomlin.

Because most high performers are interested in doing the best possible job by their own standards, they tend to be "team players" than loners. They recognise that groups can solve certain complicated problems better than individuals and are therefore eager to let others do the work. Loners, often over-concentrate on rivals, can't delegate important work or decision making. Their performance is limited because they must do everything by themselves.

"Such are the skills of the high performers. If you want to make more of your talents—to live up to your full potential—then learn to use them," says Morton Hunt.

Bring out the best in people

Have you ever wondered the way certain people bring out the best in others? Alan Loy McGinnis tells how chief executives, coaches, parents possess a knack for inspiring people. And this remarkable skill in the art of motivation makes them successful at almost everything they do. Virtually everyone is called up on to inspire others in one situation or the other. And almost everyone is capable of raising to the occasion because most often motivators are made—not born. Here are key principles that can be mastered by anyone with the desire to inspire others—in doing so experience one of life's greatest joys.

1. *Expect the best.* People who like people and who believe those they lead have the best of intentions will get the best from them. Robert Rosenthal, a Harvard University psychologist, and Leonord Jacobson, a San Francisco school principal, found that raising a teacher's expectations of students tended to improve the children's performances. If you expect more of a man, he is likely to expect more of himself; and come up with the best in him.

2. *Study other people's needs.* Real leaders know that if they listen long enough, people will explain how they can be motivated. If you take the trouble to find out more about a person's needs, you would be more successful in motivating him.

3. *Set high standards.* In successful families, as well as best run companies, leaders tolerate considerable amount of individuality. But they insist up on certain core beliefs and high standards. Leadership methods seem to vary greatly, but one constant among successful motivators is a devotion to ideas—and superior work.

4. *Create an environment where failure is not fatal.* It is an ability to fail that makes for lasting success. The best managers expect their people to make mistakes and, instead of replacing constantly, recognize that it is more efficient to teach people how to learn from mistakes. A motivator knows that the fear of failure can destroy creativity and initiative.

5. *Use role models to encourage.* Great persuaders are good storytellers, for they know that we are more easily influenced by individualised experiences than by general principles. While motivating people, use stories of real life heroes; give them strong values by holding up real people who embodied those values. This approach has the power to propel anyone toward success.
6. *Recognise and applaud achievement.* The complaint employees most often express is this: "I never get feedback from my boss—except when something goes wrong."

    We all want to be appreciated, and when someone thanks us, we will follow that person a long way. "The applause of a single human being," said the English critic Samuel Johnson, "is of great consequence." People are highly motivated to do their best, when their good work is admired.
7. *Place a premium on collaboration.* Good leaders do more than build allegiance to themselves—they also build into the organisation an allegiance to one another. In the best organisations people will take responsibility for ensuring high standards. The ultimate leaders develop followers who will surpass them.

Develop the Try-Again-Attitude

Success and failure are part of life of every human being. No one can achieve success in every attempt. Remember if you don't succeed in the first attempt you are running about average. "Only a mediocre person is always at his best," says W Somerset Maugham. Successful people know that very few people succeed in the first attempt. They are not discouraged by disappointments and failures. Dan Rather says that they have a philosophical approach: "don't be crushed if you fail. If you indulge yourself that way, you'll never put yourself in a pressure situation again, you'll never grow. If you do fail, go back over what happened. Think of everything, including the moment things started to go bad, and why. Work it out. Try again." Never give up. Marilyn Vos Savant said, "Being defeated is only a temporary condition. Giving up makes it permanent." The choice to try again is in your hand. "You can't advance in life without getting that old—jittery-feeling," says James Lincoln Collier. "You'll never eliminate anxiety by avoiding the things that caused it. You can't learn if you don't try."

Examine the shortcomings of your approach. Think what else could have contributed to the failure: lack of skills, efforts, methods, equipment, timing, risk. Your strong determination to achieve, disciplined working, proper tools, innovative methods, perseverance and sustained efforts are the most important factors you have to re-examine before you try again with renewed vigour. Remember the story of King Robert Bruce and the spider. Develop the try-again-attitude; it is one of those things in life you will never regret. As Vince Lombordi said, "The real glory is being knocked to your knees and then coming back."

Forget success and failure: pursue your own way
In 1930 a, letter from England posed the following question to Albert Einstein:

"If, on your death bed, you looked back on your life, by what facts would you determine whether it was a success or failure?" "Neither on my death bed nor before," replied Einstein, "will I ask myself such a question. Nature is not an engineer or contractor, and I myself am a part of nature." Dag Hammarskjold once wrote, "a successful life is doubly a lie; an error which has to be corrected, is a heavier burden than truth."

It is not necessary that every person should strive to achieve success in life. Henry David Thoreau said, "I would have each one be very careful to find out and pursue his own way. Let everyone mind his own business, and endeavour to be what he was made. Why should we be in such a desperate haste to succeed and in such desperate enterprises? If a man does not keep pace with his companions, perhaps it is because he hears a different drummer. Let him step to the music he hears, however measured or far away." He says that every person is free to choose his own way of living. Christopher Morley said, "There is only one success—to be able to spend your life in your own way."

Don't cry over spilt milk

Ann Landers once narrated a real life incident in which her English teacher taught the futility of rehashing the past: "One day, as the students filed into her classroom, we noticed on her desk a bottle of milk standing in a heavy jar. "This morning," she announced, "I'm going to teach you a lesson that has nothing to do with English, but it has a lot do with life. She picked up the bottle of milk and crashed against the inside of the stone jar. "The lesson is" she said, "don't cry over spilt milk." Then she invited us to look at the wreckage."

"I want all of you to remember this," she said. "Would any of you attempt to restore the bottle to its original form? Does it do any good to wish the bottle had not been broken? Look at this mess! You can moan about it for ever, but it won't put the bottle back together again. Remember this broken bottle of milk when something happens in your life that nothing can undo."

Everytime you think of a frustrating experience, remind your self the story of the broken bottle of milk in the stone jar. Just as you can't restore the broken bottle, you can't do anything about your frustrations. This kind of thinking can help you remain steady and calm.

Take advantage of the energies generated by frustration

When you are not getting what you want, when your expectations are not met or demands are not answered, you feel hurt and you become angry. You are angry with people, who you think have hurt you—spouse, family members, friends, and people who matter. You want to fight back and show the world what you can do. When the anger is targeted at things, they get destroyed. When directed at people you get interpersonal problems.

Immediate thing to do is to cool down and think what you can do about the thing that is frustrating. Focus on the problem, examine the causes of frustration. May be it calls for a little more patience, some more effort. Think about perceptual alternatives available to you. Think about try again strategies. Try to harness your frustration to your best advantage.

It is important to remember that every frustrating experience generates great amount of energy to fight back. But the unsuccessful people often waste these energies as they continue to pursue the unrealistic goals. This only aggravates their frustration. On the other hand, in a similar situation, the winners look for perceptual alternatives. They are clever enough to make constructive use of these released energies to other achievable goals. As a result they reap abundant success. Their secret is in their ability to harness the released energies. The trick is in *channeling the released energies to other achievable goals*. Every person who learns this trick can achieve great success.

Relish the sweet honey of your small achievements.
All of us have a lot of achievements to our credit, as well as failures. Yet, we often ponder over the failures unhappily, ignoring the triumphs that are so dear to us. Why not we bring to our mind our successful achievements to cement our feelings of self-confidence? When you have a glass of milk right in your hand, why cry over few drops of spilt milk? Doesn't it look funny? Do you know what the spilt milk contains? —your lost opportunities, failures, disappointments, frustrations, unhappy feelings. "It is not what we have lost that's important," said Christiaan Barnard. "What is important is what you have left." Forget what you have lost. Remember, happiness is not wishing for what we don't have but enjoying what we have. Learn to relish the sweet honey of your own achievements, however small they are: Your academic achievements, degrees acquired, your professional triumphs, success of the assignments handled, business success, the money you have made, the house or flat you have acquired, the car you have purchased, accomplished children you brought up, your style of living, and your creative achievements—excellent hand work you have done, your paintings, your poetry etc.

It is not necessary that you should wait for big achievements to reminisce and enjoy. Remember, no goal is too insignificant if it contributes to your sense of well-being! Even the small things have the potential to offer pleasure and joy: a dress you made for your baby, a toy you made for your son, a neatly kept house, a work done well, a beautiful drawing, a well-written letter, a beautiful sentence you wrote, the "thank you" letter you sent to a friend, flowers and vegetables you have grown in your garden, a tasty new dish you have created, a small gift you have given to a poor child. These are small achievements, no doubt; but they deserve to be appreciated, admired, enjoyed. Everytime you remember them, the joyful feelings of these small success will overwhelm you, infusing new strengths to your self esteem and confidence. They will rejuvenate you with the happy-to-be-alive attitudes. "Life is made up of small pleasures," says Norman Lear. "Happiness is made up of those tiny successes. The big ones come too infrequently. And if you don't collect all these tiny successes, the big ones don't really mean anything." Small success are indeed the building blocks of a joyful life !

Chapter 20

You Can Harness Anger and Stress

> *Stress is the spice of life.*
> **Hans Selye** (1907–1982).
> Canadian endocrinologist, A great pioneer of medicine
>
> *Anger must be the energy that has not found its right channel.*
> **Florida Scott-Maxwell** (1883-1979)
> Scottish-American psychologist.

We read a news item on April 13, 2003: '*Anger Management* rage at US box office' that says, "Millions of North American movie goers signed up for a little Anger Management therapy from Adam Sandler and Jack Nicholson over the weekend. The first collaboration between the screen stars sold a record $ 44.5 million worth of tickets in its first three days according to studio estimates. That's more than the combined total of the rest of the movies in Top 10". This reflects how serious is the problem of personal anger in modern times. Anger is all pervasive, and almost all of us are eager to know how to deal with this raging inferno within us.

"Anger. It is a peculiar yet predictable emotion," says Max Lucado. "It begins as a drop of water. An irritant. A frustration. Nothing big, just an aggravation. Some one gets your parking place. Someone pulls in front of you on the free way. A waitress is slow, you are in a hurry. The toast burns…Drops of water. Drip. Drip. Drip. Drip.

"Yet, get enough of these seemingly innocent drops of anger and before long you've got a bucketful of rage. Walking revenge, Blind bitterness, Unharnessed hatred. We trust no one and bare our teeth at anyone who gets near. We become walking time bombs that, given the right tension and fear, could explode like Mr Goetz."

"Anger only feeds on a primitive lust for revenge that feeds on our anger that feeds on revenge that feeds on our anger. You get the picture…. We're tired. We're tired of being bullied, harassed and intimidated. We're weary of serial murders, rapists and hired assassins. We're angry at someone, but we don't know who. We're scared of something, but we don't know what. We want to fight back but we don't know how …

Yet what do we do. We can't deny that our anger exists. How do we harness it."

"Now, is that any way to live. What good has hatred ever bought. What hope has anger ever created. What problems have ever been resolved by revenge," asks Max Lucado. "My point is this: uncontrolled anger won't better our world, sympathetic understanding will. Once we see the world and ourselves for what we are, we can help. Once we understand ourselves, we begin to operate not from a posture of anger but of compassion and concern. We look at the world not with bitter frowns but with extended hands. We realise that the lights are out, and a lot of people are in the darkness. So we light the candles."

To understand anger, we better know its evolutionary roots. Psychologist Martin E P Seligman explains: "A fight to death (—eat or be eaten) is the quintessential win-loss game in the evolution and as such arouses the panoply of negative emotions in their most extreme forms. These negative emotions—fear, sadness and anger, are the first line of defense against external threats, calling us to battle stations. Fear is a signal that danger is lurking, sadness is a signal that loss is impending, and anger signals that someone is trespassing us. In the evolution, danger, loss, and trespass are all threats to survival itself. More than that these threats are all win-loss games, where whatever one person wins is exactly balanced by a loss for the other person."

"At one time in our evolutionary past, anger was important for survival," says psychologist Aron Seigman. "It prepared us to fight and defeat the target of our anger." Alexander was known to be "swift in anger, and under the strain of his long campaigns this side of his character grew more pronounced." Yet, it prepared him to fight and defeat the target of his anger—his enemies. His anger did not come in the way of his victories; in fact, it helped him to harness his hidden energies.

Psychologists explain that anger and resentment are 'responses' to external 'stimuli' such as unmet expectations and unanswered demands. And that anger is a cyclical phenomena. Starting with threats the cycle comes back to threats: *Threats—Assumptions—Power assessment—Anger—*(and back to) *Threats*. In the first stage the individual perceives a *threat* to his physical or psychological well-being. In the second stage he *assumes* possible *danger*. He does not know what is threatening, but he knows that 'anger' is one letter less than 'danger', nonetheless dangerous. In the next stage he *assesses his personal power*, his ability to deal with the threatening situation. If he thinks that the threat is mild, he deals with it with confidence. On the other hand if he thinks that he is not powerful enough to deal with the dangerous situation, he feels miserable and helpless. This leads to the last stage of *anger*. The more he feels insecure, the more he is threatened. That is how the anger cycle goes on and on.

The angry person thinks he is powerless, he can't handle the situation. Feels helpless, tense, hurt, and frustrated. Displays polarisation, gunny sacking, sulking, guilt, depression. Desires to protect his assumed impotency. Wants to destroy or reduce the personal threat. This madness to destroy anything that threatens, sometimes results in suicide. His external behaviour displays the defence mechanism of displacement. Resorts to blaming and name calling. Sees the whole world as hostile. Has the impulse to say wrathful words. Ready to reach a boiling point. Adopts aggressive and attacking style. Has the impulse to commit violence, even on innocent third parties. Angry behaviour has several psychological effects: distorted perception, dysfunctional behaviour, poor reasoning, poor problem-solving ability, strained interpersonal relations, and poor effectiveness.

Suppression of anger is not advisable in certain circumstances. Mara Julius of University of Michigan concluded in a study that suppressing anger after receiving insult or unjustified verbal attack was unhealthful. She says, "It's unhealthful not to be angry if some one tells you you're stupid."

Anger does not necessarily lead to unhappy relationships. John Gottman, professor of psychology at University of Washington in Seattle, found in a ten-year study that couples who are extremely volatile can have very successful relationships as long as they don't blame or insult each other. "These couples have intensely emotional marriages, says Gottman. "There is laughter, tension, affection, and anger."

Sometimes displaying anger is needed when you are supervising a group of people. It is indeed a good strategy to get things done. Displaying anger at home can be safe and therapeutic if it is done appropriately. Anger is not only inevitable, it is necessary. Its absence means indifference, the most disastrous of human failings.

Dealing with personal anger

"Next time you feel the surge of anger, say to yourself 'is it really worth what it is going to do to me and others emotionally? I will make a fool of myself. I may hurt someone I love or I might lose a friend.' Practice realising it is not worth it to get so worked up about things, and always remember Seneca who said: The greatest cure of anger is delay." That's a sensible advice of Dr. Norman Vincent Peale. When you lose temper you really lose something. You lose the ability to think sanely and to make balanced decisions. As long as we feel personally insecure we cannot eliminate anger from our lives. Almost everybody becomes angry when hurt; to be angry is not the worst thing in the world. We can deal with anger. The costs are a little discomfort and unpleasantness; but the benefits are many. Our efforts will result in new learning, personal growth, self-strengthening, and improved interpersonal functioning. Anger, like hurt, should be handled immediately and directly.

- *Own your anger without guilt*: As a first step acknowledge your anger as your own. Locate it where it belongs—inside you. This attitude will give you some advantages. By knowing

your anger, your self-awareness increases. It prevents unwarranted blaming of others. It will develop a sense of personal power.
- *Learn to calibrate*: Differentiate between the levels of your anger—mild, medium, intense. It will help you to assess your capacity accurately for dealing with it. When you assess the intensity of your anger, you may soon discover that it may not be really life threatening and that you are not really in a helpless situation. Then you can deal with it in a realistic manner.
- *Reason with yourself, diagnose the threat* : Being rational helps you regain perspective. Focus on solving the problem that prompted the anger. Ask, what is frightening ? What you stand to lose? The cause of threat is often unknown. Diagnosis may reveal that it is simply difference in values, opinions, upbringing, or styles of behaving. The perceived threat may not be real. Your insecurity may not be justified. Have the courage to admit. Once you realise this, you will probably laugh at yourself.
- *Share the perceived threat* : Share your anger and make it public. Let your spouse or close friend know that you recognise the threat and you intend to control your anger. The intensity of bad feeling diffuses. Your perceptions are clarified. It permits you to receive feedback and consensual validation.
- *Assert yourself positively* : As a normal person it is natural to be angry when badly mistreated. But whatever happened, please do not lash out aggressively. If offending individual is a stranger, stay away from that person. If the other person is someone that you cannot avoid, let him/her know calmly, what is bothering you, and why. Tell him so, right away. This approach provides an opportunity for the other person to change without offending him/her unnecessarily.
- *Think like the other guy*: If you put yourself in other man's shoes and walk a mile with him, you will know how he felt. Then you are less likely to blame. Understand other's point of view, it will help you to see the world with realistic

perspective. Once you empathise with the other person, you will see your anger slipping away!

- *Learn to laugh at yourself*: Try to accept the absurdities of life. Don't try to find a scapegoat for your misunderstanding. Learn to laugh at yourself and make fun of your suspicious nature. Humour can shake off your mistrust of the other person. It can diffuse your anger. In a moment of frustration Charles de Gaulle is said to have asked, "How can you govern a nation that has 350 kinds of cheese." Bill Cosby said, "You can turn a painful situation around through laughter. If you can find humour in anything—even in poverty—you can survive it".

- *Practise forgiveness* : "He who cannot forgive others breaks the very bridge which one must pass himself," says George Herbert. Forgiveness is a magnanimous gesture that increases your personal power. Cancel charges against yourself and others. Forget the perceived wrong, open the way for future transactions. "Forgiveness is not an occasional act but a permanent attitude," says Martin Luther King Jr. "Indeed, showing 'grace under pressure' is often the best revenge," says Sue Broeder.

- *Practise trust:* Look for opportunities to trust someone. You don't have to control everything in this world. Stop suspecting people, it will reduce your insecurity. Have a trusting heart! Remember, trust begets trust and understanding. It increases your interpersonal relations.

- *Practise kindness:* Learn to withdraw hostile responses. Treat the other person with kindness. "Be kind, everyone is fighting a hard battle," says Ian MacLaren. Be considerate. Kindness reciprocates kindness. It can win people. That's the best remedy for strained interpersonal problems.

- *Realise the consequences of your anger:* Bottling up anger is a real problem. It is important to understand and manage it. Your anger hurts you most, just as the acid eats the container first, before damaging anything else. Suppressed anger some times manifests in heart attack if not suicide. Start realising the consequences. Don't wait until anything happens to you.

Fear triggers reaction of involuntary nervous system.
When we face a threatening situation, we try to cope with the help of three mental habits(fundamental subconscious thought patterns). These patterns are: the minimisation of fear, the protection of self-image, the protection of personal space. Tony Plummer says, "People who normally seek to minimise fear will feel the fear very acutely; those who seek to protect their self-image will respond to the fear by projecting hostility; and those who seek to protect their personal space will respond to fear by becoming angry."

In the evolutionary past, fear is linked to the urge to escape and anger to the urge to attack the threatening object. When you see a threat to life, your senses send an SOS message with lightening speed : "Master's life is in danger. Alert all forces for immediate action." Your brain reacts immediately. That's when you recognise the danger. The CEO of disaster management takes over. Nerve impulses trigger hormone secretion. A gushing torrent of stress hormones—catecholamines (adrenaline is one), rush into the entire network of veins. Faced with challenge our survival instincts prompt this immediate response.

These hormones have two primary functions. First is the regulation of carbohydrate metabolism. It promotes formation of glucose in liver, to help maintain normal blood sugar levels. Lack of hormone results in low levels of blood sugar; and decrease in the entry of amino-acids into muscles. Second is the regulation of sodium metabolism. It increases the quantity of sodium into the blood. It promotes sodium retention in salivary glands, sweat glands, and large colon. Promotes excretion of magnesium. Acts up smooth muscles and raises blood pressure. Increases the rate of synthesis of enzymes required to transport these substances. Lack of hormone results in loss of sodium.

The released hormones increase your capacity for effective action in emergencies. This causes heightened physiological arousal. As a result breathing rate and depth increases, the heart beats faster than normal and blood pressure increases. Blood vessels in the muscles dilate so that the body is more prepared for action. Muscle tension in arms and legs increases. Peripheral blood vessels are constricted—

to make more blood available to the blood vessels—reducing the possibility of bleeding. Blood sugar (glucose) is mobilised from liver—making energy available for brain and muscles. Eyes are dilated and the vision becomes focused. Voice changes to a higher pitch. All this preparation is to alert the body to deal with the threatening situation. Your body gets ready to face any eventuality, with 'charged up feeling,' ready for action. Simultaneously, this physiological arousal is accompanied by anxious thoughts. The individual experiences feelings of panic at being overwhelmed by anger and fear.

Unconscious defensive habits activated

'*Fight* or *flight*' is the usual reaction. Human body is energised to fight back with whatever is threatening. A man with strong self-image thinks, "I can deal with this threat." He tackles the situation courageously. Attacks the problem with more energy until he succeeds. On the other hand a person with poor self-image thinks, "I can't face this danger, but I can escape." His option is to run away from the threatening situation. His feelings of insecurity and helplessness induce this choice. If a person remains immobilised by fear he freezes himself. He thinks, "I can't deal with this nor I can escape. I have to suffer." He has no choice but prefers to *conserve,* he remains with *fright* until the threat is neutralised. His nervousness with frightful anxiety, is visible to others. These involuntary habits are embedded in our unconscious and are invoked whenever something is seen as frightening and threatening.

The urge to escape and the urge to attack are the primitive instinctual reactions inherited by all human beings, since the days of dinosaurs. These involuntary reactions to threats have been evolving from the age of dinosaurs. That's why they are sometimes called dinosaur responses. Though they are not required in all the situations, your body system does what it has been doing since centuries of evolution. These defensive habits behave as if they are the appointed body guards to protect their master (you) from the possible dangers.

Another purpose of these habits is to minimise energy, and free the higher powers of your mind for their proper work. These defensive habits sometimes use techniques of distorting *reality*. Dependency on these habits will mean that new unexpected items of information will be seen as threats rather than opportunities to learn. Your inability to respond to a new situation leads to automatic habitual responses of the nervous system to prepare you for *fight or flight or fright* readiness.

When you see danger, your involuntary system alerts the body. Perception of 'danger' is the main cause. It could be a potential threat or an imaginary danger. No matter what, when the alarm signal is switched on, the system acts immediately. Who is to be blamed for the false alarm when there is no danger? Human beings hate to take responsibility for their misdeeds. Whenever something undesirable happens as a result of personal actions, people are unwilling to take the blame. They are not ready to admit their faults. Upcoming dancer is not at fault, but the wrong beat. Amateur musician is not at fault, but the instrument. So, you are eager to throw the blame on somebody. The finger points at an innocent scapegoat. That's human nature. Now it is the turn of the involuntary habits to take the blame. People call them names. They call them as 'detrimental habits' as they are seen as interfering with the normal functioning of the individual. What a fate for the loyal servants! They will never say a word. They bear it in silence, and continue to be faithful as ever. Unlike the modern computers they will never rebel and say "illegal command." They will always say "Thy will be done". No matter what. You must realise that stress symptoms are not caused by the involuntary habits. They are only reactions, the effects of a cause. The cause is the alarm signal. Think, who switched it on? It is *you*. But you hate to admit and take the blame. Unless you realise this, there can never be a remedy for your stress.

Stress symptoms remain as long as alarm signal is not switched off

Alarm bell rings usually when it is switched on. But sometimes it keeps on ringing even after it was switched off. May be due to some short circuit problem. Until we rectify this defect the alarm continues to bother us. That's what exactly happens in the case of your stress. When we see danger, the nervous system alerts us. Fear induces stressful behaviour, that can easily be identified by psychosomatic symptoms. Physical symptoms include rapid breathing, sweaty palms, tightness in the chest, clenched rear teeth, stomach problems and tense muscles. Psychological symptoms include irritability, inability to concentrate, loss of sexual desire, loss of memory, and bizarre patterns of behaviour. They are likely to be accompanied by unpleasant emotions such as anger, frustration, embarrassment and depression. Prolonged and repeated stimulation may lead to migraines, hypertension, even coronary heart disease and stroke.

If the nervous system persists and keeps on producing stress symptoms, you can be sure that the alarm signal is not switched off. That only indicates that you are still in the tight grip of some *fear* and that you continue to feel seriously threatened. Perhaps, you have not come out of the Dark Zone. And that you have willingly volunteered to be tried in the House of Torture. Until that imagined fear is erased in your mind, the alarm signal keeps on ringing. The result is unceasing stress symptoms. Unless you consciously switch off that alarm signal there is no remedy. Learn to monitor them at your will, like we do with water faucets. Only then you can control the involuntary stress symptoms and the miserable feelings. Most important thing: learn to switch off the system as soon as you realise that there is *no real danger*. That is perhaps the best way to control the habits of the involuntary nervous system. Otherwise, we may end up with unresolved tension, strain, stress, psychosomatic problems, poor mental health, lack of energy and other problems. The 'stress theory' of Dr Hans Selye termed the body's response to stressors as the *general adaptation syndrome*. It consists of three stages : 1) the alarm reaction 2) the stage of resistance and 3) the stage of exhaustion. He says that continuous stress may be the root cause of the major killer diseases. Since most of stressful problems are caused by the unconscious defensive habits, we must enlist their cooperation by constant monitoring. And at the same time we must adopt practices that reduce stress.

Fear, then, is the main cause of stress. "Debilitating irrational fears are a hidden epidemic," says Jean Carper. One should develop the courage to deal with fears. It is all too often mistakenly seen as absence of fear. As Leonard Zunin put it, "Courage is seeing your fear in a realistic perspective, defining it, considering alternatives and choosing to function in spite of risk." This is what successful people do. They believe in themselves and deal with fears with realistic perspective. Only then one will be able to find solutions to the threatening problems.

"Whatever it is you are most afraid of, is never as bad in reality as your imagination makes it seem before you encounter it," says Geoffery Moorehouse. "Whatever it is you are afraid of, never turn tail and run away but go towards it. You may be surprised how easily you can handle it." Unless you deal with fear courageously, it haunts your nervous system. In *The conquest of fear* Basil King says that fear is the most paralysing of all emotions. It can stiffen the muscles and stupefy the mind and the will. His advice: *Be bold—and mighty forces will come to your aid.* Boldness means a deliberate decision, from time to time to bite off more than you are sure you can chew. Boldness can create a state of emergency to which the organism responds. Bold self-confidence and decisiveness often mark leaders in the business world. There is nothing mysterious about the mighty forces referred to. They are the latent powers all of us possess: energy, skill, sound judgement, creative ideas—yes, even physical strength and endurance in far greater measure than most of us realise.

Spiritual forces often have their counter parts in the physical world. But they are more important than the physical forces. While it was a hurtling pebble's centrifugal force that killed Goliath, it was courage that enabled David to face the Philistine. We must also consider the importance of emotional resilience. It is the ability to bounce back at whatever life throws at you. General George Patton says, "success is how high you bounce when you hit the bottom." It involves maintenance of *self control* and *flexibility* in the face of difficulties. We develop and grow when we face and overcome challenging situations. "Storms make oaks take deeper root" says, George Herbert. The more we face such situations, the more resilient we become.

Psychologist James Hillman says, humans are primarily image-makers and our psychic substance consists of images that direct our behaviour. Over-achieving, over-striving, overdoing are like a storm.

Some people are living out their lives with this storm-image. It is natural for them to be addicted to stressful life— tearing, torn; hurried and harried; driven, destructive.

Sometimes this kind of attitude may induce love for a stormy life. Psychologist Emma Boucher warns, "it is the beginning of a love affair with stress". A mistake of the intellect—like loving a state of war when peace holds the healing secrets of life. "Stress-addicts are so drunk on their self-image of the high pressured, high earning jet setter that they feel the fast deal is where it's at," she says. "They see stress related symptoms as medals of their speed and sass. One patient proudly displayed his psoriasis (rash) like they were heroic war wounds." What a foolish pride! Ask yourself whether you would like to have this image?

Be kind to yourself when you are stressful

When it comes to relieving you from stress, you have to do every thing yourself.

Understand your predicament of helplessness in stressful situations. Be kind to *yourself*. Show compassion to yourself, just as you show charity to other people. Perhaps it is a good time to stop, take a breath, and allow your good sense to prevail. Take a hard look and do what you can. First thing to do is to get rid of those unjustified fears that trigger false alarm bells. And learn to admire the good work being done by the great army of loyal soldiers—your own involuntary habits. Recognise the fact that they are the first to remind you that the first priority in life is to stay alive. They are the first servants that come to your rescue in traumatic moments. You must appreciate how instantly they work and admire how fast they alert your body. They indeed deserve a word of praise from you. You must pat your bodyguards once in a while so that they continue to protect you when you face real threats. You must create conditions that give them back their lost dignity. "The great thing then, is to make our nervous system our ally instead of our enemy," as rightly suggested by an American psychologist William James. Only then you can take care of yourself in any situation in life.

Learn to harness the energies released by anger and stress
Have you ever wondered how certain people become successful in spite of their stressful life, while others fail miserably? People often encounter failures when they attempt unrealistic goals with inappropriate actions. When frustrated our bodies release great amount of hidden energies to fight back. Unsuccessful people waste these energies to pursue unrealistic goals with dogged perseverance. It's like hitting the wall with head.

On the other hand, successful people know the value of these energies, just as a farmer knows the value of precious drops of water. Secret of their success is in their ability to harness the released energies which otherwise go waste. The trick is in *channeling the energies to other achievable goals.* It is like diverting the flood waters that can convert parched lands into green fields with abundant crops. That's what you have to learn to be successful in life. Don't spill over your energies. Learn to channel them to achievable goals. Soon you will have plenty of achievements to your credit.

You can manage stress
Everybody has setbacks in life; everyone experiences occasional losses or threats. Why do some people sail through such events, while others fall apart? Consider stress experience as a series of phases. Be aware of and monitor your 'anxiety' that causes self-defeating statements in stressful situations. Substitute them with coping statements. Bring out your courage and the resilient attitudes to deal with stress in your life. Before you take appropriate steps, consider the following points:

Determine whether you are experiencing useful stress or destructive stress
Ask yourself these questions: Do little things irritate me? Do I have trouble in sleeping, wake up tired or grouchy? Do I worry a lot? Feel trapped? Complain? Frequently snap at those I love? Do I suffer physical symptoms? If you answered "yes" to even one question you may be experiencing harmful stress. Learn to recognise when problems are developing and what the early warning signs are. Be able to manage your feelings when they threaten to go out of control. Control what you can and manage what you cannot.

Identify your stressors, and find out how they are stressing you.
There are many sources of stress in our lives, such as internal or external pressure to succeed, success itself, conflicts with children or mates, unrealistic expectations, too many people to please, too little sleep, money worries, lack of self-confidence, a conflict of values, and lack of goals. A stressor is neutral. Our reactions to it —based on personal beliefs and values—are what give it positive or negative power over our lives. Remember that it is your *perception* that determines your *stressful response*, not anything else.

Get as much information as possible about what to expect before the pressure starts. Keep everything under your perspective. You know it is going to be crazy around here for a while. There is no use inviting fears; the world is not necessarily as dangerous as your childhood experience had evidenced. You can't control everything around you, so don't try. Calm down. Think ahead. Remember, no matter what kind of pressure you are under, the sun will come up in the morning.

Often stress reactions are the result of habitual responses. Don't ever feel that you are trapped. You must learn that you *have choices* in life. You can create your own world by making appropriate choices; they can break the stress causing habits over a period of time.

Work off your anger
Consequences of anger are not good for you, as explained above. Don't "stand there and suffer;" it is a form of self-punishment. That is certainly not the way to solve your problems. If you feel like lashing out at someone, try holding off until tomorrow. Delay will help. In the mean while, get into some physical activity like gardening or carpentry, or tennis or long walk. Sometimes it helps to escape for a while. Working the anger out of your system will leave you much better prepared to deal with your problems intelligently.

Share your feelings with someone you trust
Frustration is a major cause of stress; if there is a problem, don't suffer it in silence. You don't have to hide your feelings always. Make your voice heard, and make your feelings known. Confide in a level-headed person you can trust. It works as a kind of catharsis that can give you some relief from strain. Talking things out helps you see your worry

in a clearer light, often helps you to see what you can do about it. Besides it gives a chance to your family members and friends to help you out.

Change the scene
Control your environment with the aid of scene changing skills. Learn to use your *fight* reaction in a positive way. When you are *frustrated* your body releases energies to fight back. Don't waste these energies; learn to divert them to achievable goals. Remember, the secret of success lies in harnessing these released energies. That is what many successful people do.

Flight reaction usually involves withdrawal as a way of insulating oneself from turmoil. It also cuts off your normal response of 'love' towards others. But you can use this reaction in a *positive* way. You can retreat from the threatening scene to find or create another setting conducive to your inner peace. For example, people leave a stressful job in a large company to a more satisfying small business of their own. You may need to reduce work-load and cut back commitments if they are causing pressure. Take a short break if you want. Be prepared to limit your exposure to stressful situations. *Listening* is another tool you can use to change the situation. "It is the art of tuning in to the feelings of others." Listen to people and know their intentions and feelings. You can get a clear perspective and change your attitudes and ways of adjustment with others.

Change your mind
Think of things that annoy you most and try to workout how you can solve the problems before they develop. You can manage your stress by taking control of your attitudes, using some techniques. *Relabelling* is the art of seeing promise in every problem. Learn to visualise your problems from different perspectives. See how you can convert a problem into an opportunity. *Whispering* is the art of giving yourself the positive messages when things are going wrong. You must believe that there are advantages in every situation; try to make the best use of them. Use your *Imagination* to accept and appreciate the incongruities of life. Go easy with criticism. Be prepared to give in occasionally. If you can laugh at yourself; it sets you apart from your problem. Then you can tackle it from a new perspective.

Increase physical strength and personal resources to cope with stress
All of us have internal resources to cope with stress. We, however, sometimes feel the overwhelming physical symptoms. Then, it is clear that our regular resources or energies are not sufficient to deal with the situation. So we need to develop new stock pile of energisers, as they will be handy when you need them most. Build up your stamina to withstand stress. Balanced diet contributes to physical strength and good health. Fitness expert Debby Mandel believes, "a sedentary life is deadly." She says that physical workouts are necessary to alleviate stress and promoting fitness. Increase your physical resources by keeping yourself physically fit to the extent possible. Get in the habit of regular exercising. Follow a regular fitness regime. Do some physical workouts and breathing exercises. They need not be strenuous. Walking and jogging offer many benefits and can put one into a good cardiovascular condition.

Increase your social resources by being in touch with friends, colleagues and family relatives. You can contact people over phone; or have a party at your home. Develop your intellectual resources by reading books, listening to music or watching TV. Increase your spiritual resources by admiring the beauty around you. Do some positive self-talk or spend some time alone in meditation. Sit with your eyes closed and day-dream. Postulate your philosophies and explore your soul. Explore and try to find the truth about yourself.

You can spend leisure time on one or two hobbies like painting, singing, dancing, collecting stamps or coins, gardening, bonsai, ikebana etc. Try some cross-word puzzles, or indoor games or any other thing that interests you. An absorbing hobby is a meaningful diversion that can help drain out pent up tensions. The key to effective energiser is that it should give you a new perspective on life.

Human beings, are primarily image-makers and our psychic substance consists of images that direct our behaviour. Research shows that an image in the mind fires the nervous system the same way as actually doing something. We can take advantage of this phenomenon, and energise our mind with positive images of courageous actions, so that our mind comes to our rescue while actually facing tough situations. Never underestimate the power of your mind and your hidden energies. Make peaceful images so that they can direct your behaviour to be at peace.

Don't turn to alcohol under pressure
It gives the illusion of control, but *only* the illusion. The next day it takes its toll, leaving your body and mind weaker. Learn to cope with the pressures; but don't seek this escape. Remember the pressures will haunt you wherever you go; escapes do not solve any problem.

Find some stability zones in your life
Everyone needs stability and comfort in life. Seek solace in the loving care of your spouse. Learn to share your moments of joy and sorrow with your family members. Firm bonds of family and friends can give you psychological comfort. You can't survive pressures in life without the support and honest appraisal of your family and friends. Enlist their emotional support and enjoy their company. You need someone you can be totally frank with; and someone who will be totally frank with you.

Learn to plan your life more efficiently. Look after yourself through maintaining good work and living habits. Develop stability inducing habits. Have a fixed daily schedule. Have a steady residence. Do anything that helps you find rootedness, comfort and emotional stability.

Keep up your self-esteem
Typically, a crisis undermines one's self-esteem, which in turn, makes it difficult to deal with the situation. Robert and Jeanette Lauer found that "those who were able to affirm a sense of self-worth were less likely to feel helpless and more likely to influence events—and explore options—when faced with adversity."

"Effective coping involves a capacity to maintain psychological equilibrium without experiencing undue or prolonged neuroendocrine arousal," says Dr James Henry. "And this is enormously dependent on a person's self-esteem and social assets, the ties that bind him to others".

Everything in life revolves around your self-esteem; if you lose it you lose everything. Low levels of self-esteem often trigger insecurity and stressful reactions. Your self-esteem, your sense of personal worth, can uphold you as long as you hold on to it as your saviour. Learn to keep it up. You can be rest assured that it can make you immune to every stress and strain in life.

Be courageous to face the ravages of life
We all know the plight of our hurry and scurry world. "The feeling of being hurried is not usually the result of living a full life and having no time," says Eric Hoffer. "It is, rather, born of a vague fear that we are wasting our life." "Our banal daily life makes banal demands on our patience, our devotion, endurance and self-sacrifice," wrote psychotherapist Carl R Rogers, "which we must fulfil modestly and without heroic gestures, and which actually need a heroism not seen from without". All growth requires this kind of invisible courage.

We also know that reality is not kind to anyone; and that life is not a bed of roses. "Life sees you coming," wrote novelist Alan Paton in a poem, "She lies in wait for you; she cannot but hurt you." You need to be brave to sustain life's griefs and failures without being thrown by them. "Disappointment, in life, is inevitable. Pain is the common lot, sorrow is not given to us alone that we may mourn. It is given us that, having felt, suffered, wept, we may be able to understand, love, bless," says Anna Robertson Brown. Since pain and pleasure are part of life, learn to experience both with a sense of dignity. The more you experience the more you become resilient.

"There are more storms within ourselves than over either land and sea," says Marques de Marcia. You have to learn to calm your inner world with self-confidence and a sense of courage.

"Expect trouble as an inevitable part of life and, when it comes, look it squarely in the eye and say, 'I will be bigger than you. You cannot defeat me.' Then repeat yourself the most comforting of all words, 'This too shall pass.'" advises Ann Landers.

Love life and be cheerful
Love joyful life. Be grateful for it always. And show your gratitude by not shying away from its challenges. Always try to live a little bit beyond your capacities—and you will find your capacities are greater than you ever dreamt. Develop happy-to-be-alive attitude.

"Cheerfulness, like spring opens all the blossoms of inward man," says Jean Paul Richter. It promises happiness throughout your life. Besides, it's the best shield against stress. No threat can hurt you. The soft cushion of cheerfulness can uphold you when you are pushed around. Abraham Lincoln once said, "Gentlemen, why don't you laugh? With the fearful strain that is upon me night and day, if I did not laugh, I should die. You need this medicine as much as I do."

Get sufficient refreshing sleep
Human beings who were denied sleep for several days get striking psychopathological symptoms. Hallucinations are common. Even mild deprivation of sleep can cause fatigue, tension and apprehension. Insufficient sleep is often the main cause of stress. Dr Hans Selye says, "Lack of sleep itself is stress." Recharge your body with sufficient rest and sleep.

J D Ratcliff gives a general rule to follow: "Sleep should be sufficient to allow us to wake up spontaneously, refreshed and ready to do a day's job. It should be sufficient to permit a high level of work performance without undue fatigue."

Enjoy your free time, do things that help you relax
The desire to spend a quiet evening and not want to do things all the time is not a sign of growing old, but fostering a balanced, youthful, stress-proof life style. Take a break at least once a week. When you have a holiday make sure it is a proper holiday. Enjoy the nature with your family and friends. Listen to the subtle rustle of the green leaves, feel the soothing cool breeze, please yourself with the sight of beautiful flowers in brilliant hues, and enjoy their heavenly fragrance. Enjoy beauty wherever you see and appreciate the goodness in whatever you find.

Relaxation can relieve you from stress. It can peel away layers of tension and anxiety, and lift up your spirits. Know the difference between feelings of tension and feelings of relaxation. Learn to relax your mind and body. Arrange daily relaxation times. Learn how to relax your mind when under pressure. By learning to relax your muscles in private, you will be able to relax them in public when you are under pressure.

Have faith

Faith is, basically, what gives your life its "meaning". "Strong, serene, unquenchable faith, in the loving kindness of God will enable us to look fearlessly towards the end of the temporal existence and the beginning of the eternal, and make it possible for us to live our lives effectively, grandly," says Anna Robertson Brown.

Realise that you need something to believe in—something bigger than yourself, beyond yourself. "Whether it is God or Buddha or that there is a higher logic in life—whatever it is, just about every one needs it," says Dan Rather. "In truth, it is hard to bear up under pressure without the steadying effects of someone's hand on your shoulder." Again, don't lose faith in yourself. Believe in your self-worth and the hidden potential. Believe in your goals and your success.

Don't reorganise yourself until things calm down

Don't change your life radically when you are under pressure or know you are about to be. Don't force yourself to adjust to new people or habits. Don't buy a new house. A pressure situation isn't the time to do such things. Wait until things calm down.

Learn to reorganise your life style, so that it is free from stress. Do a SWOT analysis and understand your core competencies and weakness. An honest evaluation will convince you the kind of life style appropriate for you. You have to examine several options: You may have to reformulate your goals; reset your priorities, change your plans, vocation, or residence. Examine the conflicts of perceptions, values, opinions, interests, attitudes etc. Isolate your realistic goals, and then draw up a time bound action plan listing specific actions with priorities to achieve those goals. You have to evaluate and monitor progress as you proceed. As you grow in age, your priorities change, you may have to make flexible changes to suit your requirements. Discuss your goals with family members and trusted friends; they can give you emotional and financial support when needed.

Take control of the way you spend your time; learn to avoid spending $ 1000 worth of energy on a $ 10 problem. You must know that life is nothing but conscious structuring of time for a meaningful, productive and satisfying life. Success lies in your realistic choices and timely actions.

We all need a little bit of nice stress in life
When Dr Hans Selye said "stress is the spice of life", he was referring to a kind of useful stress that is different from the stress we discussed above. Michele Hanson calls it "nice stress" as opposed to the "nasty stress" we all know. "Nice stress probably includes ruling the world, earning a fortune, having a tight schedule, knowing what you are doing for every minute of the day, having a purpose, and knowing where and what you are. This is the lovely, buzzy-type of stress – the sort that produces a hormone called dehydroepiandro-sterone-S or DHEA-S for short. This leads to better brain and memory function, strengthens body defences, boosts the immune system, improves complexion and lengthens your life". This is the kind of stress that we all need to prepare us to meet the challenging situations in life. At the same time we should be aware that rushing things in a hurry induces the nasty stress that disturbs the normal functioning of the body. Problems arise only when the amount of stress is excessive. Once we know our optimum limits of stress and its breaking point we will be able to harness it to our advantage.

Don't have a love affair with stressful life
Celebrities love to live a stormy life. Brazen on the surface, they might say "I am fine;" yet they lead tangled lives underneath. They get addicted to stressful life, with jet set busy schedules, in order to become popular. Don't get enamoured by such a life. That's not the kind of life to be emulated by peace loving people like you and me. Remember, it is dangerous to have a love affair with stressful life. An Italian proverb says, "The best armour is to keep out of range."

Take crisis management steps in advance
Disasters may strike any time, you never know. Initiate measures to save you from any possible danger. Create a disaster plan. It involves three things: rescue, relief and rehabilitation. A lot of money may be needed. It's prudent to be prepared for the worst. Keep some savings if not a reserve fund. Take an insurance policy. Think what all other

precautionary steps you can take in advance. These things can give you some peace of mind.

Antidote for stress

Dr Hans Selye suggested a recipe for the best antidote to the stresses of life:

> "The first ingredient is to decide whether you're a race horse or a turtle and to live accordingly. The second is to choose your goals and make sure they're really your own, not something imposed on you by others. And the third ingredient to this recipe is altruistic egotism—looking out for yourself by being necessary to others."

In other words, live a structured and active life pursuing your own goals at your own pace, leading a joyful life, while being useful to the society.

Chapter 21

Take Charge : Win Your Emotional Battles

Life does not accommodate you. It shatters you. It is meant to, and it couldn't do better. Every seed destroys its container or else there is no fruition.

                          Florida Scott-Maxwell (1883 – 1979)
                          Scottish-American psychologist

People need trouble...a little bit of frustration to sharpen the spirit on, toughen it...

Artists do; I do not mean you need to live in a rat hole or gutter, but you have to learn fortitude, endurance. Only vegetables are happy.

                          William Faulkner (1897 –1962)
                        American novelist, Nobel Prize for literature 1949

"Win your home ground before you conquer the world," is an old saying that is relevant here. We must learn to eliminate our emotional clutter and remove the internal barriers before we try to win the external world. This is absolutely necessary because no one can ever be happy without making peace with unpleasant emotions.

    Emotions and feelings are the distinctive feature of all human beings. Our emotions are originally neutral; nothing is positive or negative until we evaluate it. When they pass through our mental prism they split into positive and negative emotions. We call pleasant feelings as positive and the unpleasant ones negative. "Life is part positive and part negative," says Jim Rohn, "suppose you went to hear a symphony orchestra and all they played were the little, happy, high notes. Would you leave soon? Let me hear the rumble of the bass, the crash of cymbals, and minor keys."

It is indeed a painful experience to bear with negative feelings. But you must not forget that, "Life demands from you the strength you possess. Only one feat is possible not to have run away," said Dag Hammarskjold." Remember, "Happiness comes from being a little uncomfortable as often as possible so you are always learning and growing," as Rich Hatch put it. Psychiatrist David Viscott appeals, "Tune into your emotions, it allows you to find your natural expression and grow toward a new life of accomplishment and greater emotional freedom."

Negative emotions are inevitable and sometimes useful

Origin of negative emotions is rooted in our evolutionary past, when man had to face life threatening situations. For a long time these emotions were part of our survival kit. Over time they became part of our emotional repertoire. "Experiences of negative emotions are inevitable and at times useful," says psychologist Barbara Frederickson of the University of Michigan. "Even so, when extreme, prolonged or contextually inappropriate negative emotions can trigger wide array of problems for individuals and society." Fear and anxiety, for instance, fuel phobias and other anxiety disorders.; and together with acute or chronic stress may compromise immune functioning and create susceptibilities to stress related physical disorders. For some individuals, sadness and grief may swell into unipolar depression. In severe cases it can lead to immune suppression, loss of work productivity and even suicide. Anger and its poor management has been implicated in the etiology of heart diseases and some cancers as well as in aggression and violence especially in boys and men.

Hallmark feature of negative emotions is that they promote and support specific actions. Fear for example, is linked to the urge to escape, anger with urge to attack, disgust with urge to expel and so on. They narrow a person's momentary thought–action repertoire. They do so by calling to mind and body time tested, ancestrally adaptive actions represented by specific action tendencies. This effect is clearly adaptive in life threatening situations that require quick action to survive.

All emotions have a feeling component, sensory component, thinking component and action component. The feeling part of the negative emotions is aversion—disgust, fear, repulsion, hatred and the like. These feelings like sights, sounds, smells, intrude our consciousness and override whatever is going on. Acting like sensory alarms that a win-loss game is looming. Negative feelings mobilise all the individuals to find out what is wrong and eliminate it. The type of thinking such emotions ineluctably engender is focused and intolerant, narrowing our attention to the weapon and not the hair style of our assailant. All this culminates in quick decisive action: fight, flight or conserve.

Overcome your unpleasant feelings

Our negative feelings originate from different sources. One of the culprits is our unrealistic expectations in life. They are the result of wide gap between our *beliefs* and the *reality*. These unrealistic expectations, lead to inappropriate actions and the negative consequences. These in turn trigger our unconscious defensive habits. When they fail to get any relief, negative emotions—such as fear, hostility, frustration, anger and stress—are invoked. Simultaneously, our reactions are reflected in our negative feelings. Other sources of negative feelings are in our attitudes, prejudices, and assumptions about people and our expectations from them. When people do not meet our expectations or answer our demands we tend to feel angry and miserable.

The problem with negative emotions is that we cannot get rid of them. But one good thing about them is that, you can be aware of them just as you feel the breeze. Once you identify them and realise how they are affecting your actions or performance, you can get them under control. Since your feelings belong to you, you have the power to control them. It is important to note that if you can control your negative feelings, your psychological strengths such as your intelligence, self-confidence, courage, resilience, will take care of your actions and performance.

"Our feelings, especially the unpleasant ones, have to run their natural course," says Dr David Viscott. "This takes emotional energy—something we do not have in unlimited supply. When a child loses a pet, for example, we don't expect him to perform well in school—for a while. The child must grieve and loosen his ties with the lost pet; when this is accomplished, his energies will once again be free to invest in work and play. It's the same with adults. If we use emotional energy to push away unpleasant feelings, we will have little energy left for life itself." Be sensitive to your negative feelings as well as your positive ones. If you stand your ground and face a difficult feeling—such as anxiety or depression—it has a way of shrinking to manageable size.

The first step towards managing your moods is try to understand your feelings, by admitting where they come from. And you have to learn two important things: that there was a reason for the way you felt and that unless you got control of your mood, it would control you. It all depends on who is in charge. Whenever possible try to identify your moods. Being absorbed in work, for example, or taking pleasure in physical exertion –these are positive feelings. Most people don't pay much attention to such feelings. They should! It is good to recognise how often you're happy with yourself.

On the other hand, "Negative feelings are a different matter. When you are in a bad mood, try to characterize it," says David Viscott. "Sit down in a quiet room, close your eyes, and let your mind go blank for a few minutes. Then concentrate on your feelings. What am I feeling? Am I snappy, short-tempered, weepy, dissatisfied with myself?" Write down the adjectives that best describe the way you feel, and try to group them under one general mood, such as angry, hurt, anxious. Now probe... No matter what you call them, most of our bad moods are merely manifestations of certain basic feelings, such as hurt, anger, guilt." Even envy and jealousy come under the category of unpleasant feelings if they hinge on 'hurt' feelings.

What is going on inside you? Have you ever felt like this before? What caused similar bad feelings? What could you do now that would make you better. What would make you change if you could change anything you wanted? If you can't change, why can't you? It is not how long you have had negative feelings that count, but how sincerely you want to overcome them and how much effort you put in to deal with them.

Dealing with hurt feelings

"Healing hurt feelings is another art," says psychotherapist Tina Tessina, "that can be learned in intimate relationships. Human beings are imperfect and clumsy; we often stumble and hurt each other. The closer we get, the more likely we are to bruise each other emotionally. It is almost guaranteed that your feelings will be hurt in intimate relationships. With practise, you can learn to heal yourself individually and you and your partner can work together, to heal each other.

"Whenever you are hurt or upset in a relationship situation track your pain through self-awareness, discover its source, get as clear as you can about it. Find out where your hurt comes from. Once you understand your hurt feelings, share them gently with your partner—no accusations, just a statement of your experience.

"Sometimes sharing your clarity becomes the feeling. After sharing and talking, figure out a way to protect yourself next time. You will find that as soon as you know how to protect yourself, all the anger and hurt fade quickly."

Dealing with insults

In our daily life we often encounter deflating insults and put downs, and get caught in a vicious circle of attack and counter attacks. You must find ways to deflect the barb and boost your self esteem. Jennifer James tells how you can deal with such hurt feelings:

Look behind the insult
People who criticise have a lot of hurt to unload. If you can't figure out what's *really* bothering the critic, ask. Remember, not every criticism has your name on it. So step back and consider the source. When you give people the benefit of doubt like this, you will feel soothed by your grace.

Analyse the remark
Divide an attack into its parts and respond to the unspoken assumption—without playing the victim. The secret is to examine

what was said—and unsaid—before you get emotionally involved. Don't take the bait if you can avoid it.

Face your critic
It's not easy to stand up to insults. One trick is to be direct. Defuse the negative comment with retorts such as "Is there any reason you would want to hurt my feelings? Or "Are you aware how your remark might sound to other people." As an alternative, ask the person to clarify his or her statement: "What did you mean by that?" or "I want to make sure I understood what you said?" As soon as critics know you are on to their game they will leave you alone. Nothing shames more than being caught in the act.

Use humour
Making light of life is one of the best weapons against insults. Humour often defuses the hurt, and transforms the unpleasant feelings into pleasant ones. A quick wit can cope with almost anyone.

Set up signals
A woman realised that her husband criticised her, only in public. She began carrying a towel, and whenever he made a remark she put it on her head. He was so embarrassed that he stopped. Another family came up with a phrase that served the same purpose. Once, after Sunday dinner their guest commented, "Oh, that was wonderful! Chicken is cheap these days, isn't it?" Now, whenever one of them makes a cutting remark, someone says, "Chicken is cheap," and they all laugh.

Brush it off
Go along with whatever is said. If your wife says, "You've gained about ten kilos, haven't you dear?" respond: "Actually it is closer to 12." If she persists, "aren't you going to do anything about it?" try: "Probably not. Just be fat for a while." A remark has power only if you grant it power. By being agreeable, you immobilise it.

Ignore it
Note the comment, and realise it does not "belong" to you and simply let it go. The ability to forgive is one of the most important survival skills you can cultivate. If you are not quite ready for that, let the

speaker know that you registered the remark but won't respond. Next time some one zaps you, wipe an imaginary spot off your shirt. When the person asks what you are doing say, Oh, I thought something hit me, but I must have mistaken. When *they* know you know, criticisers are much more careful.

Add ten per cent
You will never be able to stop all hurtful comments from reaching you. Try to accept some verbal assaults as the normal venting of the frustration we encounter. Most of us try not to hurt others, but on occasion we make mistakes. So, defend yourself when it seems appropriate, but also consider the ten-per-cent solution: Ten per cent of the time the thing you just bought turn out to be cheaper elsewhere. Ten per cent of the time, something you have lent will come back damaged. Ten per cent of the time, even your best friend may say something thoughtless and regret it. In other words, develop a thick skin. It is often easier to assume that people are doing the best they can, and that many are simply unaware of the impact of their behaviour. It costs far more to defend yourself constantly, to be in need to be right and in control. Try forgiving, and you will get much more than ten per cent in return.

"The world is full of people who establish their worth by degrading others. They have pockets and purses full of insults—and they'll hand them to anyone," says Jennifer James. "Refuse to accept their jibes, even when hurled under the guise of love. By ignoring them, you'll reduce tension, strengthen your relationships and increase joy."

Don't nurse grievances
Sometimes we lie at night brooding over the bitter humiliating experiences in our daily life; we keep remembering the old grudges, humiliations, rejections. These are the things that lie at the root of most of our bitter feelings. In an article "The High Cost of Hurt Feelings" Ardis Whitman says "Someone is promoted over us unfairly—or so we think; our husbands or wives or children don't appreciate us; someone we have "done so much for" proves ungrateful; we hear that a friend has spoken ill of us. So we lie awake at night

brooding. Indeed the bitterness can affect our lives as though it has poisoned the blood stream, the cells, the tissues. There might be some reason to bear a grudge if doing so solved any problem. But it never does."

"Whatever our reason, bitterness is never worth it," says Whitman. "Much that is lovely in life is destroyed by the insults we cherish, the cold wounds we keep open, the humiliations we hug to ourselves. On the other hand, as surely as hate and bitterness destroy, love and compassion invigorate." "Magnanimity is medicine", says Dr Harry Emerson Fosdick. "Goodwill, even towards the ungrateful and hostile, is an indispensable element of emotional health."

"The first step in overcoming feelings of resentment is to locate their source," says Whitman. "Nine times out of ten, if we are honest, we will discover that the source is very close to home. It is human nature to overlook our own failures and weaknesses; whenever we can we transmute them into resentment or blame of others. Psychologists tell us there is really no innocent victim. Once we have found the source of our bitterness, and done our best to cope with it, next thing to do is—forget it".

"Our bodies take a beating when we put ourselves through an emotional wringer," says Ann Landers. "So, when you find that some one 'has done you wrong,' refuse to allow yourself to be consumed with hatred or bitterness. Hatred is like acid. It can do more harm in which it is stored than to the object on which it is poured."

Consider what might be accomplished if the time and energy we spend nursing grievances were put to profitable use.

Stop feeling guilty

Most of us are subject to guilt feelings. We feel guilty that we did not do what should have been done. We feel guilty that we have done something which should not have been done. Roy Baumeister of Case Western University studied guilt; he found that the average person spends approximately two hours of a day feeling guilty.

"Guilt for the most part is very constructive," Baumeister points out. "It's an important civilising influence that keeps people from hurting, distressing or disappointing others." However, "the system that works for good can also malfunction," says Rabbi Harlan J Weschler, professor of philosophy at Jewish Theological Seminary in New York.

If your guilt feelings don't lessen after you've tried to make amends, or if you are feeling guilty for things you can't control, you are probably suffering from false guilt, which can be self-destructive.

This unrelieved guilt can be very stressful, says Georgia Witkin of the Stress program at Mount Senai Medical Center. The stress can weaken your immune system and make you more susceptible to illness. If you are feeling guilty about anything, you can do something about it:

Make amends
Suppose you are not in a position to attend the marriage of a friend, when your presence is required to look after your father who was admitted for serious heart surgery. Probably your friend will understand, but you may be feeling guilty about it. You may be feeling miserable for letting your friend down. You can make amends to it by organising a get together or inviting the couple to your home. It allows you to show how much you value friendship.

Sometimes things happen unintentionally; and you have a nagging feeling that someone you love is not happy with what you have done. Best thing to do is to clear the doubts and you can always apologise. Your thoughtful amendment can relieve both parties from avoidable bad feelings. It will certainly reinforce same old kind relationships.

Learn from your mistakes
You can't change the past, but you can always learn to conduct yourself so that you can avoid suffering from guilt feelings.

Accept your limitations
We need to accept the fact that we are not powerful enough to control everything that happens. Expecting perfection is no-win situation. Guilt sufferers need to accept their basic human fallibility.

Disable guilt buttons
Many of us have people in our lives who can manipulate us into feeling guilty. But there are ways to deal with this situation. First

identify the "guilt buttons"—the things you're insecure about such as work, your children, your ability to give to your friends. Next, identify the people who can push those buttons—and take the power away from them. "Recognise who you are, which is not a child, and recognise that the other person is not God," says Herbert Strean. "Accept that he isn't always right." Finally set your own standards. Decide you are going to be the one in control of your life.

Since guilt tends to fester in an environment of secrecy it is also important to get your guilt buttons out in the open. Talk about them. Laugh at them with other people.

Sometimes just hearing yourself confess to your agonising guilt over failing to do trivial things —to put the cap back on the tooth paste—can make you realise how inconsequential it is.

Banish ghosts

If you find yourself haunted by past, confront what is really going on in your life. "Old guilt generally comes back because it resonates with something current," says Joy Browne. Thoughts of ancient misdeeds reflect a current problem of never being able to say no. Don't allow memories of your guilty experiences influence the present. Banish them for ever. Forget the *past*, and deal with *present*.

Count your blessings

Guilt-stricken people hide from their success because they feel they don't deserve it. To stop this self-defeating behaviour, give yourself credit when you do something right and realise that your success does not cause others to fail. If others try to make you feel guilty for that trip to Europe, keep in mind that your going is not what is preventing them from going.

Forgive yourself

A working mother sometimes feels guilty that she is not able to spend more time with her children. But she has to learn to forgive herself for not being a supermom. As long as you are doing the best you can, your feelings of guilt are not justified. Yes, most of us feel we are not doing much to our children; but that is not an occasion to blame yourself. Learn to forgive yourself for your inability to do all the things you wanted to do. After all you are doing the best you can!

Drop worry

"Worry is a circle of inefficient thoughts whirling about a point of fear," says Dr Austen Riggs. It is the fear of future events and consequences. It is a kind of crying for tomorrow's woes. Some one said, "Worry is today's mouse eating tomorrow's cheese". Anna Robertson Brown says, "Worry is spiritual nearsightedness, a fumbling way of looking at little things and of magnifying their value."

You may say, "I have plenty of reasons to worry". You may give a lot of reasons for your failure, but that should not be the reason to worry. "Worry is less work than doing something to fix the worry. Everybody wants to save the earth; nobody wants to help mom with dishes," says PJ O'Rourke. Instead of wasting time worrying about it, look for alternative choices and do something to make the failure a success.

You can manage anxiety

Let me tell you my own anxiety about this book. When I was teaching in our Staff College we used to discuss about the wonder of the playful mind. But only recently, after fifteen years, I developed this paradigm of experience with the wandering mind. My anxiety was how to put it in the form of a book.

When I got down to work my computer went out of order. The power cuts almost everyday scared me like hell—I had to retype all that was erased. Important social functions robbed my time—several times I had to go out of the city for days. And I was not able to find the books in the libraries, which I read previously. My anxiety started mounting.

I was determined, I should not give up this project under any circumstances. Then I told myself now that I am retired I don't have to worry about time. Other difficulties are part of life—not so insurmountable; and the task is within my reach. Then came out the hidden energy to complete this task at any cost.

For some of us, the anxiety is so severe that it is incapacitating. Many of us are handicapped by social phobias. Nearly everyone has experienced mild forms of social anxiety. Psychiatrist Dr David Burns says that any one can increase his social confidence, even in the most stressful situations. He gives some helpful tips:

Take off the false front
When you are anxious, sometimes you will have the urge to deny your uneasy feelings. Denying how you feel will only add to the tension; besides it makes you appear phoney. Your frankness about your insecure feelings brings others closer to you. Our openness makes us feel more comfortable.

Tackle your fears one step at a time
Impact of anxiety on gymnasts at the US Olympic Team trials was investigated by psychologist Michael Mahoney and coach Marshal Avener. The researchers found that everybody experienced anxiety before competition; what distinguished the winners from losers was how they coped.

Less successful athletes dwelt on their fears, arousing themselves to near-panic states as they imagined disastrous performance. The winners typically ignored their anxiety, concentrating instead on what they had to do: *Take a deep breath, or now I'll reach up and grip the bar.* "They controlled their fears by breaking the task down into a series of small steps," Dr Burns says. "This technique will work with virtually anything you have to accomplish."

Anxiety creates the myth that we cannot function properly. It is vitally important that you should not give up when you're nervous. No matter how nervous you become, you should keep working. Once you start working you'll find you can do much better than you thought.

Ask people questions
Sometimes all of us are forced to talk to people in uncomfortable situations, when we become nervous. You must realise that what most people want is your 'attention.' You don't have to talk, just listen. To make other person focus on the conversation you may ask a few questions: "How did you get interested in such-and-such?" or "Will you tell me more about it?" What all you have to do is to pay attention and listen to them.

Turn anxiety into energy
Everybody becomes nervous before performing in public, whether making a business presentation or acting in a school play. We freeze

up and lose spontaneity; the harder we try to relax the more nervous we get.

The trick is to let your nerves work for you. The moment you focus on presenting your ideas, with force and conviction they deserve, you will find yourself energised, loving every minute of your performance.

Therapists call this concept 'positive reframing,' which means viewing a problem differently—as "good" rather than "bad." You reduce anxiety by believing in yourself and having the courage to express your feelings. Once you use your nervousness—that jolt of extra adrenaline—as a form of energy, you will be able to come on strong.

Stop comparing yourself

"One of our biggest social cripplers is the fear of not measuring up," Dr Burns says, "Perhaps you feel you won't impress others because they are more confident, successful, intelligent or attractive than you are. Such thinking is wrong-headed. The secret of doing well with others is acceptance of yourself. No matter what you're like –whether you are rich or poor, insecure or outgoing, brilliant or average, attractive or plain—some people will like you and others couldn't care less. *Nobody* gets accepted by everyone. But if you accept your self, then far more people will be attracted to you."

Avoid depression

In an article "Think Your Way Out of Depression," Edward Ziegler says "It is the common cold of psychological disorders. Almost every one experiences it at sometime. Each year, millions are spent on medicines to alleviate the withering melancholy, blighted hopes and dismal inner weather are the symptoms of depression."

Joanne Carson, an American metabolic therapist, believes that most depression is due to hormonal imbalance. She says "It's not depression, but depletion.". One of the side effects of hormonal deficiency is depression. Many prescription drugs can cause depression as a side effect. Check your thyroid function, and ask your doctor if this could be the culprit.

Alfie Kohn points out that unhappy people often drive away the very people whose support they need thereby worsening their depression and intensifying their need for support.

Dr David Burns and Dr Aaron Beck of University of Pennsylvania, School of Medicine, and their colleagues arrived at a basic discovery: "Our moods don't decree our thoughts. It's the other way around. Our thoughts govern our moods. Therefore if you think right, you'll feel right."

"All the negative thoughts tend to distort reality", says Dr Beck." By correcting erroneous beliefs, we clamp down or alter excessive, inappropriate emotional reactions".

He gives three principles of *Cognitive Therapy:*

1. All your moods are created by your thoughts, or "cognitions." "You feel the way you do because of the thoughts you have at this moment."
2. When you feel depressed, it's because your thoughts are dominated by a "pervasive negativity." The whole world looks shadowed in gloom. "What is worse—you'll come to believe that things *really are* bad as you believe them to be."
3. Negative thoughts nearly always contain gross distortions. "Twisted thinking is the *exclusive cause* of nearly all your sufferings. Here are ten self-defeating thought patterns: All or nothing thinking; Over-generalisation; Mental filter; Automatic discounting; Jumping to conclusions; Magnification and minimisation; Emotional reasoning; 'Should' statements; Labeling and mislabeling; Personalisation.

Beck and Burns think the technique can be applied on a self help basis. In his book *Feeling Good*, Burns offers a sampling of provocative positive insights:

- Your *feelings* are *not facts*! "Your feelings don't even count, except to mirror your thinking. If your thoughts make no sense, feelings they create will be just as absurd."
- You *can* cope. Even with genuine sadness due to real loss or disappointment, a substantial portion comes from thought

distortion. "When you eliminate these distortions, coping with the real problem becomes less difficult."
- Don't base your opinion of yourself on your achievements. In the end, *your own sense of self-worth determines how you feel.*

And that is the main lesson of Cognitive Therapy: *self-esteem.* Like yourself better and you will feel better. "Self-esteem can be viewed as your decision to treat yourself like a beloved friend," says Burns. He asks: "If a famous visitor came to stay with you, would you insult him? Would you peck a way at his weakness and imperfections? Of course not. You would do everything you could to make your guest feel comfortable. Now – why not treat yourself like that? Do it all the time."

Beat your bad moods for good

Psychologists now believe that *acting* a part can help us feel the way we want to *feel*—more self-assured in a trying situation, more cheerful when things go wrong.

You can make yourself feel happy, relaxed, and confident by acting that way.

For decades psychologists and psychotherapists believed that patients generally can't change their behaviour until they change their feelings. This type of therapy is often essential in treating serious psychological problems. But for people with everyday emotional problems, the connection between body and emotions can work the other way around.

Evidence came from the University of California School of Medicine in San Francisco. There, psychologist Paul Eckman and two colleagues had volunteers make six facial expressions, each signifying a specific emotion: surprise, disgust, sadness, anger, fear, and happiness. Surprisingly, when volunteers looked afraid, their bodies reacted as if they *were* afraid. Their heart rates speeded up and their skin temperature dropped. In varying degrees the same thing happened with other five emotions. When volunteers simulated anger, for example, their heart rates and skin temperature rose; with disgust their heart rates dropped.

Many of us already apply this principle without realising it," says Morton Hunt.

"'Smile' we urge a tearful child, and unwillingly the child smiles—and is cheered up." How can you put this principle to work in your own life? Hunt tells a systematic way to do it:

Smile to cheer yourself up

But don't be half-hearted about it. False smile—one that is too sudden, too brief, uses the mouth but not the eyes—does not convey happy feelings. So make real effort. Start with gentle smile, then slowly broaden it into a big glowing grin. Next, laugh. If you can't think of something funny, pretend. This does not mean you should laugh off real troubles. The key is to use the technique when you simply need a lift to get on with the day.

Reading aloud also helps. Read with expression—and read something that conveys a mood other than sadness. In a study in Philadelphia's University of Pennsylvania, depressed patients who read aloud with expression showed considerable improvement in their moods.

Relax to reduce anxiety or fear

A typical body-relaxation technique is to tense muscles of hand and gently let it go. Then the muscles of the arm, and let go. Do the same with muscles in the neck and the face and so on, working through the body, all the way down the toes. Or picture yourself relaxing in a relaxing place—on a beach in a shady park. Such relaxation techniques can quickly bring a marked reduction in heart and breathing rates, oxygen consumption, and levels of blood lactate, a substance suspected of stimulating anxiety attacks.

One of the best ways to dispel gloom is to play a word game with acted clues, such as charades. Or see a funny movie—and be sure to laugh out aloud. It's not the distraction that helps. Your own laughter will make you feel better.

Look your best to increase self-confidence

Groom yourself, dress up, stand erect, before you do anything important—before interview for a job, asking for a raise or speaking in public. Research shows that looking good will make others readier to accept your message—but more important, it will also help you accept yourself. Practise the part you would like to play. You can rehearse in front of a mirror or, for best results, with a friend or spouse.

Keep cool in a crisis
Suppose you lose some important papers or your home is threatened by a raging storm, to remain calm. Keep your movements smooth and steady, not hasty and jerky. Keep your voice even, your speech crisp but unhurried. Panic is contagious; so is calmness. If you panic a crisis can put you down; if you keep your calm it will seem like a challenging adventure, which you can handle with confidence.

"Using our bodies and actions to change the way we feel can be a useful tool in helping us through difficult times," says Hunt. "As George Eliot wrote a century ago, "our deeds determine us, as much as we determine our deeds." People who remember that—and *act* upon it – can only be richer and happier for experience."

Other approaches
"There are some natural methods of treatments which have been demonstrated to work for milder forms of depressions. It doesn't make sense to ignore them any more", says clinical psychiatrist Dr David Servan Schrieber, author of *Healing Without Freud or Prozac.* "What many people don't realise, however, is that scientists have discovered the effectiveness of several non-drug approaches to pry you loose from an unwanted mood." says Catherine Houck. "These can be just as useful as prescription drugs, and have the added benefit of being non-toxic and non-addictive. So next time you feel out of sorts, don't head for the chemist—try one of these techniques:

Exercise: Aerobic exercises, cycling, running, walking. Dr Robert Brown of University of Virginia School of Medicine says, "It changes the level of hormones in the blood that may elevate your beta-endorphins (mood-effecting brain chemicals). Exercise may also improve the autonomic system".

Use colour: Colour Psychologist Patricia Szezerba suggests some ways to lift your moods: To diffuse irritability and anger it may help stay away from red. To counteract depression, avoid wearing or surrounding yourself with colours that make you feel down—black, dark blue, for instance. Go for warm, bright, active colours that lighten your mood. To help alleviate anxiety and tension, choose neutral colours that have soothing and calming effect. Soft shades of blue, for example, are often used in hospitals to calm patients.

Try music: Music therapists suggest that, first you match your music to the existing mood; then gradually change the music to reflect the mood you want to attain. Try three or four sessions, gradually heading towards your desired mood.

Eat right: Scientists confirm the link between food and mood. Especially vitamins and amino acids have important effect on emotional health. Even a single nutritional deficiency can cause depression. Carbohydrates eaten alone are a sort of 'comfort food' with tranquilising effect. Eating protein tend to sustain alertness and mental energy. There seems to be a strong connection between high caffeine intake and increased depression, irritability, and anxiety.

Think positive : Many studies suggest the pessimist's feeling of helplessness undermines the body's natural defences, the immune system. Think positive and develop optimistic attitudes. It would be like inoculation against negative feelings. Your own optimism can help you to be happier, healthier, and more successful. "The message seems to be : think positive thoughts, and you're actually more likely to *feel* happy," says Deborah Steinberg of New York's Institute for Emotive Therapy. She adds, "Try to take an interest in someone else. Not only will you delight that person; you may lift yourself out of your own self-defeating mood." In his book *Learned Optimism*, Martin E P Seligman of University of Pennsylvania says that we can learn and cultivate optimistic way of life.

Try humour: Mel Brooks says, "Humour is another defense against the universe." "The more one suffers, the more I believe one has a sense of comic. It is only by the deepest suffering that one acquires the authority in the art of comic", says Soren Kierkegaard.

Yes indeed it is natural for people suffering from unpleasant feelings to look for pleasant humour. "A sense of humour can help you overlook the unattractive, tolerate the unpleasant, cope with the unexpected, and smile through the unbearable", says Moshe Waldoks. It creates pleasant atmosphere to have a fresh look at the problems on hand. Humour can transform the unpleasant situations into joyful moments.

Positive emotions broaden and build resources

Given the suffering and loss that stem from negative emotions, the press to understand them is immense. In part reflecting this press, scientific literature on emotions includes far more publications on negative emotions, like fear, anger, and sadness than on positive emotions. It is only recently psychologists have woken up to revive interest in positive emotions under the leadership of professor Martin E P Seligman of University of Pennsylvania. Recent focus on positive emotions have identified at least three emotions: joy, interest, and contentment.

Joy

Joy arises in contexts appraised as safe and familiar as requiring low effort; and in some cases, by events construed as accomplishments or progress toward one's goals. It is part aimless unasked for readiness to engaging in whatever interaction presents itself and in part readiness to engage in enjoyment. In other words, joy creates the urge to play and be playful; in the broadest sense joy is a generic non-action tendency. Joy and related positive emotions (e.g., exhilaration and amusement) can thus be described as broadening an individual's thought-action repertoire.

Joy not only broadens an individual's momentary thought –action repertoire through the urge to play, but also, over time as a product of recurrent play, can have incidental effect of building an individual's physical, intellectual, and social resources. Importantly, these resources are durable and can be drawn later – long after the instigating experience of joy has subsided.

Interest

Interest is the emotion experienced most frequently. Interest and related states (e.g., curiosity, wonder, excitement, intrinsic motivation and flow) arise in contexts appraised as safe and offering novelty, change, a sense of possibility, challenge and mystery. The momentary thought-action tendency sparked by interest, according to psychologist CE Izard is exploration, explicitly and actively aimed at increasing knowledge of and experience with the target of interest. Interest generates a feeling of wanting to investigate, become involved or extend or expand the self by incorporating new information and having new experience with the person or object that stimulated the interest.

Although interest may or may not be accompanied by overt physical action; it is nonetheless associated with the feeling animated and enlivened. Another psychologist SS Tomkins characterised interest as thinking with excitement. Importantly, the openness to new ideas, experience and actions is what characterises the mindset of interest as broadened rather than narrowed.

Although interested individuals explore for intrinsic reasons, to satisfy their own inner curiosity, such exploration has reliable outcomes. Interest inspired exploration increases an individual's knowledge. Interest and related states appear to foster "psychological complexity," the ability to integrate and differentiate complex relationships with people and among concepts and strivings.

According to CE Izard interest is the primary instigator of personal growth, creative endeavour, and development of intelligence. Interest then, not only broadens an individual's momentary thought-action repertoire as the individual is enticed to explore, but as a product of sustained exploration, interest also builds an individual's store of knowledge and cognitive abilities. Again these become durable resources that can be accessed in later moments and in other emotional states.

Contentment

Contentment and related emotions (e.g., serenity, tranquility, relief) arise in situations appraised as safe and as having high degree of certainty and low degree of effort. This emotion is distinct from mere satisfaction or the pleasure that derives from good meal or otherwise meeting bodily needs. It may also be the positive emotion least appreciated in Western cultures. In part, contentment is captured by the Japanese emotional form *amae* which refer to the sense of being accepted and cared for by others in a passive relationship of reciprocal dependence.

Contentment appears to have no real action tendency. It may be, however, that the changes sparked by contentment are more cognitive than physical. Psychologists suggest that this emotion prompts individuals to savour the moment or recent experiences, feel "oneness" with others, with the world around them, and integrate current and recent experiences into their overall self-concept and world-view. Contentment is not simply behavioural passivity but a reflective broadening of a person's self-views and world views.

Contentment is a mindful emotion. It involves full awareness of, and openness to momentary experiences. It carries the urge to savour and integrate these experiences, which in turn creates a new sense of self and world view. These links to mindfulness, receptivity, integration self complexity and insight characterise contentment as an emotion that broadens individual" momentary thought-action repertoire and builds their personal resources.

Cultivate positive emotions to optimise health and well-being

Positive emotions have a profound purpose far beyond the delightful way they makes us feel. Psychologist Barbara Frederickson of University of Michigan claims that positive emotions have a grand purpose in evolution. They broaden our abiding intellectual, physical resources, building reserves we can draw up on when a threat or opportunity presents itself. When we are in a positive mood, people like us better, and friendship, love, and coalitions are more likely to cement. In contrast to the constrictions of negative emotions our mind set is expansive, tolerant, and creative. We are open to new ideas and new experiences.

She points out that not only do joy, interest and contentment share the feature of broadening an individual's momentary thought –action repertoire but they also share the feature of building the individual's personal resources ranging from physical, intellectual and social resources. Importantly these resources are more durable than the transient emotional states that led to their acquisition. By consequence, then, the often incidental effect of experiencing a positive emotion is an increment in enduring personal resources that can be drawn later, in other contexts and in other emotional states.

This is what Frederickson calls broaden-and-build model of positive emotions; and there is sufficient empirical evidence to support this view.

According to this model the form and function of positive and negative emotions are distinct and complementary. Negative emotions (fear, anger, sadness) narrow an individual's memory thought-action repertoire toward specific actions that served the ancestral function of survival. By contrast positive emotions (joy, interest, and contentment) broaden an individual's enduring personal resources, resources that also served the ancestral function of survival. One implication of broaden-and-build model is that the positive emotions have an undoing effect on negative emotions. By broadening the momentary thought-action repertoire, positive emotions loosen the hold, the negative emotions gain on individual's mind and body by undoing the narrowed psychological and physiological preparation for specific action. Indeed, the empirical studies have shown that contentment and joy speed recovery from cardiovascular after effects of negative emotions.

Frederickson developed the hypothesis that intervention strategies that cultivate positive emotions are particularly suited for preventing and treating problems rooted in negative emotions, such as anxiety, aggression and stress-related health problems. She suggests that this approach can be combined with other intervention strategies : Relaxation therapies, Behavioural therapies aimed at increasing rates of pleasant activities, Cognitive therapies aimed at teaching optimism, and Coping strategies marked by finding positive meaning. These strategies optimise health and well-being to the extent that they cultivate positive emotions. Cultivated positive emotions not only counteract negative emotions but also broaden individual's habitual modes of thinking and build their personal resources for coping.

Chapter 22

Choose to be Happy : Living is Joy Enough

Happiness is the meaning and purpose of life, the whole aim and end of human existence.

Aristotle (384 BC – 322 BC)
Greek philosopher

> My creed is this :
> Happiness is the only good
> The place to be happy is here
> The time to be happy is now
> The way to be happy is to make others so.

Robert Ingersoll (1833-1899)
US Attorney, Orator

Happiness: the very purpose of life

"Happiness is not transitory joy but a longevity of secret power," explained Johann wolfgang von Goethe. Everyone wants to feel happy. That's what we want in our lives, without exception, because that's the ultimate purpose. No wonder, "The thirst for happiness is never extinguished in the heart of man" as said by Jean Jacques Rousseau. But William Saroyan warns, "The greatest happiness you can have is knowing that you do not necessarily require happiness."

Human beings are endowed with the wonderful gift of feelings—an ability unique to human beings. No other living beings can feel the way we do. Happiness is one of the many feelings we are capable of experiencing; yet, we prefer happy feelings over the others. In fact, happiness is a philosophical abstraction from happy feelings. In grammar, they call it an abstract noun, derived from the adjective 'happy.' It qualifies any noun—anything, that gives happy feelings. The dictionary meaning of happiness is: "feeling of joy and happiness mingled together. A feeling of happiness is more than just the experience of joy or pleasure; it is a state of mind where the individual feels that life is good." Happiness, then, is rooted in our feelings. It does not come into being until you feel it. If you don't feel happy, happiness does not come into the picture. It is not conceived until you evaluate an event as a happy event. The secret of happiness then is in our feelings.

Feelings are, in fact, after effects. They appear on the mental horizon only after the occurrence of an event. That too after we evaluate an event as pleasant or unpleasant. If the event is what we wanted or expected we feel happy, otherwise we feel unhappy. If an event is unexpected but pleasant, we feel extremely happy. If it is expected but the unpleasant happens, we feel miserable. Happiness follows successful deeds just as the effect follows a cause. But unfortunately human beings want to feel the effect without the cause. For some reason or the other, we prefer effortless achievement. That's the problem with us. When that is not possible, we are distancing ourselves from possible happiness.

Samuel Johnson gives another reason:

> "Such is the condition of life that something is always wanting to happiness. In youth we have warm hopes, which are soon blasted by rashness and negligence, great designs defeated by inexperience. In old age, we have knowledge and prudence, without spirit to exert, or motives to prompt them; we are able to plan schemes, and regulate measures, but have no time remaining to bring them to completion."

Such is our predicament that makes us want happiness.

Happiness is the most prized state of mind

June Callwood says, "Happiness is the rarest, and most prized and most misunderstood state of man. Actually, lasting happiness depends on how much maturity a man has been able to assemble—some of it derived from being desperately unhappy. It is a consequence of at least a moderate amount of education or training, because happiness requires a decently stocked mind. It is bound up with the ability to work, and to be readily interested in the world around you."

Happiness is the state of mind. "Happiness must come from within in order to respond to that which comes from without," says Ella Wheeler Wilcox, "just as there is a musical ear and the temperament to enjoy music. Cultivate happiness as an art or science." "Your *own expectations* are the key to this whole business of mental health. If you expect to be happy, healthy and fulfilled in life, then most likely it will work out that way," says PSYCHOTHERAPIST Wayne W Dyer.

"Living should be a happy vocation," says Maxwell Maltz, the psycho-cybernetics guru. "People should be useful to themselves and others. Pleasure must be part of us—like our heart, our eyes, our hands, our feet. It should know no race, no creed, no colour, no status, no age. The good feelings in life belongs to us and there is no moral aspect to it except that it is immoral for people to fester in unhappiness."

Robert Harrington developed a questionnaire *How happy are you?* Based on his research, he arrived at a general conception of a happy person: "The happy person likes to do useful, productive work, to use his abilities fully. He enjoys helping people, but is not self-sacrificing. At night, sleep researchers have found, he has little trouble falling asleep. He tends to be self-sufficient and can enjoy both solitude and company but is dependent on neither. Generally he's orderly and punctual. Though tolerant of people's minor flaws, the happy person dislikes cruelty and destructiveness. He is healthy, has no complex about prosperity and refuses to participate in other people's negative emotions— *or* cling to his own. When choosing a mate, he will pick a congenial, compatible figure rather than someone romantic and glamorous. Like many busy, absorbed people, he feels days pass quickly, though in large units—weeks, months, years—time may seem endless. Finally, the happy person has a sense of progress, improvement, of getting somewhere."

Myths about happiness

Psychotherapist Wayne W Dyer wrote an interesting article "Happiness—It's Only Natural *Reader's Digest*, Jan.1978). His suggestions are absolutely relevant today, as they were 25 years ago. He points out that it is only *natural* for human beings to be happy; but there are five myths that come in the way. These myths were created by psychiatrists and social workers; and even educators were instrumental in establishing these myths.

First myth is that we all believe that *it is only natural to be depressed, angry, guilty.* "*Who* says that adults have to be unhappy?" asks Dyer. "For it is *not* 'only natural' to be depressed and miserable. It is, in fact, "only neurotic." The natural state of human beings is a healthy and happy one. Most of us as children were spontaneous and cheerful. And then we *learned* our self-defeating patterns.

Second, *it takes a long time to change a habit.* If you believe that the process of change is going to take a long time, then it will. But if you work at living your life a moment—instead of a decade—at a time, then you can cope with your problems. Though it is not possible to bring change in a split second, you can definitely accomplish it with positive attitudes.

Third, *you have to work on yourself and your relationships to be happy.* Happiness comes from doing things, rather than wondering if you are doing the *right* things. When you make life hard work by constantly searching for happiness it will elude you. An old proverb says "Happiness is a journey not a destination." Similarly, if you're working on your relationships trying to understand the other person, analysing every move, you will probably miss the very thing you want. That is, simple *happiness* which flows from every normal activity in life—if you just let it happen.

Fourth, *the answers to your problems are located in your past.* The most you can get from lengthy excursions into your past is a let down. If your parents were cruel or lacking in understanding, that's the way they were; you can't change it. But the answers to your current problems are available right now. Begin by erasing all traces of self-pity that makes you blame your past for what you are today. Whatever your past you'll have to make your decisions *now* if you want your *present* to be happier.

Lastly, *external factors made you what you are today.* People often cite the fact that they lived in a poor family, or that they were born a middle child, as the reason for their present unhappiness. "If you cannot get rid of the family skeleton, you may as well make it dance," said George Bernard Shaw. People look for excuses to explain their self-defeating behaviour. All "externals," of course, are just that—excuses. Once you see these factors as simply the unchangeable realities of earlier life, rather than problems, you can put the responsibility for change where it belongs: on *you* today, not on your background.

Impediments to happiness

Ignorance
Many times it so happens, we live our life in chains; we never even know we have the key. We don't realise that the key to happiness lies within ourselves. Instead of looking within, we look out for things that make false promises of happiness. This is something that no individual can afford to ignore. As pop star Celine Dion put it, "the only failure is not knowing how to be happy."

Sometimes we are ignorant about ourselves, people, things and situations. Without sufficient knowledge of this world it is impossible to arrange actions to bring about our own happiness or other's happiness. By cultivating fine awareness, acquiring knowledge and learning new skills we can transcend our limitations and improve ourselves and others.

Closed-mindedness
Closed-mindedness narrows thinking, restricts perspective. We become rigid in our approach. When we are not open to possibilities and opportunities, we are likely to miss all the fun in life. Open-mindedness can widen the horizon of happiness in our lives. Flexibility of our choices can increase the chances of a joyful life.

Immersion
Most of the time when we are immersed in some activity, many important things get out of focus. When our focus is narrowed on

few things, we lose the broader perspective. We have no awareness of the big picture, though we look into the minute details of the present context. Small gains and short-term happiness may be possible; but certainly not the deep, broad, more secure, lasting happiness.

Comparison

Comparison is a useful perceptual device available to man that helps in understanding the nature of things. It also helps us in determining the qualities of an object, such as beauty, quality, height, weight, speed etc. But unfortunately the same device can deceive the true nature of things. When we compare ourselves with others we are often misguided because our assessment of ourselves or other people is often faulty because of our limited knowledge.

Comparing ourselves with the wealth of the rich people we often feel miserable. On the other hand, we are pleased to see ourselves better off when we compare with the poor. But while assessing how happy you are compared to anyone in this world you are likely to be wrong; because you don't know the other person's state of happiness. Even if you try to compare your happiness with that of the known people like friends or neighbours you will never be right. This is because, what all we see is what is physically visible. Based on this, if you try to assess the subjective feelings of joy and happiness of others, you will never be right. Comparison, then, is not an appropriate way to guide our actions to achieve happiness.

Conditioning

As children we used to express our happiness very freely. But in our upbringing we are gradually conditioned. Rewards and punishments are linked up with our happiness or unhappiness. By the time we grow up into adults, happiness has become a conditioned response. People condition themselves saying, "If I get this I feel *happy*". "If I don't get that I will be *unhappy*." People generally associate happiness with the occurrence of an event. That is what conditioning is. As Arthur Rubinstein pointed out, "Most people ask for happiness on condition. Happiness can only be felt if you don't set any condition."

The Nobel Prize winning Russian physiologist Ivan Pavlov was the first to use the terms "conditioning" and "de-conditioning" and "conditioned reflexes." According to him we can learn to de-condition our habitual responses to external stimuli. We have the ability to feel happy whenever we want, if only we get rid of the conditioned stimuli that are chained to our feelings. Make effort to get rid of those chains of habit. You have nothing to lose but your chains. We can de-condition socially desirable things and events that were linked to our happiness. And we can condition our happiness to our own small achievements. If we can do this, our actions do not require approval from others. Nobody can stop you feeling what you want to feel. Then, whatever we do will be the source of joy. The choice is yours. It is all up to you. Even in sadness one can get some relief. P B Shelly says, "Our sweetest thoughts are those that tell of saddest thought."

How to go about

Several psychologists offer suggestions as to how to change yourself to achieve happiness. Let us consider some suggestions of PSYCHOTHERAPIST Wayne Dyer that should help:

1. Eliminate all *roles* that you've adopted in your life; behave as you want to rather than in terms of how you feel you're *supposed* to. If your behaviour has been circumscribed by a role, then you as a *person* have been negated, and the *role* has taken over. There is no "right" way for people to behave. Be *you* each moment and rid yourself of the *roles*. Elizabeth Coatsworth said "I was anxious to be what someone else wanted me to be. Now I have given up that struggle, I am what I am." There is joy in being what you are. Be yourself, not the role.

2. Take constructive risks in life. If you've always been shy and reserved, introduce yourself to a stranger. If you want to tell your mother how you feel about her behaviour, do it. Most risks involve no danger, only anxiety. And you will find that the more you muster courage to do the things you truly want for yourself, however risky, the more effective you will become.

3. Eliminate all blame sentences from your vocabulary. Stop saying, "They're to blame" for your *unhappiness*. Replace

blame sentences such as: "She made me feel bad" with "I made myself feel bad when I heard what she said."
4. Be assertive. You are an adult, responsible for your own life. You never need ask anyone, how you ought to lead that life. While you may want to see how your behaviour will affect people, that doesn't mean you must seek their permission.
5. Several times a day, stop thinking and analysing, and let your brain slip in to neutral. Take a minute to concentrate on a colour, pushing out all other thoughts. Or go for a walk, with your thoughts "free wheeling." Just as the body needs the rest and exercise periods, so does the mind.
6. Stop looking outside yourself for validation of your worth, beauty, intellect and personality. When you fish your compliments ask yourself if *you* are satisfied with your performance or looks. If so, ask yourself why you need anyone else to say so. You will soon discover the less approval you seek the more you will receive.
7. Decide to appreciate life even when cynics and grumps are determined to drag you down. Surround yourself with happy faces. And stop feeling it is *your* responsibility to change those who insist on being unhappy.
8. Your *own expectations* are the key to this whole business of mental health. If you expect to be happy, healthy and fulfilled in life, then most likely it will work out that way.

You can find happiness

"The constitution only guarantees the American people the right to happiness. You catch it yourself," said Benjamin Franklin. That's it. The responsibility to catch happiness lies with the individual. Many people seek happiness as if it is out there in this world; and try to reach out in search of it. Because happiness is an abstract concept, it appears to be elusive.

"Happiness is like a cat," says William Bennet. "If you try to coax it or call, it will avoid you. It will never come. But if you pay no attention to it and go about your business you will find it rubbing against your legs and jumping into your lap." Nathaniel Howthorne says, "Happiness is a butterfly, which when pursued, is always beyond the grasp; but which if you sit down quietly may alight upon you." Seeking happiness is like chasing the butterfly.

"Pursuit of happiness is a ridiculous phrase; if you pursue happiness you will never find it," observed C P Snow. "Most people are searching for happiness. They are looking for it," says Wayne W Dyer. "They try to find it in someone or something outside of themselves. This is a fundamental mistake. Happiness is something that you are, and it comes from the way you think." Remember, happiness is not there in the world outside you. The truth is, it is there right inside you. But the eyes that are designed to see the outer world cannot see what is inside. You need special glasses to focus on the inner world. Only then the source of happiness can be located. It is hiding in our *feelings*. "An ecstasy is a thing that will not go into words, it feels like music," says Mark Twain. Yes, joy, happiness and ecstasy are in our feelings—and the words fail to express them.

June Callwood narrated a story how the historian Will Durant discovered the true nature of happiness. He looked for happiness in knowledge, and found only disillusionment. He then sought happiness in travel, he found weariness. He looked for happiness in writing and was only fatigued. One day he saw a woman waiting in a car with a sleeping child in arms. A man descended from a train and came over and gently kissed the woman and then the baby, very softly so as not to awaken him. The family drove off together, and left Durant with a stunning realisation of the real nature of happiness. He relaxed and discovered that "every normal function of life holds some delight." Looking for happiness is like shouting "where are my glasses," when you are wearing them. Samuel Taylor Coleridge says, "Happiness of life is made up of minute fractions—the little, soon forgotten charities of a kiss or smile, a kind look or heartfelt compliment"

Avenues for achieving happiness

Scientists believe that a natural capacity for enjoying the world exists in everyone of us. This is because our ancestors evolved on this earth in this environment. The world is sufficient in its abundant resources to provide contexts for every possible happiness. Every wonderful thing that can be experienced and every means for attaining it are already existing in this world. That is the hope we have as individuals, as species; that is the reason we can be confident in our approach. We are determined to increase our ability to enjoy life, and be happy over time.

As Charles Caleb Colton put it, "Happiness the grand mistress of the ceremonies in the dance of life, impels us through all its mazes and meanderings but leads none of us by the same route." This indeed is true because each human being is unique; and as such each person deals with life differently. Let us list some important avenues available to human beings to experience joy and happiness in life:

In accepting life as it is
Respecting reality means accepting life as it is. Werner Erhard says, "happiness is a function of accepting what is". We have already discussed this subject (chapter 13). Realising the errors of reality and correcting oneself leads to sane and happy living. Otherwise, the fine we have to pay for our negligence would be very heavy; it could be poor mental health, insanity or schizophrenia.

In deep and broad harmony of life
Being at peace with oneself and the world around us is perhaps the highest form of happiness. Deep and broad harmony of life arises from unity, congruence, and wholeness of inner directions; as opposed to inner conflicts and turmoil (that cause self-doubt, cross purposes, self-destructive behaviour.) Our own character and moral conduct in life, with firm practise of sublime qualities such as love, kindness, truthfulness, honesty, integrity etc., will endow inner peace. "He who is plenteously provided from within needs but little from without," says Johann Wolfgang von Goethe. When our whole mind is unified, harmonious, at peace with oneself, all the different things we do, think and feel work together to create greatest possible happiness for us.

"Being happy is something you have to learn," says famous Hollywood actor Harrison Ford. "I often surprise myself by saying 'wow, this is it. I guess I'm happy. I got a home I love. A career that I love. I am even feeling more at peace with myself.' If there is something else to happiness, let me know. I am ambitious for that, too."

In seeking happiness in every moment in life.

> Yesterday is history
> Tomorrow is mystery
> Today is a gift
> That is why it is called the present
> Enjoy it.
> *Allan Johnson*

"Concentrate for a moment all that you see, hear, smell and feel for one exquisite moment, you may sense the meaning of life," says Jean Bell Mosley. "Present moment living, getting in touch with your "now", is at the heart of effective living," says Psychotherapist Wane W Dyer. "When you think about it, there is really no other moment you can live. Now is all there is, and the future is just another moment to live when it arrives. One thing is certain, you cannot live it until it does appear." We have already discussed the importance of the present, the impact of past and future on the present, and the importance of living in the present to enjoy life on earth (chapter 5). Buddhist tradition of meditation is originally meant to increase mindfulness of the present. Gautama Buddha himself extolled the importance of living in the present: "The secret of health for body and mind is not to mourn for the past, nor worry about future nor anticipate trouble, but to live the present moment wisely and earnestly."

Happiness is in the *present* but not in the distant future. We can find happy moments everyday, just as we look forward to happy days in a year. "If you are not happy today, you will never be happy!" said Anna Robertson Brown. "Strive to be patient, unselfish, purposeful, strong, eager and work mightily! If you do these things with grateful heart, you will be happy—at least as happy as it is given man to be on earth."

Look for blissful moments in everyday living. This sort of enjoyment begins in the present—in enjoying what we have now and what we are now. It means we take time to notice the beauty of everyday things and we are not too focused on our goals to do. We are vividly aware of all the good things and good potentials in the world around us and are able to see things in their best positive light.

"Nobody is ever happy 24 hours a day, seven days a week," says James E Faust." Rather than thinking in terms of a day, we perhaps need to snatch happiness in little pieces, learning to recognise the elements of happiness and then treasuring them while they last." This is important for your happiness.

Happiness is all around us, if only we are determined to find it with open mind. "Many seemingly humdrum aspects of everyday living can give us pleasure if we but take the time to contemplate them: the comforting tick of a clock, the colours of flowers, the smell of a freshly – brewed coffee, relaxation of hot bath, the drifting off to sleep when tired and the refreshed awakening," says Elizabeth Starr Hill. "We all have a second chance to appreciate life – while we live it, beginning now". Remember the words of Richard Bach, popular American writer: "The best way to pay for a lovely moment is to enjoy it."

> Each day has a gift to give
> Small joys and great ones, too.
> Beauty to see and songs to hear
> And wonderful things to do
> Enjoy each to the fullest
> For they add up to nothing less
> Than a life time of lovely moments
> And here full of happiness.
>
> *Constance Parker Graham*

In seeking to satisfy biological, social and spiritual needs

"What we call happiness in the strict sense comes from the(preferably sudden) satisfaction of needs which have been damned up to a higher degree," explained Sigmund Freud, an Austrian psychiatrist. We have already dealt with the subject of satisfaction of needs (Chapter 14). As Professor Bernard Meltzer said, "success is getting what you want. Happiness is wanting and being content with what you get."

"The first step to getting the things you want out of life is this: decide what you want," said Ben Stein. Then you strive to get what you want. One thing is certain: you don't get what all you want. That is why Bertrand Russel, a British Nobel-Laureate, said, "To be without some of the things you want is an indispensable part of happiness."

Money, because of its exchange value, plays an important role as a 'means' to get what we want in life. Because of this reason, acquisition of money in itself has acquired the status of the supreme need, superseding all other needs. We have already discussed the need for money (Chapter 15), and noted the fact that it may provide some comforts but does not guarantee happiness. As Benjamin Franklin rightly observed, "Money never made a man happy yet, nor will it. There is nothing in its nature to produce happiness. The more a man has, the more he wants. Instead of its filling a vacuum, it makes one." Kin Hubbard observed, "It is pretty hard to tell what does bring happiness, poverty and wealth both have failed."

In seeking more gratifications than pleasures.

Happiness in the present moment consists of very different states of happiness about the past or future. Psychologist Martin E P Seligman says it embraces two different kinds of things: pleasures and gratifications.

"The pleasures are delights that have clear sensory and strong emotional components; what philosophers call raw 'feels': ecstasy, thrills, orgasm, delight, mirth, exuberance and comfort." Self-esteem peddlers in our society shout, "Get in touch with feelings;" and our youth have absorbed this message. Pleasures are evanescent and they involve little, if any, thinking.

The gratifications are activities, we very much like doing, but they are not necessarily accompanied by any raw feelings at all. Rather, the gratifications engage us fully, we become immersed and absorbed in them, we lose self-consciousness. Enjoying a great conversation, rock climbing, reading a good book, dancing are all examples of activities, in which time stops for us, our skills match the challenge, and we are in touch with our (signature) strengths—intelligence, creative abilities, talents, special skills. They involve a lot of thinking and interpretation. They do not habituate easily(unlike pleasures), and they are under girded by our strengths and virtues. The gratifications last longer than pleasures.

Bodily pleasures are delights that are immediate, come through the senses and are momentary. George Santayana says, "A string of excited, fugitive, miscellaneous pleasures is not happiness." "Don't mistake pleasure for happiness. They are different breed of dogs," says Josh Billings. Pleasures are short cuts to happiness, and they are short-lived. Seligman says "over-reliance on short cuts to happiness may be the cause of the modern epidemic of depression. These short cuts require no skill, no effort. What would happen if my entire life were made up of such easy pleasures, never calling on my strengths, never presenting challenges? Such a life sets me for depression. The strengths and virtues may whither during the life of taking short cuts rather than choosing a life made full through the pursuit of gratifications".

In contrast to getting in touch with feelings, the defining criterion for gratification is absence of feeling, loss of consciousness, and total engagement. Gratification dispels self-absorption, the more one has the *flow* that gratification produces, the less depressed one is. Here then is a powerful antidote to the epidemic of depression in youth: "Strive for more gratifications while toning down the pursuit of pleasure. The pleasures come easily, and the gratifications(which come from the exercise of personal strengths) are hard-won."

"Pleasure is a powerful source of motivation, but it does not produce challenge.; it is a conservative force that makes us want to satisfy existing needs, achieve comfort and relaxation," says psychologist Mihaly Csikszentmihalyi(pronounced ' cheeks sent me high'). "Enjoyment (gratification) on the other hand is not always present, and it can be utterly stressful at times. A mountain climber may be close to freezing, utterly exhausted, in danger of falling into bottomless crevasse, yet wouldn't want to be anywhere else. Sipping a cocktail under a palm tree at the edge of turquoise ocean is nice, but it just doesn't compare to the exhilaration he feels on the freezing ridge."

"The question of enhancing gratifications is nothing less than and nothing more than the venerable question: 'What is the good life?'"says Seligman. The belief that we can rely on short cuts to gratification and bypass the exercise of personal strengths and virtues is folly. It leads to legions of humanity who are depressed in the middle of great wealth and starving to death spiritually. Such people ask, "how can I be happy?" This is the wrong question, because without the distinction between pleasure and gratification, it leads all to easily to total reliance on short cuts, to a life of snatching up as many easy pleasures as possible.

Pleasures are our psychological capital. When we engage in pleasures, we are just consuming. The smell of perfume, taste of raspberries, sensitivity of a scalp rub or massage are all momentary delights, but they do not do anything for the future. They are not investments, nothing is accumulated for the future.

In contrast when we are engaged (or absorbed in *flow*), perhaps we are investing, building psychological capital for the future. Perhaps the flow is the state that marks growth. Absorption, the loss of consciousness, and stopping time may be evolution's way of telling us that we are stocking up reserves for the future. In this analogy, pleasure marks the achievement of biological satiation, whereas gratification marks the achievement of growth. Lawana Blackwell says, "I have grown to realize that the joy that comes from little victories is preferable to the fun that comes from ease and pursuit of pleasure."

In doing things that make us happy
"We act as though comfort and luxury were the chief requirements of life; when all that we need to be happy is something to be enthusiastic about," says Charles Kingsley. Yes, doing things with enthusiasm gives a lot of pleasure. "The secret of happiness is doing things with curiosity," says Norman Douglas. Happiness comes on its own when we do things with interest and curiosity; but they need not be lofty projects. We have already discussed about actions and accomplishments that contribute to our joy and happiness (Chapter 18).

Doing things means being engrossed in activities and processes that we enjoy. It includes having fun, exercising inherent abilities, and constructively employing our strengths. It also means that we are aware of meaningful things and people in our lives we appreciate and value them. Doing things means doing what pleases you." If you observe a really happy man you will find him building a boat, writing a symphony, growing double dahlias in his garden, or looking for dinosaur eggs in Gobi desert," says Dr Bern Wolfe. "He will not be searching for happiness as if it were a collar button that has rolled under a radiator. He will not be striving for it as a goal in life. He will have become aware that he is happy in the course of living life 24 crowded hours of day." When we are engrossed in doing things we love to do, we experience what psychologists call *flow*—overflowing joy that comes with such experience.

Doing things for others is indeed a more rewarding experience. Dick Gregory says, "One of the things I keep learning, is that the secret of being happy is doing things for others." "Our happiness is greatest when we contribute to the happiness of others," says Harriet Shephard.

In realising dreams and achieving goals
Dreaming is one thing and daring to realise dreams is another. The pleasure of dreaming in itself is a happy event; but the joy we derive from realising the dreams is totally overwhelming. We have already discussed about realising dreams and achieving goals (Chapter 16).

Goals can provide happiness that derives from both setting goals and as well as striving to attain them. When we set realistic goals that match our abilities, we can get the most enjoyment out of working toward them and achieving them. We are happy in setting goals, because then we have heightened expectations for enjoyment. Looking forward to a goal is the happiness of a process. When we achieve our aim we experience happiness about what we have achieved.; then we can be proud of ourselves. If our expectations are not met, even after achieving the goals set by us, we are not discouraged or disappointed; we may decide to change it or decide to set higher goals. This is an indication that we have grown, we were better than we were before, we have better things to look forward to.

While endeavouring to realise our dreams or achieve our goals we are often required to look for opportunities. Capturing opportunities in itself is a joyful activity. We have already discussed this subject (Chapter 17). Successful actress Sarah Jessica Parker says, "It is a great challenge to be better than your opportunities."

In seeking joy in family life

"He is happiest, be he king or peasant who finds peace in his home," observed Johann Wolfgang von Goethe. "To be happy at home is the ultimate end of all ambition the end to which every enterprise and labor tends, and of which every desire prompts the prosecution" says Samuel Johnson. We have already discussed the virtues of family and the happiness one can derive from family life (Chapter 12). "Happiness is having a large loving, caring, close-knit family in another city," says George Burns.

In seeking joy in the company of friends.

"Friends are the family we choose," says Jennifer Aniston. In fact they are the secret to a longer life. "Celebrate the happiness that friends are always giving. Make everyday a holiday and celebrate just living!" says, Amanda Bradley. We have already discussed the importance of friends in everybody's life (Chapter 12). "Have social contacts, a good network of friends," says Laura Cartensen of Stanford University. "Most crucial is having close friends—the kind of people you can't imagine life without. Quality beats quantity all the time." Another secret of happiness is to make others believe they are the cause of it.

In seeking contentment and absence of suffering.

Joy, interest, and contentment are positive emotions. Contentment is a broader concept distinct from mere satisfaction or pleasure that derives from good meal or otherwise meeting bodily needs. In part it is a sense of being accepted and cared for by others in a passive reciprocal dependence. Changes sparked by contentment are more cognitive than physical. Psychologists suggest that this is a mindful emotion. It involves full awareness of, and openness to momentary experiences, which in turn creates a new sense of self and world view. Barbara Frederickson says "these links to mindfulness, receptivity, integration, self-complexity and insight characterise contentment as an emotion that broadens individual's momentary thought –action repertoire and builds their personal resources." She advocates cultivation of positive emotions like contentment to optimise health and well-being. "Happiness is a habit cultivate it," says Elbert Hubbard. Lin Yutang, a Chinese-American writer says, "The secret of contentment is knowing how to enjoy what you have, and then be able to lose all desire for things beyond reach."

Relief from pain and suffering (physical and mental) is another form of happiness. We find ways to stop pain, cure illness, heal injuries. We get a lot of peace when we get relief from mental anguish—inner conflicts of passion, fighting against ourselves, trouble dealing with the changing world, depression, anxiety, mental disorders, minor neuroses, major mental illness. As Lord Tennyson put it, "Happiness of a man in this life does not consist in the absence but in the mastery of his passions." Without relief from physical or mental problems there can be no happiness. Focusing on happy elements in your life will help dilute or decrease the impact of negative elements. By bringing the positives into light we can build on them. Make sure you look for the good in circumstances and people to help keep yourself positive.

What more can you do

Be cheerful and choose to be happy

"Happiness can exist only in acceptance," as said by Denis De Rougamont. We must accept the fact that the only reason to live is to enjoy it. We must therefore be cheerful and learn to live joyfully.

"Merry heart has a cheerful countenance, a merry heart has a continual feast," says an ancient proverb. "Start each day affirming peaceful, contented and happy attitudes and your days will tend to be pleasant," says Dr Norman Vincent Peale. Another best advice comes from Dan Millman: "Act happy, feel happy, without reason in this world. Then you can love, and do what you will."

Never delay happiness

Unhappiness is nurtured by the habit of putting off living until some fictional future day. Dale Carnegie says, "One of the most tragic things I know about human nature is that all of us tend to put off living. We are all dreaming of some magical rose garden over the horizon—instead of enjoying the roses that are blooming outside our windows today."

Sadly, many of us postpone our happiness indefinitely. It is not that we consciously set out to do so, but we keep convincing ourselves,

"Someday I'll be happy." This point is well taken up by Crystal Boyd. Let us consider a passage titled "Happiness on hold," from her book *Midnight Muse*:

"We convince ourselves that life will be better after we get married, have a baby then another. Then we are frustrated that the kids aren't old enough, and we will be content when they grow. After that, we are frustrated that we have teenagers to deal with. We will certainly be happy when they are out of that stage. We tell ourselves that our life will be complete when our spouse gets his or her act together, when we get a nice car, are able to go on a nice vacation or when we retire.

"One of my favorite quotes comes from Alfred D'souza. He said, "For a long time it had seemed to me that life was about to begin—real life. But there was always some obstacle on the way, some unfinished business, time still to be served, a debt to be paid. Then life would begin. At last it dawned on me that these obstacles were my life."

This perspective has helped me to see that there is no way to happiness.

The truth is, there is no better way to be happy than right now.

If not now when?

Your life will always be filled with challenges.

It is best to admit this to yourself and decide to be happy any way.

Happiness is the way!

"So, treasure every moment that you have, and treasure it more because you shared it with someone special, special enough to spend your time. And remember, that time waits for no one. So, stop waiting until your car or home loan is paid off, until you get a new car or home, until your kids leave the house, until you finish school, until you go back to the school, until you lose 10 lbs., until you gain 10 lbs., until you get married, until you get a divorce, until you have kids, until you start work, until you retire, until Friday night, until Sunday morning, until summer, until fall, until winter, until spring, until you are off welfare, until your song comes on, until you had a drink, until you are sobered up, until you die, until you are born again to decide *there is no better time than right now to be happy.*

"Happiness is a journey, not a destination.
So work like you don't need money.
Love like you've never been hurt.
And dance like no one is watching" says Crystal Boyd.

So, "If you want to be happy, be," says Leo Tolstoy.

Don't delay—remember, your time is running out!

Pause to enjoy

Jerome K Jerome says, "Opportunities fly while we sit regretting chances we have lost, and happiness we heed not, because of happiness that is gone." Yes, "Plenty of people miss their share of happiness not because they never found it. But because they didn't stop to enjoy it," observes the Nobel-laureate William Faulkner. So, pause to enjoy life, however busy you are. In the journey of life, stop for a while to enjoy the beauty of the mini-stations on the way. Find out what you might be missing in life.

Savour every pleasant experience

"Understanding the unique strength and beauty of all living things is the heart of happiness," says June Callwood. "You have to sharpen your wits and when you observe man and nature." Yes, we have to learn to pause to enjoy. "Happiness isn't something you experience, it's something you remember," says Oscar Levant. It is in savouring pleasant experiences that we find lasting happiness.

But the sheer speed of modern life and our extreme future-mindedness can sneak up on us and impoverish our present. Almost every technological advance in modern times—from telephone to Internet has been about doing more and doing faster. We think that there is great advantage in saving time, as we place high value in planning for future.

Saving time (for what) and planning for future (that arrived yesterday and never comes), we lose acres of present. Abdul-Baha once said, "if we are not happy and joyous at this season, for what other season shall we wait and for what other time shall we look?"

To counter this malady, Fred B Bryant and Joseph Verloff of Layola University advocate a technique called *savouring*. It is the awareness of pleasure and of the deliberate conscious attention to experience of pleasure. There are four kinds of savouring: 1. Basking—receiving praise and congratulations; 2. Thanks giving—expressing gratitude for blessings. 3. Marvelling—losing self in the wonder of the moment. 4. Luxuri-ating—indulging the senses.

They recommend five techniques for promoting savouring: 1. Sharing with others – sharing how you value the moment; 2. Memory building—taking a mental photograph or collecting a physical souvenir as a reminder of the pleasurable moment. 3. Self-congratulation 4. Sharpening perceptions 5. Absorption—letting yourself totally immersed, sensing the pleasure; not reminding yourself of other things you should be doing; wonder what comes next or consider ways in which it can be improved upon.

Ellen Langer of Harvard University advocates another technique called *mindfulness*. It begins with the observation that mindlessness pervades much of human activity. We fail to notice huge swaths of experience; we act and interact automatically without much thinking. Professor Langer developed a set of techniques for making us more mindful, allowing us to see the *present* anew. Underlying these techniques is the principle of shifting perspective to make a stale situation fresh.

You can enhance your happiness

By sharing

We all know that by sharing our joyful moments with family members and friends we virtually distribute happiness. Sharing joy, in fact, is sharing life with others. On the other hand, by telling our woes to our close friends and relatives we get a sigh of relief that lightens the burden on our hearts. Consider how beautifully this wonderful phenomenon is captured by a Swedish proverb: "Shared joy is double joy, shared sorrow is half sorrow."

Let us consider to apply this rule. Suppose that happiness and unhappiness have equal chances of knocking at your door every day; let us give equal points to each, say 100. By sharing with others, 100 units of happiness will become 200 units, while 100 units of unhappiness 50. By another round of sharing 200 units of happiness will become 400, and the 50 units of unhappiness 25. The sharing process can go on until the proportion of unhappiness is reduced to a very insignificant level. "Happiness adds and multiplies as we divide it with others", says A Nielsen. That is the secret of enhancing happiness.

By optimal spacing and surprising

Psychologist Martin E P Seligman reminds about the negative effects of habituation.

Once the external stimulus is gone the positive emotion sinks beneath the wave of ongoing experience with little trace. Habituation or adaptation is an inviolable fact of life.

Pleasures fade quickly and even have negative aftermath. Seligman says, "Inject into your life as many events that produce pleasure as you can, but spread them out, letting more time elapse between them than you normally do." If you find that your desire to engage in a particular pleasure diminishes to zero (or below, to aversion), when you space it enough apart, you are probably dealing with an addiction as a pleasure. You can keep habituation of your pleasures at bay, by trying to find the optimal spacing.

Seligman recommends pleasures by surprise. Try to take yourself by surprise or arrange it so that people you live with or otherwise see frequently surprise each other with 'presents' of the pleasures. It does not need to be a dozen roses from the florist. An unexpected cup of coffee will do; but it is worth five minutes each day to create a pleasing little surprise for the spouse, your children, or a coworker. Such acts are reciprocally contagious.

Never fear to use yourself up

Anyone who wants to live a fulfilled life, must be prepared to use all the energies at his command to achieve a happy life. The great elixir of life according to George Bernard Shaw, is "to be thoroughly worn out before being discarded on the scrap heap—a force of nature, instead of a feverish, selfish cold of ailments and grievances."

Express your happiness through smiling and laughing.

Scientists believe that there is a chemical 'reward system' located in the brain, in which emotions reward the attention centre 'for a job well done,' creating a feeling of satisfaction and well-being. This is what we call the feeling of happiness, usually expressed by the body through smiles and laughs.

"Man is distinguished from all other creations by the faculty of laughter," says Joseph Addison. "Mirth is like a flash of lightening that breaks through the gloom of clouds and glitters for a moment." This is, indeed, one quality that makes us special, because no other living being is capable of laughing. It is a vehicle for expression of joyful feelings, and happiness in life.

"A smile enriches those who receive without making poorer those who give," says an anonymous philosopher "It takes a moment but the memory of it sometimes last forever. None is so rich that he can get along without it and none is so poor that he cannot be made rich by it. A smile creates happiness in the home, fosters goodwill in business and is the counter sign of friendship. It brings rest to the weary, cheer to the discouraged, sunshine to the sad, and nature's best antidote for trouble. Yet it cannot be bought, begged, borrowed or stolen, for it is something that is of no value to anyone until it is given away. Some people are too tired to give you a smile. Give them one of yours, as none needs a smile so much as who has no more to give."

Our smiles and laughs help us in keeping ourselves healthy. "Hysterical laughter" says Will Stanton, is a "Good sign. Releases nervous tension. Relieves frustrations." Laughter is indeed an antidote for anger and stress. Mort Sahl says, "I found people looked better when they laughed." Andrew Mason says, "If you laugh a lot, when you get older your wrinkles will be in the right places." "People who laugh live longer than people who don't laugh," says James S Walsh. "Few persons realize that health actually varies according to the amount of laughter."

"A smile is a universal welcome," says Max Eastman. You are never fully dressed without a smile," says Martin Charnin. "A smile is a light on your face to let some one know you are at home," says Allen Klein. Mother Teresa said, "The fruit of love is service. The fruit of service is peace. And peace begins with a smile." "When people are smiling they are almost receptive to almost anything you want to teach them" says Allen Funt "To get them listening get them laughing" says Allen Klein. We win people by smiles and laughs.

It is said, it takes fourteen muscles to smile and seventy two to frown; it is easier to smile than frown. A smile is the effortless way to display happiness. A smile costs nothing but gives much. "A smile is an inexpensive way to improve your looks," says Charles Gordy. "A man isn't poor if he can laugh," says Raymond Hitchcock.

Psychologists now believe that *acting* a part can help us feel the way we want to *feel*—more self-assured in a trying situation, more cheerful when things go wrong. This is one of the most amazing phenomena of the mind you can experience and practise. By *acting* how you feel happy, you can actually experience happy feelings. That drives home the point that the source of happiness is within you; and you have the power to make yourself happy. You can apply this principle in your own life. We have already discussed about it in the previous chapter.

Let me tell you the real life story of Bruce Willis, a Hollywood hero of blockbuster movies. He was originally a blue collar guy with a horrible stutter. "And then a miraculous thing happened when I was in the high school," he explained. "I was acting in a production of *A Connecticut Yankee in King Arthur's Court*. When I got on stage, I stopped stuttering. When I stepped off the stage, I started stuttering again. I said, "This is a miracle", I got to investigate this." His stutter went away when he became the entertainer!

"To laugh often and much, to win respect of intelligent people and affection of children, to leave the world a better place to know even one life has breathed easier because you have lived. This is to have succeeded," says Ralph Waldo Emerson. He insists that we should learn to smile and laugh as often as we can because that is the essence of joyful living.

"I want to tell you to keep laughing," says Alan Alda. "You gurgle when you laugh. Be sure to laugh three times a day for your own well-being. And if you can get other people to join you in your laughter, you may help keep this shaky world afloat. When people are laughing, they're generally not killing one another. Above all, to laugh and enjoy your life of your own choosing and in a world of your making." Your own laughter will make you feel better. According to Peter Michelmore, "The foundations of good health lie in love, laughter, and faith in oneself." Laughter had been a lifelong drug for Sir Peter Ustinov. It was said that he was "always seeing the bright side of every thing".

"Laugh, the world laughs with you;
Weep, and you weep alone;
For the sad old earth has to borrow its mirth;
It has trouble enough of its own.

Ella Wheeler Wilcox

Count your blessings
We must see the bright side of everything in life; and treasure the memories for pleasant reminiscence. Every person experiences happiness on several occasions; he must learn to count his blessings, expressing gratitude for pleasant moments in life. Anyone can beat the blues by refreshing oneself with the memories of the happiest events in life; it is one of the best ways to keep oneself in good spirits. Your 'happiness collection' can always create a heaven on earth.

Keep a happiness calendar
John Culhane devised a Happiness Calendar for organised counting of blessings—as one of the ways to keep off the problems.

He bought a calendar with big blank squares for every day of the year, and on it he began to record when, where and with whom he has been most happy. Based on the daily appointment calendars he has kept for years, this master calendar will eventually register the 365 happiest days of his life.

From the start his method was simple. At the top of his Happiness Calendar, he wrote: "I Count Only the Sunny Days," Then he went on a hunt for happy days through all the journals and engagement calendars, he has kept for a long time. Out of this raw material, he compiled a list of the happiest days of his life, from childhood up to 1982. Then he worked out a simple three-step plan for keeping such a calendar up-to-date.

First, at the end of the each month, he will select from current appointment calendar three or four days on which he was happiest. These become headlines at the top of that month's page. Here, for example, are the headlines for January 1982: "Michael and T H Play for Holiday Parties." And "Hind and I celebrate Virgil's Birthday" He explains, Michael and T H—for Thomas Henry—are his sons and they played their guitars for parties on January 1 and 2. Hind is his wife, and they had a birthday party on January 11 for their friend Virgil Burnett.

Step two takes place on New Year's Day of the following year, when he sorts through the monthly headlines and add their dates to the Happiness Calendar. The third step starts when he has already recorded a happiest day on a certain date. He jots down the new happy day on the back of the calendar. When he completes this happiest year of his life, he will start another one. He says "After all you can't have too many happier years. Here are some of his entries to demonstrate what you can do with Happiness Calendar:

January "The 30th was the happiest in 1966. His calendar says: "Riverdale. Sledding with sons, Michael, 4; T H 3." He and his sons slid down the snowy hill from the statue of Henry Hudson to the fence.

February "My birthday is February 7, which is also Charles Dickens's Birthday."

He had a costume party celebrating Charles Dickens's Birthday. "It was a splendid evening, and it confirmed my belief that where good friends are, happiness is sure to go."

March "On March 27,1985, I saw gray whales spouting off the coast of California, and my heart leapt. I can't explain why the sight made that day one of the happiest of my life, but it did".

April "One of the happiest working days of my life was April 9, 1959. As a press reporter, I was covering poet Carl Sandburag, as he received a honorary degree from Rockford College in Illinois. On a visit to a local museum he admired the wood carvings of a farmer Alex Farb. I learnt the value of making time to show appreciation".

May "On May 7, 1959, my paper sent me to review a college production of *Antigone*. The title role was played by a student from Baghdad, Iraq, named Hind Rassam. I gave her a good review, and backed up my judgement by marrying her. Talk about paving the way for happy days!"

June "It was a happy day when I graduated from college on June 2, 1956—also my mother's birthday. Twenty nine months passed. Like all months they contained happy and unhappy days. Then, suddenly, it was 1985. Hind and I took my mother to see T H graduate from Harvard on the happiest June 6.

July "On the Fourth of July in 1980 I was flying to New York from California. The day offered clear blue skies all the way, and I spent five hours aloft with nose pressed to a jet window celebrating America's Independence Day by drinking in this country from sea to shining sea."

August "Hind and I arrived in London on August 15, 1984. On August 16 jet lag got us up before dawn. We caught a night-prowling taxi and went to Waterloo bridge to watch the dawn come up over London. Then we had an early breakfast and went back to hotel and slept like babies."

September "On September 27, 1985, my wife and I walked down to the Hudson River as Hurricane Gloria was slowly clearing. Everything was grey and white and scudding clouds, and then gradually blue again There was another person in our waterfront park. "This is the kind of weather!" he called to us, "I love blustery days." A local barber told him that his grand father once shouted : 'My kind of weather Jimmy! I love blustery days.' "I wish I knew the date my grand father said that. I'd put it on my calendar on his behalf."

October "On the sixteenth, in 1965, Hind and I were taking our young sons for a walk, and suddenly she said," Listen everyone! Do you hear the leaves rustle?" I jotted her words on an envelope, found it among some papers some 17 years later., and registered October 16 as the quintessential 'Perfect autumn day.'"

November "On November 4, 1984, I heard a mocking bird singing in a tree across from our building. I counted seven separate songs and then it started all over. I ran to get my tape recorder, but by the time I got back outside, the bird was gone. I learnt a good lesson from that: *Listen to the mocking bird!* Don't miss the moment.

December "Like most of us, I have enough happy holidays to fill dozens of happy calendars. But the one catches my eye is the day after Christmas, 1985. We were having our annual family charades tournament, and my niece, Yasmeen Rassam was participating for the first time in ten years. Great Charades Victory"

That brings to his 13th example—the miserable March 12, 1980. When I looked at My Happiness Calendar that day I re-read a six-year-old entry. On March 12, 1980 I drove my younger son and his girl friend to New York to see a revival of Charlie Chaplin film. Then, after watching the orangutans at the Bronx Zoo, we had dinner at a restaurant overlooking the Hudson. My calendar reminded me that this grey day was once graced by sunny events."

This last entry shows how the calendar helps when the miseries come – as they inevitably will. "Here was proof that no matter how miserable this day of this month of this year may have been, I had already been happy on this date," says Culhane. "And chances are, in some future year this day will be even happier." Happiness indeed depends on your ability to count on blessings and enjoy life.

Be grateful: Thank heaven for the joy of life
George Herbert once said a prayer of thanksgiving: "O Thou who has given us so much, mercifully grant us one thing more—a grateful heart." That reminds the following poem of thanksgiving:

We thank you, Lord of Heaven,
For all the joys that greet us,
For all that you have given
To help us and delight us
In earth and sky and seas;
The sunlight on the meadows,
The rainbow's fleeting wonder,
The cloud with cooling shadows,
The stars that shine in splendour—
We thank you, Lord, for these.

For swift and gallant horses,
For lambs in pastures springing,
For dogs with friendly faces,
For birds with music thronging
Their chantries in the trees;
For herbs to cool our fever,
For flowers of field and garden,
For bees among the clover
With stolen sweetness laden—
We thank you, Lord, for these.

For homely dwelling places
Where childhood's visions linger
For friends and kindly voices,
For bread to stay our hunger
And sleep to bring us ease;
For zeal and zest of living,
For faith and understanding,
For words to tell our loving.
For hope of peace unending—
We thank you, Lord, for these.

—*Enlarged Songs of Praise*

Chapter 23

Enjoy Life to the Full

> *Be happy. It is a way of being wise.*
> **Colette (Sidonie Gabrielle Claude 1873- 1954)**
> French author

> *Try to enjoy the festival of life with other men.*
> **Epictetus (55- 135 CE)**
> Roman stoic philosopher

Thus, we are introduced to a new paradigm of experience. We are reminded of the fact that the divisions of past, present and future of human life do not exist in the passage of infinite time. In fact, they are created by human mind. Yet, paradoxically, our thinking about past and future makes a considerable impact on our present behaviour. Human living here and now is influenced by past memories and future concerns. Human mind always wanders playfully in the microcosm it has created. It plays with ideas, creates beautiful dreams and wonderful visions. It can tune in the hidden energies to help us realise our dreams. In the process, it raises hopes of bright future of sunny days and addresses apprehensions of frightening events and unhappy consequences. It is totally committed to help us in our struggle to be happy every day. It also stops its pendulum once in a while for a few moments to give us some glimpses of the abundant joy in the eternal now.

All of us are busy with many activities to satisfy basic needs, achieve personal goals, capture opportunities, eke out a living, earn money and make our lives happy. Sometimes we succeed and other times fail. In the process we encounter frustration, anger, stress and all the unpleasant feelings. We often forget that all of us are born with precious gifts of life that can make our lives happy, but we hardly make use of their full potential. If we make realistic expectations and take appropriate actions our goals can be within our reach. If we learn from our failures and mistakes, endeavour with sustained effort, we can be successful. Our achievements, how ever small, can give us immense happiness. If only we realise this we all can enjoy life.

The main idea is that the very purpose of our lives is to be happy. Though happiness appears to be elusive we can experience it through our actions. We all seek happiness as if it is out there in the world. It is indeed like chasing the wind. In point of fact, it is 'so far yet so near'. The truth is, it is here *within* us. But the eyes that are designed to see the outer world cannot see what is behind them. You need special glasses to focus on the inner world. Only then the source of happiness can be located. In fact, it is hiding in our positive feelings. Happiness generally follows successful deeds just as the effect follows a cause. But unfortunately sometimes, we human beings want to feel the effect without the cause. We want effortless achievement. That's the problem with us. So often times it happens we live our lives in chains, we never even know we have the key. Yes, we have the ability to feel happy whenever we want, if only we get rid of the conditioned stimuli that are chained to our feelings. Make effort to get rid of those chains of habit, and win your freedom. Only then you are free to express your true self and feel happy.

No one is born happy. Psychoanalyst Eric Fromm says "Happiness is not a gift of Gods." June Callwood believes that "serene and lasting joy comes not by accident, nor is it a gift of gods. It is an achievement brought about by inner productiveness. People succeed at being happy in the same way they succeed at loving, by building a liking for themselves, for true reasons." It is something each of us must construct oneself. Happiness is a proof of one's success in the art of living.

That reminds a thoughtful saying by Ella Wheeler Wilcox: "The truest greatness lies in being kind. The truest wisdom in a happy mind." How right she was! Think about this for a while. This could be a defining moment of truth, if not a turning point in life. Be kind to yourself, and have a happy mind. Remember, you can command your mind, the genie within you; it will never disobey you, because you are the master. With its powerful help you can overcome this world where you are born to be happy.

Happiness comes by choice not by chance. Yes, "you can choose to think and feel as you desire," says PSYCHOTHERAPIST Wayne W Dyer. Listen carefully to the words of the Nobel laureate Aleksander Solzhenitsyn: "It is not the level of prosperity that makes for happiness but in kinship of heart to heart and the way we look at the world. Both attributes are within our power, so that a man is happy so long as he chooses to be happy; and no one can stop him."

That's the point : *the attributes that can make you happy are within your power.* You are powerful enough to wield influence over your attitudes. Agony and ecstasy, misery and happiness are at your command. John Milton says, "The mind is in its own place and in itself can make a heaven of hell and a hell of heaven." It is up to you to choose what you want. Your feelings exist to serve thy will. Remember! *A man is happy so long as he chooses to be happy.* You will be happy as long as you wish to be happy! No one can stop you. Now that you have every reason to be happy, what stops you from being happy?

Life is a banquet, but most people are starving to death. "No fire, no heroism, no intensity of thought and feeling can preserve an individual beyond grave," reminds Bertrand Russell. Remember, no one gets a second chance to live again. Nobody! That is the bitter truth about human life. When you lose a thing you realise how valuable it was; though you take it lightly when you have it. But unfortunately you won't be there to realise the value of your life, when you lose it. Life indeed is the most precious thing in the world.

Christiaan Barnard, the famous South African heart surgeon once survived a terrible car accident that almost crushed him. It was a great feeling for him to know he was still alive. He wrote, "Suddenly, I realised... a profound lesson in getting on with the business of living.

Because the business of living is joy in the real sense of the word, not just something for pleasure, amusement, recreation. The business of living is the celebration of being alive!" Joy indeed is the nectar of life! Let us learn to celebrate, as long as we live, for being alive! And for the joy of living the life of a unique human being.

"To live is to be happy, to be care free, to be overwhelmed by the glory of it all. Not to be happy is living death," says Everett Ruess. Listen to the advice of another great soul, Will Durant: "Drink the brimming cup of life to the full and to the end—and thank God and nature for its trials and challenges, its punishments and rewards, its gifts of beauty, wisdom, labour and love." You live only one life; why not make it joyful!

"Be grateful for yourself," says William Saroyan, a Pulitzer Prize winning humanitarian writer "Yes, for yourself. Be thankful. Understand what a man is, is something he can be grateful for and ought to be grateful for." You must be thankful and grateful as well for what life offers you — and above all, for the joy and happiness of living! Realise, the only reason to live is to enjoy it. Be cheerful and learn to live joyfully.

Soon today's door is going to close softly between us.

So long my friend, enjoy life!

References

Adler, Mortimer. 'Success Means Never Feeling Tired', *Reader's Digest*, February 1980.

Alda, Alan. 'Dig into the World', *Reader's Digest*, December 1981.

Amos, Wayne. 'Eternity's Sunrise', *Reader's Digest*, April 1965.

Barnard, Christiaan. 'In Celebration of being alive', *Reader's Digest*, December 1980.

Bartocci, Barbara. 'Dare to Change Your Life', *Reader's Digest*, February 1987.

Bechtel, Stephan. 'How to do Today What You Could Put Off until Tomorrow.' *Reader's Digest*, June 1984.

Bliss, Edwin. 'Ten Tips to Help You Manage Your Time', Reader's Digest, September 1977.

Bolch, Jennifer. 'How to Manage Stress', *Reader's Digest*, January 1981.

Boyd, Crystal. *Midnight muse.*

Bruner, Jerome K. *On knowing : Essays for the left hand.*

Buck, Pearl. 'Joy of children'. *Reader's Digest*, November 1965.

Buckley, 'William Thomas.' You Can Beat Depression, *Reader's Digest*, September 1990.

Burgess, Gelette. 'The Delightful Game of Conversation', *Reader's Digest*, July 1967.

Burns, David. 'Aim for Success not Perfection', *Reader's Digest*, October 1985.

Burns, David. 'You Can Conquer Anxiety', *Reader's Digest*, September 1991.

Caffiere, Blanche. 'The Boy with the Billion Dollar Secret' *Reader's Digest*, December 1995.

Callwood, June. 'The One Sure Way to Happiness', *Reader's Digest*, January 1965.

Campion, Nordi Reeder 'The Knack of Asking', *Reader's Digest*, October 1966.

Campion, Nordi Reeder. 'What Really is Worthwhile', *Reader's Digest*, May 1995.

Carnegie, Dale. 'How to Win Friends and Influence People', *Reader's Digest*, April 1977.

Cherry, Laurence. 'Why You Need to Dream', *Reader's Digest*, September 1978.

Cherry, Laurence. 'The Brain Slowly Yields its Secrets, *Reader's Digest*, April 1983.

Clark, Blake. 'What You Can Learn from Your Dreams', *Reader's Digest*, December 1972.

Covey, Stephen R. *The Seven Habits of Highly Effective People.* Simon & Schuster, New York, 1989.

Coudert, Jo. 'Excuse Me, Your Manners Are Missing', *Reader's Digest*, June 1986.

Culhane, John. 'Keep a Happiness Calendar,' *Reader's Digest*, June 1987.

Davis, Elise Miller. 'Short Cut to Set You free,' *Reader's Digest*, June 1970.

De Bono, Edward. *Opportunities.*

Dobson, James. 'The Greatest Gift You Can Give Your Child', *Reader's Digest*, June 1988.

Drury, Michael. 'Release the Breaks on Your Brain', *Reader's Digest*, December 1975.

Dukas, Helen and Banesh Hoffman. 'Yours' sincerely, Albert Einstein, *Reader's Digest*, October 1979.

Durant, Will. 'Man is Wiser than Any Man', *Reader's Digest*, March 1969.

Dyer, Wayne. 'Happiness – It's Only Natural,' *Reader's Digest*, June 1978.

Ellis, William. 'Your Ideas May Be Your Future', *Reader's Digest*, March 1975.

Encyclopaedia Britannica. (10.618). Seleucus Nicator.

Enlarged songs of praise. 'Hymn of Thanksgiving', *Reader's Digest*, October 1975.

Epstein, Joseph. 'The New Tyranny of Sex', *Reader's Digest*, May 1975.

Frank, Ellen and Carol Anderson. 'How Important is Sex to a Happy Marriage', *Reader's Digest*, January 1960.

Franklin, Jon and Alan Doelp. 'A Breathtaking Journey into the Mysterious World of the Human Brain, *Reader's Digest*, November 1984.

Frazier, John. 'Meet Your Memory'. *Reader's Digest*, February 1973.

Furlong, William Barry. 'Why fun is fun', *Reader's Digest*, September 1977.

Gallup, Jr. George, Alec Gallup with William Proctor. 'What Successful People Have in Common', *Reader's Digest*, November 1987.

Gordon, Arthur. 'The Best Advice I Ever Had', *Reader's Digest*, August 1987.

Gotlieb, Annie. 'Dare to Live Your Dream', *Reader's Digest*, May 1985.

Gregory, Stephanie and Brad Wetzler. 'How fast are you going When You're Standing Still', *Reader's Digest*, August 2002.

Harrington, Robert. 'How Happy Are You', *Reader's Digest*, November 1979.

Hill, Elizabeth Starr. 'The Time to be Happy', *Reader's Digest*, August 1966.

Houck, Catherine. 'How to Beat a Bad Mood', *Reader's Digest*, December 1989.

Hunt, Morton. 'Seven Secrets of Peak Performers', *Reader's Digest*, November 1982.

Hunt, Morton. 'Seven Steps to Better Thinking', *Reader's Digest*, August, 1983.

Hunt, Morton. 'Get Your Own Way – The Easy Way', *Reader's Digest*, July 1984.

Hunt, Morton. 'Beat Your Bad Moods for Good', *Reader's Digest*, January 1987.

James, Jennifer. 'When Words Hurt', *Reader's Digest*, January 1991.

Kalidas. *Ritusamhara*.

Kennedy, Father Eugene. 'Sex isn't Everything,' Reader's Digest, December, 1972.

Kingston, W. *Innovations*.

Korda, Michael. 'Why manners'? *Reader's Digest*, March 1989.

Kreisler, Kristin Von. 'Why We Dream What We Dream', *Reader's Digest*, March 1995.

Kriegel, Robert with Louis Patler. 'Do you risk enough to succeed'. *Reader's Digest*, February 1992.

Lagemann, John Kord. 'Don't Be Afraid to Let Your Feelings Show', *Reader's Digest*, September 1976.

Landers, Ann. 'Say No to Your Children', *Reader's Digest*, November 1968.

Landers, Ann. 'Coping with crisis', *Reader's Digest*, April 1981.

Lane, Margaret. 'Are You Really Listening', *Reader's Digest*, July 1981.

Le Boeuf, Michael. 'Realize Your Creative Potential', *Reader's Digest*, January 1982.

Lucado, Max. *No Wonder They Call Him the Savior*, Multnomah Publisher's Inc.

Maltz, Maxwell. *Creative Living for Today*. Pocket Books, New York, 1967.

Mann, Thomas. *The magic mountain*.

Mc. Ginnis, Alan Loy. 'Bringing Out the Best in People', *Reader's Digest*, October 1987.

Michelmore, Peter. 'Emotions Do Rule Our Health', *Reader's Digest*, June 1984.

Miller, James Nathan. 'The Art of Intelligent Listening', *Reader's Digest*, November 1965.

Mills, Joan. 'Sweet Uses of Solitude', *Reader's Digest*, October 1970.

Mills, Joan. 'My Wonderful Whirligig Time Machine', *Reader's Digest*, April 1979.

Mills, Joan. 'When Love Begins Again', *Reader's Digest*, April 1985.

Morgan, Clifford.T. et al. *Introduction to Psychology*. Mc. Graw-Hill Book Co. New York, 1986.

Mosley, Jean Bell. 'Take It from the Here and Now', *Reader's Digest*, September 1968.

Newman, Mildred and Bernard Berkowitz. 'You Can Take Care of Your Life'. *Reader's Digest*, September 1979.

Nicholas, William. 'Is Sexual Freedom Becoming a Bore', *Reader's Digest*, October 1966.

Oech, Roger Von. 'Unlock Your Own Creativity', *Reader's Digest*, February 1987.

Peale, Norman Vincent. 'You Can Do It Now', *Reader's Digest*, April 1972.

Peale, Norman Vincent. 'Manners Mark the Difference', *Reader's Digest*, May 1974.

Peale, Norman Vincent. 'Make Your Dreams Come true', *Reader's Digest*, December 1983.

Peale, Ruth Stafford. 'Adventures in Being a Wife', *Reader's Digest*, October, 1966.

Peterson, Wilfred, 'Happily Ever After', *Reader's Digest*, July 1967.

Pfeiffer, John. 'How We Remember, Why We Forget', *Reader's Digest*, January 1964.

Pierce, Ponchitta. 'Three Steps to Self-confidence', *Reader's Digest*, August 1976.

Ratcliff, J.D. 'I am John's Brain', *Reader's Digest*, June 1974.

Rather, Dan. 'How to Handle Pressure', *Reader's Digest*, March 1984.

Rowan, Roy. 'The Filing System Inside Your Head', *Reader's Digest*, February 1980.

Safran, Claire. 'You Are what you think', *Reader's Digest*, January 1988.

Sagan, Carl. 'A Cosmic Calendar', *Reader's Digest*, April 1978.

Schisgall, Oscar. 'What You Can do with an Hour a Day', *Reader's Digest*, August 1965.

Seligman, Martin E.P. *Authentic happiness: using the new positive psychology for lasting fulfillment,* Free press, New York. 2002.

Sellers, Patricia. 'What's so good about failure', *Reader's Digest*, September 1995.

Selye, Hans *interviewed* by Laurence Cherry. 'Straight talk about stress', *Reader's Digest*, December, 1982.

Schreiner, Jr. Samuel. 'How to Do Better at Almost Everything', *Reader's Digest*, June 1982.

Singer, Jerome. 'Don't Be Afraid to Day-dream', *Reader's Digest*, October 1976.

Sircar, D.C, *Inscriptions of Asoka*, The Publications Division, Government of India, New Delhi, 1957.

Sussman, Vic. 'Don't Fear Failure', *Reader's Digest*, January 1991.

Tagore, Rabindranath. *Personality,* Lectures delivered in America. Macmillan, London, 1926.

Tavris, Carol. 'Anger: The Misunderstood Emotion'. *Reader's Digest*, January 1984.

Tessina, Tina. *It ends with you: Grow up and out of disfunction.*

The Hindu Business Line (March 10, 2003). They sleep on diamonds and go hungry to bed.

Thomas, Lewis. 'The Way the World Works', *Reader's Digest*, February 1982.

Thoreau, Henry David. 'Simplify, simplify', *Reader's Digest*, May 1978.

Toffler, Alvin. 'Coping with Future Shock', *Reader's Digest*, December 1971.

Turner, Dale. 'How to Find Time', *Reader's Digest*, November 1989.

Viscott, David. 'Ways to Manage Your Moods' *Reader's Digest*, May 1975.

Ward, Barbara. 'Is the Future Possible', *Reader's Digest*, November 1977.

Whitman, Ardis. 'The High Cost of Hurt Feelings', *Reader's Digest*, August 1958.

Whitman, Ardis. 'Change is to Live', *Reader's Digest*, March 1966.

Whitman, Ardis. 'Five enduring Values for Your Child', *Reader's Digest*, December 1981.

Whitman, Ardis. 'The Awesome Power to be Ourselves', *Reader's Digest*, July 1983.

Whitman, Ardis. 'Secret Joys of Solitude', *Reader's Digest*, November 1983.

Wolfe, John. 'You Can Speak in Public', *Reader's Digest*, October 1983.

Wylie, Max. 'When Faced with Grief', *Reader's Digest*, December 1971.

Zeigler, Edward. 'Think Your Way Out of Depression', *Reader's Digest*, June 1981.

Zeigler, Edward. 'Dreams: The Genie within', *Reader's Digest*, February 1986.

Of Allied Interest